"The authors highlight key issues and concerns shaping people's conceptions of Europe and point to the tension between diversity being seen as preventing a European identity while also considered core to it, acknowledging mobility as both "an answer and a challenge to politics of belonging". In doing so from an insightful interdisciplinary perspective, they are diagnosing a major issue for future research across the broad field of European Studies."

 – *Ullrich Kockel, Professor of Cultural Ecology and Sustainability, Heriot-Watt University*

"We speak more than ever about identity politics. This book will be the most authoritative study of the European Union's effort to provide European citizens with a European identity through its cultural policies. With its ethnographic approach, the book takes us beyond the top-down policy studies and analyse the many different ideas of Europe expressed by ordinary citizens."

 – *Jan Ifversen, Associate Professor of European Studies, Aarhus University*

Europe from Below

European Studies

AN INTERDISCIPLINARY SERIES IN EUROPEAN CULTURE,
HISTORY AND POLITICS

The titles published in this series are listed at *brill.com/es*

Europe from Below

Notions of Europe and the European among Participants in EU Cultural Initiatives

By

Tuuli Lähdesmäki, Katja Mäkinen, Viktorija L. A. Čeginskas, and Sigrid Kaasik-Krogerus

BRILL

LEIDEN | BOSTON

This work was supported by the European Research Council (ERC) under the EU's Horizon 2020 Research and Innovation Programme under Grant 636177 (EUROHERIT), the Academy of Finland under Grant SA137650 (ID-ECC), and the Kone Foundation under Grant 46–11423 (the project Politics of participation and democratic legitimation in European Union). The content of this work does not reflect the official opinion of the European Union. Responsibility for the information and views expressed in the work lies entirely with the authors.

Library of Congress Cataloging-in-Publication Data

Names: Lähdesmäki, Tuuli, author. | Mäkinen, Katja, author. | Čeginskas, Viktorija L. A., author. | Kaasik-Krogerus, Sigrid, author.

Title: Europe from below : notions of Europe and the European among participants in EU cultural initiatives / by Tuuli Lähdesmäki, Katja Mäkinen, Viktorija Linda Čeginskas, and Sigrid Kaasik-Krogerus.

Other titles: Notions of Europe and the European among participants in EU cultural initiatives

Description: Leiden ; Boston : Brill, [2021] | Series: European studies, 1568-1858 ; vol. 38 | Includes index.

Identifiers: LCCN 2020056528 (print) | LCCN 2020056529 (ebook) | ISBN 9789004396876 (paperback) | ISBN 9789004449800 (ebook)

Subjects: LCSH: European Union countries–Cultural policy. | European Union countries–Influence. | Group identity–European Union countries. | National characteristics, European. | Politics and culture–European Union countries.

Classification: LCC D2021 .L34 2021 (print) | LCC D2021 (ebook) | DDC 306.094–dc23

LC record available at https://lccn.loc.gov/2020056528

LC ebook record available at https://lccn.loc.gov/2020056529

Typeface for the Latin, Greek, and Cyrillic scripts: "Brill". See and download: brill.com/brill-typeface.

ISSN 1568-1858
ISBN 978-90-04-39687-6 (paperback)
ISBN 978-90-04-44980-0 (e-book)

Folk dance performers dancing with the audience in Pécs, Hungary, as part of the European Capital of Culture year in 2010

Contents

Preface

Notions of Europe and understandings of features and elements that characterize it form a complex research topic that can never be exhausted or reach a definitive conclusion. Through transforming culture, politics, the environment, and social reality, Europe is never standing still but is rather constantly on the move to become something else than it used to be. Even within a single moment, Europe is always plural. For different people, in different discourses, and from different points of view, these 'Europes' differ – even radically. Several transnational actors, such as the European Union (EU), seek to bring these different 'Europes' closer together by attempting to create a common cultural space in Europe. This book focuses on these attempts by exploring the EU's cultural initiatives and how Europe and the 'European' are understood in their context, particularly by people participating in these various initiatives and activities.

Our book arose from three separate research projects that have all explored different EU cultural initiatives, in order to understand how these initiatives communicate the meanings of Europe and construct Europe in their implementation and practices. This book not only brings together the data and findings from these projects but also combines our expertise from various disciplines including heritage studies, cultural studies, European ethnology, history, media and communication studies, art history, sociology, and political science. Our approach builds on a rich disciplinary background as well as our overlapping research interests, which are brought together by a common theme – Europe, and its construction by participants in the EU's cultural initiatives.

The idea for this book was triggered by our informal discussions where we noted that all our three research projects – despite their distinct thematic focuses on the EU's cultural, urban, and heritage actions and policies and culture and citizenship programmes – explored the idea of Europe and were based on field research among people participating in EU cultural initiatives that deal with this idea. The first of these projects was Tuuli Lähdesmäki's postdoctoral project 'Identity politics in Pécs, Tallinn and Turku as European Capitals of Culture' (ID-ECC) based at the Department of Art and Culture Studies in the University of Jyväskylä. The project was made possible by a grant from the Academy of Finland between 2011 and 2013, and it included funds for field research in Tallinn, Estonia, and Turku, Finland in 2011. The research related to this project had already started in autumn 2009, with funding by the Faculty of Humanities at the University of Jyväskylä, Finland which continued until the beginning of 2011. The financial support of the University of Jyväskylä enabled

Lähdesmäki's field research in Pécs, Hungary, in 2010. This project resulted in a variety of publications with a wide range of foci from exploring transformations in cultural policy discourses to identity politics. The issues it addressed ranged from cultural activism to cultural regeneration of urban space in the EU initiative, European Capital of Culture.

Chronologically, the next project was Katja Mäkinen's and Marko Nousiainen's postdoctoral project 'Politics of participation and democratic legitimation in European Union', funded by the Kone Foundation, Finland, between 2013 and 2015. Based at the Department of Social Sciences and Philosophy, University of Jyväskylä, they scrutinized the forms and political meanings of civic participation in EU policies. Mäkinen and Nousiainen developed an ethnographic approach to politics and the EU's participatory governance. In the project, Mäkinen led research line A: 'Spaces and cultures of participation in EU programmes', which investigated participation in the context of projects funded by EU culture and citizenship programmes. Funding from the Kone Foundation enabled Mäkinen to conduct field research on one such project in Strasbourg, France, and Antwerp, Belgium. This project has produced several publications exploring participation and participatory governance as a part of the EU's policies and their contradictory implications for democracy, citizenship, and understandings of the EU as a polity.

The third, and the most recent project contributing to this book is 'Legitimation of European Cultural Heritage and the Dynamics of Identity Politics in the EU' (EUROHERIT), funded by the European Research Council (ERC) between 2015 and 2020. This ERC Starting Grant project was led by Tuuli Lähdesmäki, and all the other authors of this book have worked in it as postdoctoral or senior researchers at the Department of Music, Art and Culture Studies at the University of Jyväskylä. In the project, we broadly explored EU heritage policies and politics through analysing different EU heritage and history initiatives, with the main empirical focus on the most recent EU heritage action, the European Heritage Label. Funding from the ERC enabled us to conduct extensive field research at selected heritage sites awarded the European Heritage Label in ten countries: Austria, Belgium, Estonia, France, Germany, Hungary, Italy, Netherlands, Poland, and Portugal. The publications written in the context of the project have explored the construction of European cultural heritage from various perspectives, such as governance, borders and practices of bordering, participation and community building, the affective nature of heritage, and gender. The main framework of our research on this project has been critical heritage studies.

These three projects could not have succeeded without the involvement of various experts and collaborators. Moreover, several research assistants have helped us during our field research, collecting data, and communicating with visitors in languages that we were not able to speak. Tuuli Lähdesmäki would particularly like to thank Péter Müller, Beáta Thomka, and Adrienn Bognár from the University of Pécs and Kristóf Fenyvesi from the University of Jyväskylä for their help in implementing the field research in Pécs and for providing 'insider' views of the year when Pécs was European Capital of Culture. She also thanks the coordinators of the European Capital of Culture Volunteer Programmes and all the volunteers who assisted in collecting and translating the data in Pécs, Tallinn, and Turku. Katja Mäkinen warmly thanks the organizers of the European Citizen Campus project for their good cooperation and support for the research and for providing the access to relevant sources of information. She particularly thanks Janine Fleck for granting permission to use her research interviews with the participants in the European Citizen Campus project in Freiburg, Germany.

We all want to thank the many research assistants and project researchers who helped us to collect, translate, and transcribe our field research data in the EUROHERIT project. We thank following people for their hard work: Maria Bogdan, Elina Jääskeläinen, Riikka Kalajoki, Miro Keränen, Aino-Kaisa Koistinen, Sofia Kotilainen, Quentin Labégorre, Lorenzo Leonardelli, Bella Lerch, Mila Oiva, Ave Tikkanen, Camille Troquet, Urho Tulonen, Rita Vargas de Freitas Matias, and Anne Vera Veen. Equally, all our contacts who helped to facilitate our field research deserve special thanks. But most importantly, we would like to thank all the people we interviewed, surveyed, and observed for agreeing to participate in our research projects, and thus making our research possible.

This book has been proofread by Kate Sotejeff-Wilson, who deserves thanks for her detailed work. We also wish to thank our editor Wendel Scholma and the whole team at Brill for our smooth cooperation in the publishing process, as well as Brill's anonymous reviewers for their fruitful comments, which helped us to develop the book by sharpening our argumentation.

Tuuli Lähdesmäki, Katja Mäkinen, Viktorija L. A. Čeginskas,
Sigrid Kaasik-Krogerus
28 February 2020, Jyväskylä, Munich, and Helsinki

Figures and Tables

Figures

Tables

Notes on the Authors

Viktorija L. A. Čeginskas
(Ph.D.) is a Postdoctoral Researcher at the Department of Music, Art and Culture Studies, University of Jyväskylä, Finland. She has previously worked on the EUROHERIT project as well as in the private and public sectors and published in a number of peer-reviewed journals on (multilingual and European) belonging and (transnational) identity, cultural heritage, and Europe. Čeginskas is editor of the open access journal *Ethnologia Fennica* and a co-editor of the volume *Challenges and Solutions in Ethnographic Research: Ethnography with a Twist* (Routledge, 2020). ORCiD: 0000-0002-5794-9503

Sigrid Kaasik-Krogerus
(DSocSc) is a University Lecturer at the Faculty of Arts, University of Helsinki, Finland. She has previously worked as a Postdoctoral Researcher on the EUROHERIT project at the University of Jyväskylä, Finland. She specializes in media and communication; identity and belonging; heritage; critical geopolitics; and European studies in the EU context, especially in Central and East European countries. From 2015 to 2018, she was a member of the Jean Monnet Module, East within Europe, funded by Erasmus+ at the Aleksanteri Institute, University of Helsinki. ORCiD: 0000-0002-6424-5520

Tuuli Lähdesmäki
(Ph.D., DSocSc) is an Associate Professor at the Department of Music, Art and Culture Studies, University of Jyväskylä, Finland. Her research focuses on cultural identities; belonging; cultural heritage; strategies of representing, narrating, and interpreting the past; and governance of diversities. Between 2015 and 2020, Lähdesmäki led the EUROHERIT project (Legitimation of European Cultural Heritage and the Dynamics of Identity Politics in the EU), funded by the European Research Council. The project members jointly authored the monograph *Creating and Governing Cultural Heritage in the European Union: The European Heritage Label* (Routledge, 2020). Lähdesmäki co-leads the University of Jyväskylä's research profiling area CRISIS (Crises Redefined: Historical Continuity and Societal Change). ORCiD: 0000-0002-5166-489X

Katja Mäkinen
(Ph.D.) is an Adjunct Professor and Senior Researcher at the Department of Music, Art and Culture Studies, University of Jyväskylä, Finland. Mäkinen's research focuses on citizenship, participation, identities, and cultural heritage;

she specializes in a conceptual approach to analysing EU programmes on culture and citizenship. She has worked as a lecturer in political science and cultural policy at the University of Jyväskylä. She has previously worked in several research projects, such as EUROHERIT and Muddy Waters: Democracy and Governance in a Multilateral State, funded by the Academy of Finland. ORCiD: 0000-0002-1107-4801

CHAPTER 1

Introduction: Europe from Below

1 Constructing the EU as a Cultural Community

From its inception, the principal idea of the European project was to unite people and to form a 'community of Europeans' based on the values of peace and reconciliation, which would make it possible to move beyond a national perspective and instead foster better relations among European nations by promoting cooperation and tolerance (see Monnet 1955; Schuman 1963). The preamble to the Treaty of Paris (1951), formally establishing the European Coal and Steel Community, expressed precisely this aspiration:

> to substitute for age-old rivalries the merging of their essential interests; to create by establishing an economic community, the basis for a broader and deeper community among peoples divided by the bloody conflicts; and to lay the foundations for institutions which will give direction to a destiny henceforward shared.

The founders of the European Coal and Steel Community were clear about their intentions for the Treaty, namely that it was the first step towards European integration resulting in close collaboration between its member states and culminating in the idea of a united Europe.

Culture can be considered as one of the underlying ideas that have motivated the creation and building of the European Community (EC) and, later, the European Union (EU) (e.g. Rosamond 2000; Sassatelli 2006; Näss 2009). The EC started its culture-focused activities in the 1970s, and has used cultural aspects as central elements in promoting integration since the mid-1980s (Shore 1993; Shore 2000, 25). With the Maastricht Treaty in 1992, culture was made an official policy field of the EU. Since then, cultural policy has been perceived as an increasingly central area for the Union (Näss 2010; O'Callaghan 2011). The establishment of European cultural, heritage, and remembrance policies over the last few decades can be interpreted as extending and deepening the European project by emphasizing the cultural-historical underpinning of the Union that has long been viewed mainly from economic and political perspectives (Prutsch 2013, 36). Scholars have discussed this process with the concept of 'cultural Europeanization', which refers to policies and practices dealing with being or becoming European through culture. It has been interpreted as the third wave of the integration process, in which European integration broadens from economic and political spheres to encompass culture (Delanty 2005; Sassatelli 2006, 2008, 2009; Jarausch 2010; Karlsson 2010; Patel 2013; Lähdesmäki 2017). In these views, cultural Europeanization is mainly understood as a top-down process initiated by the EU.

Since the 1990s, the EU has increasingly developed a particular European discourse based on a transnational 'European' interpretation of culture and heritage across national differences. It began to narrate this amalgam of a multitude of types of knowledge, attitudes, and values to a wider public as the story of 'Europe'– of what Europe is, who Europeans are, and the elements which make up their 'Europeanness' (see Karlsson 2010; Lähdesmäki 2017a; Lähdesmäki et al. 2020). Since then, the EU has been increasingly interested in its own and Europe's past – pasts that are commonly paralleled in EU policy rhetoric. While 'flirting' with the imagination of a shared European past and heritage, this EU discourse is simultaneously extremely future-orientated. The narrations of Europe's past and common heritage function as building blocks which the EU uses to create a particular image of itself and 'its' citizens, and to educate future 'Europeans' (Lähdesmäki 2014a).

The EU's need for a narrative that would increase unity in Europe and promote acceptance of European integration has become urgent during the past decade due to the serious economic, political, and humanitarian challenges that the continent and the Union have faced. These challenges range from struggles of the Eurozone and European financial markets to the dispute among EU member states regarding further integration and enlargement of the Union, and include diverse political crises stemming from the EU's legitimation and democratic deficits, which connect to the rise of Eurosceptic political parties demanding to exit the common currency zone and/or the European single market and political institutions. Diverse populist, nationalist and radical right-wing parties and groups, and their increasing public acceptance across Europe, have caused additional challenges. The sudden arrival of a great number of people fleeing violent conflicts and harsh living conditions to Europe in 2015 has exacerbated the political crisis, as contradictory views on how to deal with this mobility exist within the EU and its member states. At the same time, the EU has struggled with its own identity crisis (Jenkins 2008), which stems from the difficulty of narrating a common story of Europe (Lähdesmäki et al. 2020). The EU cultural policy discourses, with their emphasis on constructing a common cultural area and a feeling of belonging to Europe and the EU, can be perceived as the Union's response to these diverse challenges. The EU's interest in tackling these challenges is reflected in its policy discourses in various sectors and concretized in EU cultural initiatives that seek to implement these policies and move their discourses into practice.

In this book, we scrutinize EU cultural policy as politics of belonging (Yuval-Davis 2006, 2011), particularly from the perspective of participants in the EU's cultural initiatives. In this context, we understand politics of belonging as attempts to create a cultural narrative for Europe in order to promote a sense of belonging to Europe and the Union in terms of a cultural community among EU citizens and to strengthen their identification with the EU through the means of participation in culture. We view the EU's politics of belonging as an act of power based on the utilization of diverse discursive, narrative, and cultural resources to construct Europe and the 'European' and as a means to justify specific policies to do so (Lähdesmäki 2020; Lähdesmäki et al. 2020).

The EU's cultural initiatives can be seen as instruments in the EU's politics of belonging. Through them, the EU constructs and creates the idea of Europe, a category of Europeans, and a set of features that define them. This goal is often explicitly stated in the EU's cultural policy documents. For instance, by defining the objective to create a "common cultural area" and strengthen a "feeling of belonging" to it among citizens (e.g. EP&C 2006, 2, 4; EP&C 2013, 3), such policy documents provide evidence of how, in the EU's politics of belonging, cultural initiatives are used to both define and convey notions about Europe and the 'European' to a wider public.

Since the turn of the millennium, the EU has governed its cultural sector through large funding programmes that typically run in seven-year intervals. The first of these programmes, Culture 2000, ran from 2000 to 2007, and was followed by the second Culture programme from 2007 to 2013. The current programme is called Creative Europe and is running from 2014 to 2020. From these programmes, the EU finances various temporary projects organized by micro and meso level actors. One of our case studies in this book, the European Citizen Campus (ECC), is an example of these small-scale temporary projects. In addition, the EU allocates some funds from its cultural programmes to cultural initiatives that the European Commission itself regularly runs. Two of these initiatives, the European Capital of Culture (ECOC) and the European Heritage Label (EHL), are selected as cases for this book.

In terms of budget, culture represents a tiny EU policy sector. The Union does not have similar legal authority in this area compared to its core policy sectors, such as economy and trade. Even though the culture article in the Maastricht Treaty, adopted in 1992, and the following EU treaties allow the EU to develop overarching cultural policies, its member states are responsible for their own cultural policies according to the subsidiarity principle. Hence, the EU cannot exert direct influence on cultural policy at the national level. The whole idea of an EU cultural policy has therefore been considered controversial. Scholars have emphasized the complexity of decision- and policy-making in EU cultural policy as well as its symbolic nature due to its "soft law" instruments, such as non-enforceable recommendations and incentives (Dewey 2010). Several researchers of EU cultural policy have scrutinized its discourses and rhetoric, and identified vagueness, limitations, or conceptual contradictions (e.g. Shore 2006; Gordon 2010; Cooke and Propris 2011; Lähdesmäki 2012). Others have critically discussed weak links between ambitious goals and idealistic rhetoric in EU policies and the reality of their implementation (e.g. Mattocks 2017).

Nevertheless, the EU's cultural agendas, initiatives, actions, programmes, and policy goals affect both the cultural sector and cultural actors in the member states (e.g. Dewey 2010, 116). EU cultural policy has an important role in producing images, representations, narratives, cultural meanings, sentiments, and emotional bonds regarding the EU and Europe – in other words, it has an important role in the EU's politics of belonging. Being simultaneously cognitive and affective, the EU's cultural policy discourses and initiatives seek to appeal to cultural and social attachments and identity by disseminating knowledge, as well as by touching people on the emotional level (Lähdesmäki 2014b, 2017, forthcoming). For example, the rhetoric of EU cultural policy is characterized by eloquent usage of broad and abstract but rarely explicitly explained concepts of culture, heritage, values, and their supposedly shared features (Lähdesmäki 2017b; Lähdesmäki et al. 2020). This symbolic nature has been conceived as the key to the power of EU cultural policy: its seeks to 'touch' people's emotions, raise interest in and curiosity towards Europe' past and present, enhance positive attitudes towards the EU, and make Europeans feel European – in brief, to 'win the hearts and minds' of Europeans (see Patel 2013; Lähdesmäki 2017b). Young people are the explicit target audience of some EU cultural initiatives, such as the EHL; the aim is to advance their belonging to Europe and the EU.

The power of EU cultural policy is embedded in the way it is used to govern cultural matters. EU cultural policy is based on the model of multilevel governance that characterizes EU policy-making in general (e.g. Hooghe and Marks 2001; Bache and Flinders 2004; Nousiainen and Mäkinen 2015; Lähdesmäki et al. 2020). This means that governance is not centralized but is based on interdependent and simultaneous acts of governing at different levels, including diverse formal and informal networks of actors in the processes of governance. Moreover, the EU has recently emphasized participatory governance in its cultural policies (Lähdesmäki et al. 2020). This model of governance seeks to include diverse non-governmental actors in policy-making processes, such as cultural stakeholders, scholars, experts, representatives of civil society organizations, and citizens.

Even though both multilevel and participatory governance of culture aim at involving citizens in policy-making, both governance models present challenges. While multilevel governance seeks to encourage various actors to participate in the processes of governance, it may simultaneously complicate governance by spreading it to different levels (Piattoni 2009, 164). Similarly, participatory governance seeks to encourage citizens to get involved in various participatory practices. This may be mere tokenism, however, as someone else at a 'higher' level defines the conditions of participation and continues to hold the decision-making power (Lähdesmäki et al. 2020).

Nevertheless, the multilevel and participatory governance in EU cultural initiatives mingles top-down and bottom-up dynamics between the EU and local cultural actors, and thereby increases the variety of 'voices' included in the implementation of these initiatives (see Sassatelli 2006; Lähdesmäki 2014b; Lähdesmäki et al. 2020). The EU cultural initiatives seek to influence EU citizens' notions of Europe, co-construct a shared European culture and heritage, and affect a feeling of belonging through top-down policies with specific procedures and listed criteria for local actors implementing the initiatives. However, these local implementors have the power to interpret the identity-political aims of these initiatives from their own perspectives.

We argue in this book that cultural Europeanization – policies and practices dealing with being or becoming European – is an interrelated process that emerges in networked diversity and connectivity between various actors, in which they actively participate (see Chapters 2 and 8). For analytical reasons, we identify these actors and their discourses as representing macro, meso, and micro levels to distinguish the different institutional contexts and horizons of expectation from which the notions, discourses, and narratives of Europe are constructed. We perceive the EU as a macro-level actor that seeks to explicate and transmit specific notions of Europe to the wider European public through the conceptualizations and expressions used in its cultural policy discourses. Even though the EU itself is a composition of several institutions, which rarely take unanimous decisions, its policy discourses form a single 'voice' that represents the view of the EU as a political actor. The meso-level actors in EU cultural policy include national and local cultural managers, directors, and other facilitators who implement these policies in practice by organizing cultural events under EU cultural initiatives. These actors need to follow the macro-level 'voice' but at the same time they are both able and expected to fill open, empty, or undefined contents of the EU discourse with their own 'voices'. We mean by micro-level actors people who participate in the cultural activities funded and governed through the cultural initiatives of the EU. These actors do not have any official role in meso- or macro-level practices. The identification of these three levels aims at clarifying our analysis and arguments. It does not seek to suggest that these levels are stable or actors could not move between them. Our analysis focuses on actors who represent the micro level in our categorization, and who in our case studies are 'ordinary' citizens who participate in and visit three selected cultural initiatives.

What kind of 'voices' exist and can be heard at the micro level? In this book, we argue that the constructions of the ideas of Europe and the 'European' in EU cultural initiatives need to be scrutinized not only from above but also from below. We use flexible and multifaceted methodology to analyze how the participants of the EU cultural initiatives construct perceptions of Europe and the 'European' and their own relations to them. Our aim is not to study the reception of the notions of Europe constructed in EU cultural policy. However, our case studies enable scrutinizing how people's personal conceptions of 'a community of Europeans' relate to the 'voices' and discourses at the macro and meso levels. Our research thus also brings new understanding on how the EU's politics of belonging is perceived and functions at the micro level. We continue this introduction by backing up our argument through a review of the existing literature on EU cultural policy and pointing out gaps in it. After this, we introduce our three cases embedded in the EU's cultural policy – the ECOC, ECC, and EHL. The examination of these case studies is based on broad ethnographic field research, which generated manifold data. After that, we outline how the notion of Europe has been addressed in the previous research. We end this chapter with a brief introduction to our theoretical approach, discussed more deeply in Chapter 2, and an overview of the book's structure and contents.

2   EU Cultural Initiatives – Often Approached from Above

In the scholarly literature discussing the development, conceptual choices, and thematic foci of EU cultural policy (e.g. Shore 1993; 2000; Sassatelli 2006; 2009; O'Callaghan 2011; Näss 2010; Patel 2013; Lähdesmäki 2014a, 2014b, 2016; Lähdesmäki et al. 2020), the focus and theoretical approaches taken vary greatly. Researchers have explored EU cultural programmes by perceiving them as the core documents communicating the EU's cultural political views, priorities, and values (e.g. Psychogiopoulou 2008; Mäkinen 2012, 2014; Kandyla 2015; Suárez and Luz 2018). Moreover, these programmes have served as data for analyses of specific topics ranging from audience building (Potschka, Fuchs, and Królikowski 2013) to cinema (Liz 2016), and from the construction of citizenship (Mäkinen 2012) to EU enlargement (Vos 2017). However, the researchers have less approached EU cultural programmes from the perspective of participants' experiences of being part of the European project and how these experiences have an impact on their notions of Europe.

Scholars have explored EU cultural programmes and particularly some of its long-term cultural and civic initiatives, such as the European Capital of Culture. The ECOC initiative and the designated cities have been actively investigated since the 1990s. This research has particularly focused on EU cultural policies and policy discourses, cultural management in the implementation of the initiative, and views and experiences of cultural managers and decision-makers in the ECOCs (e.g. Richards 2000; Sassatelli 2002, 2006, 2009, García 2004a, 2005; Lassur, Tafel-Viia, Summatavet and Terk 2010; Bergsgard and Vassenden 2011; Patel 2013; Žilič-Fišer and Erjavec 2017). Moreover, cultural regeneration, urban transformation, regional development, and cultural and creative industries have had a strong role in the research on ECOCs (e.g. Heikkinen 2000; Richards 2000; García 2004a, 2004b; Rommetvedt 2008; Campbell 2011; Hudec and Džupka 2016). These studies reflect the development of urban policies during the first decades of the initiative: the ECOC was introduced at a time when culture-led approaches to urban development and ideas of cultural regeneration of economically regressed cities were about to emerge (Sassatelli 2009, 95).

Much of the previous ECOC research has focused on the impacts of the initiative at the local level. These studies have explored diverse issues ranging from the tangible cultural outcomes to the residents' and visitors' impressions of the city in question (e.g. Richards and Wilson 2004; Berg and Rommetvedt 2009), and from the networks of cultural actors (e.g. Bergsgard and Vassenden 2011; Campbell 2011) to the economic impact, measured for instance through hotel stays and tourist visits (e.g. Herrero et al. 2006; Richards and Rotariu 2011; Falk and Hagsten 2017). The impacts of the initiative have also been a key focus of the *ex post* evaluations commissioned both by local authorities and the EU. In addition, scholars have been interested in the media discourses and representations of the designated cities (e.g. Aiello and Trulow 2006; García 2005, 2010). The impacts of the ECOC initiative have typically been analyzed by taking one ECOC as a case study. However, some broader investigations have applied a comparative approach (e.g. Myerscough 1994; Palmer 2004a, 2004b; Palmer and Richards 2007, 2009; Sassatelli 2009; Palmer, Richards, and Dodd 2011, 2012). Previous explorations of the ECOC initiative have considered the construction of European identity (e.g. Hansen 2002; Reme 2002; Sassatelli 2009). Nevertheless, we still need a deeper analysis of the visitors to ECOC events and how they construct the notion of Europe and their 'Europeanness' while participating in the EU initiative that explicitly seeks to increase their belonging to Europe (see however Lähdesmäki 2014c, 2014d, 2014e).

Compared to the ECOC, the EHL is a much more recent EU initiative. This is reflected by the quantity of research exploring it. The EHL has been analyzed in some studies as part of EU cultural and heritage politics and policies (e.g. Calligaro 2010, 2013; Kaiser 2014; Lähdesmäki 2014a, 2014b, 2016, 2017b; Niklasson 2017; Jakubowski, Hausler, and Fiorentini 2019; Lähdesmäki and Mäkinen 2019; Lähdesmäki, Kaasik-Krogerus, and Mäkinen 2019; Zito, Eckersley, and Turner 2019). The authors of this book have previously published an in-depth analysis of the implementation of the EHL initiative, approaching it from various perspectives, such as governance, geopolitics, participation, and gender (Lähdesmäki et al. 2020). Our research team has also analyzed exhibition narratives at several heritage sites awarded the EHL (Kaasik-Krogerus 2019; Čeginskas and Kaasik-Krogerus 2020; Turunen 2020). In the research on the EHL initiative, there is little in-depth exploration of visitors' experiences and their perceptions of Europe and the 'European' at heritage sites that are required to emphasize a 'European dimension' of cultural heritage.

Our review of the existing literature indicates that deeper qualitative analyses of the notions of Europe and the 'European' among participants in EU cultural initiatives are few. Even fewer are studies that compare such qualitative results between different initiatives. Our book seeks to fill this research gap at the intersection between studies of EU cultural policy, European identity and belonging, and visitors. Moreover, our book offers a comparative and longitudinal approach to the construction of Europe from below. Our case studies cover the period from 2010 to 2018. Our longitudinal approach enables us to analyze transformation and stability in the notions of Europe and the 'European'. It is motivated by the recent transformations in Europe: as discussed above, the EU has begun to search for a new inclusive European narrative in order to increase belonging to and unity in Europe as a response to the various challenges of the 2010s. Our data includes material from 12 countries belonging to Western, Southern, Eastern, Northern, and Central Europe. Our comparative approach goes beyond comparing the findings from our three cases and makes it possible to explore the participants' notions of Europe in relation to various demographic factors, such as their geographical location, gender, age, education, and cultural participation.

3   Three Cases: The European Capital of Culture, European Citizen
       Campus, and European Heritage Label

The three cases discussed in our book, the ECOC, the ECC, and the EHL, share certain similarities. All three have been funded from the EU's cultural programme; thus they follow the EU's cultural political agendas and have similar policy goals, such as promoting Europe's cultural diversity and shared heritage, promoting intercultural dialogue, and strengthening a feeling of belonging to Europe and the EU. Yet, they differ in terms of implementation, funding, length, and the number of people they reach. The initiatives also represent divergent foci in EU cultural policy – urbanity, citizenship education through creativity, and cultural heritage. These cases reflect the cultural and identity political interest common to many EU cultural initiatives and offer manifold data to explore the notions of Europe among their participants. As a case study, our research does not seek to generalize our findings to cover all EU cultural initiatives.

The ECOC initiative was launched in 1985, when the ministers of cultural affairs in the member states of the European Community adopted a resolution to hold an annual event named the European City of Culture. The initiative was run as an intergovernmental scheme until 1999, when it was transformed into an official action of the European Parliament and Council and renamed the European Capital of Culture. The new official status of the initiative did not have a major impact on its EU funding but it enabled the Union to formulate a more detailed set of regulations, criteria, and guidelines for its implementation (Oerters and Mittag 2008, 75). The annual process of selecting the ECOCs is based on applications from candidate cities. They first compete for the designation at the national level. National panels in the member states suggest their final candidates to an international expert panel appointed at the European level. Based on the selection of this panel, the European Commission finally designates cities as ECOC. Since 1997, it has been possible for several cities to be designated simultaneously. By 2020, 62 cities have celebrated their designation as European City/Capital of Culture (see the list of ECOCs in Annex 2).

During the past decades, the implementation of the ECOC initiative at the local level has undergone various changes as the cities have aimed to utilize the designation to further current cultural and urban policies (Lähdesmäki 2014e). Over its history, the ECOC designation has developed from a short-term cultural festival into a year-long urban event that enables economic and social development of the city, regeneration of the city space, and participation of civil society actors in various political and cultural processes in the city (see Richards and Palmer 2010, 205–206; Sassatelli 2013, 64–66; Staiger 2013, 33). The ECOC initiative includes some funds allocated for the selected cities. Since 2007, the EU has supported each ECOC with a Melina Mercouri prize of 1.5 million euros. Yet, the EU funding still comprises only a small fraction of a city's total budget for the ECOC year.

One of the central purposes of the EU cultural programmes is to distribute financial support for multi-annual cooperation projects in the field of culture. In these programmes, the European Commission opens calls for proposals for general cooperation projects as well as thematic calls for operators in various fields of culture. The small-scale projects must include a project leader and at least two partner organizations from at least three countries, while the large-scale projects must have at least five partners in addition to the project leader from at least six countries. The maximum duration of all the projects is four years. The projects funded through the EU's cultural programmes are a central way of putting the policy discourses of these programmes into practice. As an example of the projects funded through the EU's cultural programmes, our book explores the ECC.

The ECC was an EU-funded temporary project launched in 2013. It focused on citizenship education through artistic laboratories that took place in summer 2014 in six European countries. A total of 144 students from various universities in the Netherlands, Luxemburg, France, Germany, Italy, and Portugal worked in thematic laboratories led by 12 artists. The themes and the host cities of the laboratories were: identity in Antwerp, dialogue in Luxembourg, roots in Strasbourg, home in Freiburg, conflict in Padova, and freedom in Viana do Castelo. The art forms used in the laboratories included painting, clay work, sculpture made from waste material, illustration, photography, dance, and music. Through artistic work, the students elaborated on the themes of the laboratories. The project ended with a final conference and an art exhibition organized in Antwerp in June 2015.

The EU's most recent heritage action is the European Heritage Label. The EHL is not a funding instrument as it does not include any regular financing measures for the sites but rather focuses on networking and cooperation among them. The scheme was launched in 2006 as an intergovernmental initiative run by the EU's Ministries of Culture. By 2011, 68 sites had been awarded the Label. It was considered difficult to effectively implement the initiative on an intergovernmental basis due to the lack of coordination and opportunities for operational arrangements (Lähdesmäki 2014a). Yet, the scheme was considered important by the European Parliament and Council, and in 2008 the Council adopted conclusions transforming the initiative into an official EU action. Previously awarded sites were required to reapply for the 'official' Label. The idea of heritage is understood in the EHL action both in tangible and intangible terms, as the decision defines heritage as "monuments, natural, underwater, archaeological, industrial or urban sites, cultural landscapes, places of remembrance, cultural goods and objects and intangible heritage associated with a place, including contemporary heritage" (EP&C 2011, 3).

The European Commission used the ECOC as a case in point for establishing the EHL. Therefore, the selection procedures in these two initiatives are similar. The EHL sites are first pre-selected at the national level. The final selec-tion is then made by an international expert panel appointed at the EU level, and the Labels are awarded for the selected sites by the European Commission. In contrast to the ECOCs, the EHLs are selected biannually and the award is permanent. The sites may, however, lose their Label if they do not continue to fulfil the criteria of the action during the monitoring processes. The number of labelled sites in each labelling year has ranged from four to 16. As of 2020, 48 sites from 19 EU member states have been awarded the official Label. These sites vary from well-known tourist attractions, such as the Acropolis in Athens, Greece, to lesser-known and smaller sites, such as the Franja Partisan Hospital in Slovenia, and from high cultural sites, such as Franz Liszt Music Academy in Budapest, Hungary, to sites of the EU's political history, such as places related to the negotiation of the Maastricht Treaty in the Netherlands (see the list of EHL sites in Annex 3). The sites date from Neanderthal times to recent decades.

Our case studies of these three EU cultural initiatives have been conducted as part of different research projects over the past decade. The first of them focuses on the ECOC initiative, covering three cities: Pécs in Hungary, ECOC in 2010; Tallinn in Estonia, ECOC in 2011; and Turku in Finland, ECOC in 2011. The second study explores the ECC project, focusing on its implementation in Strasbourg, France and Freiburg, Germany. Moreover, this case study includes participant observation in the final conference of the project in Antwerp, Belgium. The third study examines the EHL in 11 heritage sites: Alcide De Gasperi's House Museum, Italy; Archaeological Park Carnuntum, Austria; Camp Westerbork, The Netherlands; European District of Strasbourg, France; Franz Liszt Academy of Music, Hungary; Great Guild Hall, Estonia; Hambach Castle, Germany; Historic Gdańsk Shipyard, Poland; Mundaneum, Belgium; Robert Schuman's House, France; and Sagres Promontory, Portugal.

The analysis of the three cases is based on ethnographic field research that included various modes of observing the implementation of the initiatives and people who participated in them, or, in the case of the EHL, visited the heritage sites and their exhibitions. The field research for the ECOC and the ECC cases was conducted by only one of the authors of this book, Lähdesmäki for the ECOC in 2010 and 2011 and Mäkinen for the ECC in 2014 and 2015, respectively. In contrast, EHL case study is based on team ethnography jointly conducted by the book's four authors in 2017 and 2018. The research team included a fifth scholar, Johanna Turunen, who did not co-author this book. We have discussed our epistemological approach to team ethnography and practices, including our experiences with it, in depth elsewhere (Lähdesmäki et al. 2020; Turunen et al. 2020). Although all four of us did not participate in the field research of all three case studies, for this book, we analyzed and discussed them collaboratively, based on extensive knowledge exchange, sharing our ideas, findings, and experiences, and writing the book together.

4   Previous Discussions on the Idea of Europe

The research on the idea of European identity as such has a long tradition in academia. During the past decades, scholars have extensively explored the construction of European identity in relation to social, political, and cultural transformations in Europe, the development of the EU, and European integration (e.g. Risse 2003, 2006; Bruter 2003, 2004, 2005; Herrmann and Brewer 2004; Mayer and Palmowski 2004; Beck and Grande 2007; Antonsich 2008; Pichler 2008, 2009; Checkel and Katzenstein 2009; Kaina, Karolewski, and Kuhn 2015; Triandafyllidou and Gropas 2015; Waechter 2019). In addition, identifications of Europeans have been regularly investigated through broad surveys, such as the European Value Survey and Eurobarometer surveys.

The European integration process and the development of the EU has generated extensive academic literature on the transforming character of Europe. In this literature, Europe is commonly perceived as a conceptual rather than geographical entity that has been both historically and philosophically a "moving target" and, thus, so "elusive that it is doubtful whether [it has] any reality at all outside the imagination", as Kockel, Nic Craith, and Frykman (2012, 1) note. Instead of a factual reality, scholars have perceived Europe rather as an idea or narrative (e.g. Delanty 1995; Lee and Bideleux 2009; Stone 2014). In conceptual histories and conceptual research into its politics (e.g. Stråth 2000a; 2000b; Wiesner and Schmidt-Gleim 2014), Europe has been taken as a changing, contested, and contingent political construction that is produced in diverse political discourses and debates. Indeed, Europe has been 'imagined' in numerous ways in the course of history and continues to be constructed through imaginations in politics, media, history writing, museums, heritage sites, literature, art, and everyday practices of and interaction between people living in the continent. This is also our approach. For us, Europe is a fluid and constantly transforming idea that is constructed through and in relation to various discourses, meanings, and practices; it is intertwined with spatial and temporal scales.

In both public discourses and EU policy rhetoric, Europe is often represented as a singular and discernible unit, yet paradoxically left as an abstract and undefined entity. Yet, the continent has been, and still is, divided by various concrete physical boundaries, as well as symbolic and discursive divisions that influence people's notions of Europe, and of what and who belongs to it.

These boundaries and divisions have contributed to creating diverse political, spatial, religious, cultural, and social internal 'others' in Europe's history, such as the Roma and Jews, whose 'otherness' depends on their various positions in European societies. Due to historical and recent internal boundaries, such as the division between the Eastern and Western blocs, the idea of Europe differs considerably between different geographical European locations (Malmborg and Stråth 2002; Straczuk 2012). The ideas also vary between people belonging to different social and educational strata (Lähdesmäki 2014c).

Internal divisions are not the only factor in differing conceptions of Europe. Various scholars have noted how the idea of Europe has been and continues to be constructed in relation to Europe's external 'others' (Stråth 2000a; Brague 2002; Pagden 2002; Wiesner and Schmidt 2014; Schmidt-Gleim 2014). Ambivalence towards these 'others' has been manifested in concrete relations with non-European peoples but also through creating images of the 'other' based not on observation or personal experience but on psychological drives, as Passerini (2002, 201–202) claims (on the Eurocentric view in past studies, see also Clifford and Marcus 1986). The indivisible nature of these concrete and imaginary relations is underlined by studies that emphasize how attempts to define the idea of Europe as a mentally and culturally unified continent have strengthened in periods when the continent has been perceived as being under threat. The idea of Europe and a European identity have been commonly formulated through diverse antitheses of Europe and perceived threats to it, such as the Turks, Russians, American or Asian economic powers, or Islam, just to mention a few (Mikkeli 1998). The attempts to define Europe through its 'other' have also culminated in the views of Europe as more progressive and civilized than other continents, thus furthering perceptions of racial superiority.

Similarly to Europe, the EU has been explored and explained in various studies through its relations to the 'other' (e.g. Shore 2006; Eder 2006; Wilken 2012). As Wilken (2012, 132) notes, "the EU itself may be defined as a union of Others", as its member states have been or still are the 'other' to some other member states. Since the 1960s, policy discourses of the European Community, and later the EU, have defined a European identity in terms of common values, such as democracy, freedom, human rights, and the rule of law. In this discourse, 'Europe's other' is elicited from totalitarian and undemocratic regimes and their politics, thus as a negation of the aforementioned 'European' values (Wilken 2012).

The enlargement of the EU has transformed the concrete divisions in Europe but simultaneously created new ones between the Union and the non-EU states, and consequently fueled discussions about whether countries on the borders of the EU belong to Europe. EU enlargements have produced 'liminal positions', characterized by the ambiguity of "being Europe but not quite Europe" and by being half-insider-half-outsider, as Mälksoo (2009, 67) describes the condition of the Baltic countries after the EU's eastern enlargement in 2004.

The EU's 'others' have also been distinguished in time. In the EU's own history discourse, European integration has been justified by appealing to the need to prevent a return to Europe's warlike past, particularly the horrors of World War II and the political division of Europe during the Cold War (Lähdesmäki 2017a). In this discourse, past wars, struggles, and conflicts, such as the closed borders between the Eastern and Western blocs after World War II, are compared to the imagined presence of the EU represented by its positive virtues and values in EU policy discourse, such as peace, tolerance, solidarity, and free movement. As EU history discourse commonly narrates the difficult pasts of Europe as located in the history of nation states, this leads to the discourse positioning a 'Europe of the nation states' as the EU's 'other' (Wilken 2012, 133; see also Hellström 2006, 94; Lähdesmäki 2017a).

The terms Europe and the EU are often intertwined in the EU policy rhetoric. This intertwinement is particularly created through EU initiatives in which the idea of Europe is emphasized, constructed, and promoted – but also conditioned – by the EU. We use the term EUrope to refer to this kind of discursive intertwinement in which Europe as a geographical continent and the EU as an institutional entity are closely linked without making any clear distinction between them (Lähdesmäki et al. 2020; Turunen 2020). The discourse of EUrope is also commonly used in media discussions and everyday talk – and thus occurs in our data from the participants in EU initiatives. This is not surprising, as EUrope is a construction and an ideal that the EU cultural initiatives seek to advance.

Due to the fluidity of the notion of Europe and its nature as an imagination, idea, and narrative, it is difficult to distinguish Europe as a noun from the 'European' as an adjective. It is even more difficult to distinguish the concept of 'Europeanness' as a quality or characteristic of being European. All these different aspects of what Europe is, who belongs to it, and what is common or typical to 'Europeans', intertwine in political, cultural, and everyday discussions. This is why we do not seek to distinguish clearly between them in our book but rather perceive them are inseparable components of the same idea or imagination.

5   The Analysis of Europe and the 'European' in This Book

To scrutinize our fluid, transforming, and 'moving target', Europe, and how it is understood and given meanings from below in the context of EU cultural initiatives, our research methods need to allow different 'voices' to be heard and show the sensitivity to understand them. Ethnography enables us to approach the processes of constructing Europe and the 'European' among diverse people. Due to our thematic focus, we describe our methodology as 'ethnography of Europeanization' in which the emphasis is not (only) on participation in EU cultural initiatives but on Europe itself as an idea and an ongoing process constructed and governed by various actors at different levels. Previous ethnographic studies of EU cultural initiatives have mainly focused on actors, policy makers, and 'EU elites' operating from 'above' (e.g. Shore 2000; Sassatelli 2009), while ethnographic studies with an interest in cultural notions of Europe at the micro level do not usually deal with the EU's cultural initiatives or policies (e.g. Macdonald 2013). In our ethnography, we investigate how the participants in our three cases discursively and performatively give meanings to and construct Europe and the 'European' from below within the framework of the EU's politics of belonging. These meaning-making processes are based on finding connections and similarities between people and cultural features in Europe, but also on making distinctions between 'us' and 'them', as our analysis shows.

Our book is structured in eight chapters. Following this first introductory chapter, we discuss five core concepts of this book, culture, identity, belonging, participation, and citizenship, and their intertwined nature in Chapter 2. Our concepts and diverse meanings related to them stem from the policy discourses related to our case studies and the EU initiatives, as well as the ethnographic data created and gathered among their participants and visitors. We claim that these concepts form the core of the EU's politics of belonging. This is where we lay the theoretical and methodological foundations of our book: politics of belonging and ethnography of Europeanization.

Chapter 3 provides an overview of the development of the EU cultural policy and initiatives. Here, we introduce in more detail the EU's central programmes regarding culture (e.g. Culture 2000, Culture, and Creative Europe) that form the common policy framework for all the three cases in the book. In this chapter, we discuss the role of EU cultural policy in the Union's politics of belonging by distinguishing two entwined modes, or clusters, of creating belonging: an identity-building agenda and a participatory agenda.

The case studies follow in Chapters 4, 5, and 6, focusing on meso- and, particularly, micro-level data. Each of these chapters start by exploring the construction of Europe and the 'European' in the meso-level material, highlighting the 'voice' of local managers of these EU initiatives. This material includes ECOC bid books and promotional and information material of the ECC project and EHL sites. After this, the analysis moves to the micro level, investigating our field research data and discussing how participants in these initiatives give meanings to Europe and the 'European' in a variety of ways. The case studies share a common theoretical framework – politics of belonging – and a common methodological approach – ethnography of Europeanization – but in each case, we deal with the data and perceive themes from it in different ways. These differences stem from the contexts of the case initiatives and their implementation, as well as the type of data created and gathered during the fieldwork.

Chapter 7 compares the findings from the case studies and traces similarities and differences in participants' notions of Europe and the 'European'. These similarities and differences are interpreted in the context of the case initiatives and transforming reality in Europe in the 2010s. In this chapter, we focus on the interrelation between the social locations and views of our participants. We discuss how various background factors – such as gender, age, nationality, education, and activeness in cultural participation – affect their notions of Europe and the 'European'.

To conclude, in Chapter 8 we summarize how the notions of 'Europe' and the 'European' are constructed in EU cultural initiatives from below by perceiving Europe as characterized by diversity, mobility, nationalities, languages, politics, culture, and temporal, spatial, and social relations. Based on these results, we then formulate two dominant strands of European narratives. While the first of these emphasizes Europe in terms of cultural differences and distinct nation states, the second underlines a personal approach to belonging to Europe and is associated with affective experiences that are used to construct a notion of a transnational 'shared space' in Europe. In the conclusion, we explore the intertwined cultural and social dimensions of Europe and discuss the politics of belonging on a more abstract level. We stress the contradictory notions of belonging and non-belonging to Europe and how ideas of Europe are constructed in relation to 'others' inside and outside Europe. Our data reveals various inclusive and solidarity-based notions of 'Europe' that emphasize diversity in Europe. However, it also reveals explicitly and implicitly exclusive notions in which 'Europe' and the 'European' are based on bordering and making distinctions between 'us' and 'them'.

In this book, we examine how Europe and the 'European' are constructed from below. As this examination is grounded in research about EU-level policy discourses on Europe, we are able to explore differences and similarities between the notions of Europe from below and from above – between participants in EU cultural initiatives and EU policy discourse. Our exploration of the dynamics between EU cultural policy and the experiences of people participating in its initiatives reveals several gaps in the aims and effects of EU policies. As a core result of this exploration, we propose that 'Europe' and the 'European' are constructed in EU cultural initiatives not top-down or bottom-up but as an interrelated two-way process comprised of personal everyday experiences and interaction between Europeans and 'banal', well-known, and often-repeated representations and narratives of the continent and its inhabitants.

References

Aiello, G., and C. Thurlow. 2006. "Symbolic Capitals: Visual Discourse and Intercultural Exchange in the European Capitals of Culture Scheme." *Language and Intercultural Communication* 6 (2): 148–162.

Antonsich, M. 2008. "The Narration of Europe in 'National' and 'Post-national' Terms: Gauging the Gap between Normative Discourses and People's Views." *European Journal of Social Theory* 11 (4): 505–522.

Bache, I., and M. Flinders. 2004. "Themes and Issues in Multi-level Governance". In *Multi-level Governance*, edited by I. Bache and M. Flinders, 1–14. Oxford: Oxford University Press.

Beck, U., and E. Grande. 2007. *Cosmopolitan Europe*. Cambridge: Polity Press.

Berg, C., and H. Rommetvedt. 2009. *Stavanger-regionen som europeisk kulturhovedstad – slik innbyggerne ser det*. Rapport 203. Stavanger: International Research Institute of Stavanger.

Bergsgard, N. A., and A. Vassenden. 2011. "The Legacy of Stavanger as Capital of Culture in Europe 2008: Watershed or Puff of Wind?" *International Journal of Cultural Policy* 17 (3): 301–320.

Brague, R. 2002. *Eccentric Culture: A Theory of Western Civilization*. South Bend, Ind.: St. Augustine's Press.

Bruter, M. 2003. "Winning Hearts and Minds for Europe. The Impact of News and Symbols on Civic and Cultural European Identity." *Comparative Political Studies* 36 (10): 1148–1179.

Bruter, M. 2004. "Civic and Cultural Components of a European Identity: A Pilot Model of Measurement of Citizens' Levels." In *Transnational Identities. Becoming European in the EU*, edited by R. K. Herrmann, T. Risse, and M. B. Brewer, 186–213. Oxford: Rowman & Battlefield.

Bruter, M. 2005. *Citizens of Europe? The Emergence of a Mass European Identity*. New York: Palgrave Macmillan.

Calligaro, O. 2010. "EU Action in the Field of Heritage: A Contribution to the Discussion on the Role of Culture in the European Integration Process." In *Cultures nationales et identité communautaire: Un défi pour l'Europe?*, edited by M. Beers and J. Raflik, 87–98. Berlin: Peter Lang.

Calligaro, O. 2013. *Negotiating Europe: EU Promotion of Europeanness Since the 1950s*. New York: Palgrave Macmillan.

Campbell, P. 2011. "Creative Industries in a European Capital of Culture." *International Journal of Cultural Policy* 17 (5): 510–522.

Čeginskas, V. L. A., and S. Kaasik-Krogerus. 2020. "Politics of Solidarity in the Context of European Heritage. The Cases of the European Solidarity Centre and Hambach Castle." *International Journal of Heritage Studies* 26 (10): 998–1012. doi: 10.1080/13527258.2019.1663235.

Checkel, J. T., and P. J. Katzenstein, eds. 2009. *European Identity*. Cambridge: Cambridge University Press.

Clifford, J., and G. E. Marcus, eds. 1986. *Writing Culture. The Poetics and Politics of Ethnography*. Berkeley and Los Angeles: University of California Press.

Delanty, G. 1995. *Inventing Europe: Idea, Identity, Reality*. Basingstoke: MacMillan Press.

Eder, K. 2006. "Europe's Borders: The Narrative Construction of the Boundaries of Europe." *European Journal of Social Theory* 9 (2): 255–271.

EP&C (European Parliament and the Council). 2006. "Decision NO 1855/2006/EC of the European Parliament and of the Council of 12 December 2006 Establishing the Culture Programme (2007 to 2013)." *Official Journal of the European Union* L 372: 1–11.

EP&C (European Parliament and the Council). 2013. "Regulation (EU) NO 1295/2013 of the European Parliament and of the Council of 11 December 2013 Establishing the Creative Europe Programme (2014 to 2020) and repealing Decisions No 1718/2006/ EC, No 1855/2006/EC and No 1041/2009/EC." *Official Journal of the European Union* L 347: 221–237.

EP&C (European Parliament and the Council). 2011. "Decision No. 1194/2011/EU of the European Parliament and of the Council of 16 November 2011: Establishing a European Union Action for the European Heritage Label." *Official Journal of the European Union* L 303: 1–9.

Falk, M., and E. Hagsten. 2017. "Measuring the Impact of the European Capital of Culture Programme on Overnight Stays: Evidence for the Last Two Decades." *European Planning Studies* 25 (12): 2175–2191.

García, B. 2004a. "Cultural Policy in European Cities: Lessons from Experience, Prospects for the Future." *Local Economy* 19 (4): 312–326.

García, B. 2004b. "Urban Regeneration, Arts Programming and Major Events: Glasgow 1990, Sydney 2000 and Barcelona 2004." *International Journal for Cultural Policy* 10 (1): 103–118.

García, B. 2005. "Deconstructing the City of Culture: The Long-Term Cultural Legacies of Glasgow 1990." *Urban Studies* 42 (5): 841–868.

García, B. 2010. *Media Impact Assessment (part II): Evolving Press and Broadcast Narratives on Liverpool from 1996 to 2009*. Liverpool: University of Liverpool.

Hansen, K. 2002. "Festivals, Spatiality and the New Europe." *Ethnologia Europaea* 32 (2): 19–36.

Heikkinen, T. 2000. "In from the Margins: The City of Culture 2000 and the Image Transformation of Helsinki." *International Journal of Cultural Policy* 6 (2): 201–218.

Hellström, A. 2006. *Bringing Europe down to Earth*. Lund: Lund University Press.

Herrero, L. C., J. Á. Sanz, M. Devesa, A. Bedate, and M. J. del Barrio. 2006. "The Economic Impact of Cultural Events: A Case-Study of Salamanca 2002, European Capital of Culture." *European Urban and Regional Studies* 13 (1): 41–57.

Herrmann, R. K., and M. B. Brewer. 2004. "Identities and Institutions: Becoming European in the EU." In *Transnational Identities. Becoming European in the EU*, edited by R. K. Herrmann, T. Risse, and M. B. Brewer, 1–22. Oxford: Rowman & Battlefield.

Hooghe, L., and G. Marks. 2001. *Multi-level Governance and European Integration*. Lanham: Rowman and Littlefield.

Hudec, O., and P. Džupka. 2016. "Culture-led Regeneration through the Young Generation: Košice as the European Capital of Culture." *European Urban and Regional Studies* 23 (3): 531–538.

Jakubowski, A., K. Hausler, and F. Fiorentini, eds. 2019. *Cultural Heritage in the European Union*. Leiden: Brill.

Jenkins, R. 2008. "The Ambiguity of Europe." *European Societies* 10 (2): 153–176.

Kaasik-Krogerus, S. 2019. "Politics of Mobility and Stability in Authorizing European Heritage: Estonia's Great Guild Hall." In *Dissonant Heritages and Memories in Contemporary Europe*, edited by T. Lähdesmäki, L. Passerini, S. Kaasik-Krogerus, and I.van Huis, 157–181. New York: Palgrave Macmillan.

Kaina, V., I. P. Karolewski, and S. Kuhn, eds. 2015. *European Identity Revisited: New Approaches and Recent Empirical Evidence*. London: Routledge.

Kaiser, S. 2014. *The European Heritage Label: A Critical Review of a New EU Policy*. Unpublished MA Thesis, University of Illinois, USA.

Kandyla, A. 2015. "The Creative Europe Programme: Policy-Making Dynamics and Outcomes." In *Cultural Governance and the European Union: Protecting and Promoting Cultural Diversity in Europe*, edited by E. Psychogiopoulou, 49–60. New York: Palgrave Macmillan.

Karlsson, K.-G. 2010. "The Uses of History and the Third Wave of Europeanisation." In *A European Memory? Contested Histories and Politics of Remembrance*, edited by M. Pakier and B. Stråth, 38–55. New York: Berghahn Books.

Kockel, U., M. Nic Craith, and J. Frykman. 2012. "Introduction: The Frontiers of Europe and European Ethnology." In *A Companion to the Anthropology of Europe*, edited by U. Kockel, M. Nic Craith, and J. Frykman, 1–10. Oxford: Blackwell Publishing.

Lähdesmäki, T. 2014a. "The EU's Explicit and Implicit Heritage Politics." *European Societies* 16 (3): 401–421.

Lähdesmäki, T. 2014b. "Transnational Heritage in the Making. Strategies for Narrating Cultural Heritage as European in the Intergovernmental Initiative of the European Heritage Label." *Ethnologica Europaea* 44 (1): 75–93.

Lähdesmäki, T. 2014c. "The Influence on Cultural Competence on the Interpretations of Territorial Identities in European Capitals of Culture." *Baltic Journal of European Studies* 4 (1): 69–96.

Lähdesmäki, T. 2014d. *Identity Politics in the European Capital of Culture Initiative.* Joensuu: University of Eastern Finland.

Lähdesmäki, T. 2014e. "Discourses of Europeanness in the Reception of the European Capital of Culture Events: The Case of Pécs 2010." *European Urban and Regional Studies* 21 (2): 191–205.

Lähdesmäki, T. 2016. "Politics of Tangibility, Intangibility, and Place in the Making of European Cultural Heritage in EU Heritage Policy." *International Journal of Heritage Studies* 22 (10): 766–780.

Lähdesmäki, T. 2017a. "Narrativity and Intertextuality in the Making of a Shared European Memory." *Journal of Contemporary European Studies* 25 (1): 57–72.

Lähdesmäki, T. 2017b. "Politics of Affect in the EU Heritage Policy Discourse: An Analysis of Promotional Videos of Sites Awarded with the European Heritage Label." *International Journal of Heritage Studies* 23 (8): 709–722.

Lähdesmäki, T. 2020. "Politics of Belonging in Brussels' European Quarter." *International Journal of Heritage Studies* 26 (10): 979–997. doi: 10.1080/13527258.2019.1663237.

Lähdesmäki, T., V. L. A. Čeginskas, S. Kaasik-Krogerus, K. Mäkinen, and J. Turunen. 2020. *Creating and Governing Cultural Heritage in the European Union: The European Heritage Label.* London: Routledge.

Lähdesmäki, T., S. Kaasik-Krogerus, and K. Mäkinen. 2019. "Genealogy of the Concept of Heritage in the European Commission's Policy Discourse." *Contributions to the History of Concepts* 14 (1): 115–139.

Lähdesmäki, T., and K. Mäkinen. 2019. "The 'European Significance' of Heritage: Politics of Scale in EU Heritage Policy Discourse." In *Politics of Scale. New Directions in Critical Heritage Studies*, edited by T. Lähdesmäki, S. Thomas, and Y. Zhu, 36–49. New York: Berghahn's Books.

Lassur, S., K. Tafel-Viia, K. Summatavet, and E. Terk. 2010. "Intertwining of Drivers in Formation of New Policy Focus: Case of Creative Industries in Tallinn." *The Nordic Journal of Cultural Policy* 13 (1): 59–85.

Lee, C., and R. Bideleux. 2009. "'Europe': What kind of idea?" *The European Legacy* 14 (2): 163–176.

Liz, M. 2016. *Euro-Visions: Europe in Contemporary Cinema.* New York: Bloomsbury.

Macdonald, S., 2013. *Memorylands. Heritage and Identity in Europe Today.* London: Routledge.

Mäkinen, K. 2012. *Ohjelmoidut eurooppalaiset. Kansalaisuus ja kulttuuri EU-asiakirjoissa* [Programmed Europeans. Citizenship and Culture in EU Documents]. Jyväskylä: University of Jyväskylä.

Mäkinen, K. 2014. "Constructing Europe as an Area via EU Documents on Citizenship and Culture." In *The Meanings of Europe: Changes and Exchanges of a Contested Concept* edited by C. Wiesner and M. Schmidt-Gleim, 130–143. London: Routledge.

Mälksoo, M. 2009. "Liminality and Contested Europeanness. Conflicting Memory Politics in the Baltic Space." In *Identity and Foreign Policy. Baltic-Russian Relations and European Integration*, edited by E. Berg and P. Ehin, 65–84. London: Routledge.

Malmborg, M. af, and B. Stråth, eds. 2002. *The Meaning of Europe: Variety and Contention Within and Among Nations*. Oxford: Berg.

Mayer, F. C., and J. Palmowski. 2004. "European Identities and the EU – The Ties That Bind the People of Europe." *Journal of Common Market Studies* 42 (3): 573–598.

Mikkeli, H. 1998. *Europe as an Idea and an Identity*. Basingstoke: Palgrave Macmillan.

Monnet, J. 1955. *Les Etats-Unis d'Europe ont Commencé*. Paris: Laffont.

Myerscough, J. 1994. *European Cities of Culture and Cultural Months*. Glasgow: The Network of Cultural Cities of Europe.

Näss, H. E. 2009. *A New Agenda? The European Union and Cultural Policy*. London: Alliance Publishing Trust.

Näss, H. E. 2010. "The Ambiguities of Intercultural Dialogue: Critical Perspectives on the European Union's New Agenda for Culture." *Journal of Intercultural Communication* 23. Accessed 23 March 2020. https://www.immi.se/intercultural/nr23/nass.htm

Niklasson, E. 2017. "The Janus-Face of European Heritage: Revisiting the Rhetoric of Europe-Making in EU Cultural Politics." *Journal of Social Archaeology* 17 (2): 138–162.

Nousiainen, M., and K. Mäkinen. 2015. "Multilevel Governance and Participation: Interpreting Democracy in EU-programmes." *European Politics and Society* 16 (2): 208–223.

O'Callaghan, C. 2011. "Urban Anxieties and Creative Tensions in the European Capital of Culture 2005: 'It Couldn't Just Be about Cork, Like'." *International Journal of Cultural Policy* 18 (2): 185–204.

Oerters, K., and J. Mittag. 2008. "European Capitals of Culture as Incentives for Local Transformation and Creative Economies: Tendencies – Examples – Assessments." In *Whose Culture(s)? Proceedings of the Second Annual Conference of the University Network of European Capitals of Culture held in Liverpool 16–17 Oct 2008*, edited by W. Coudenys, 70–97. Pécs: The University Network of European Capitals of Culture.

Pagden, A., ed., 2002. *The Idea of Europe. From Antiquity to the European Union*. Cambridge: Cambridge University Press.

Palmer, R. 2004a. *European Cities and Capitals of Culture. Part I*. Brussels: European Commission & Palmer/Rae Associates.

Palmer, R. 2004b. *European Cities and Capitals of Culture: City Reports. Part II*. Brussels: European Commission & Palmer/Rae Associates.

Palmer, R., and G. Richards. 2007. *European Cultural Capital Report*. Arnhem: ATLAS.

Palmer, R., and G. Richards. 2009. *European Cultural Capital Report 2*. Arnhem: ATLAS.

Palmer, R., G. Richards, and D. Dodd. 2011. *European Cultural Capital Report 3*. Arnhem: ATLAS.

Palmer, R., G. Richards, and D. Dodd. 2012. *European Cultural Capital Report 4*. Arnhem: ATLAS.

Patel, K. K. 2013. "Introduction." In *The Cultural Politics of Europe: European Capitals of Culture and European Union Since the 1980s*, edited by K. K. Patel, 1–15. London: Routledge.

Passerini, L. 2002. "From the Ironies of Identity to the Identity of Irony." In *The Idea of Europe. From Antiquity to the European Union*, edited by A. Pagden, 191–208. Cambridge: Cambridge University Press.

Piattoni, S. 2009. "Multi-level Governance: A Historical and Conceptual Analysis." *European Integration* 31 (2): 163–180.

Pichler, F. 2008. "European Identities from Below: Meanings of Identification with Europe." *Perspectives on European Politics and Society* 9 (4): 411–430.

Pichler, F. 2009. "Cosmopolitan Europe. Views and Identity." *European Societies* 11 (1): 3–24.

Potschka, C., M. Fuchs, and A. Królikowski. 2013. "Review of European Expert Network on Culture's Audience Building and the Future Creative Europe Programme, 2012." *Cultural Trends* 22 (3/4): 265–269.

Prutsch, M. J. 2013. *European Historical Memory: Policies, Challenges and Perspectives*. Directorate-General for Internal Policies. Policy Department B: Structural and Cohesion Policies. Culture and Education. Brussels: European Parliament.

Psychogiopoulou, E. 2008. *Integration of Cultural Considerations in European Union Law and Policies*. Leiden: Martinus Nijhoff Publishers.

Reme, E. 2002. "Exhibition and Experience of Cultural Identity. The Case of Berger– European City of Culture." *Ethnologia Europaea* 32 (2): 37–46.

Richards, G. 2000. "The European Cultural Capital Event: Strategic Weapon in the Cultural Arms Race?" *Cultural Policy* 6 (2): 159–181.

Richards, G., and R. Palmer. 2010. *Eventful Cities: Cultural Management and Urban Revitalisation*. London: Routledge.

Richards, G., and I. Rotariu. 2011. *Ten Years of Cultural Development in Sibiu: The European Cultural Capital and Beyond*. Arnhem: ATLAS.

Richards, G., and J. Wilson. 2004. "The Impact of Cultural Events on City Image: Rotterdam, Cultural Capital of Europe 2001." *Urban Studies* 41 (10): 1931–1951.

Risse, T. 2003. "European Identity and the Heritage of National Culture." In *Rethinking Heritage. Cultures and Politics in Europe*, edited by R. S. Peckham, 74–89. London: I.B.Tauris.

Risse, T. 2006. "Neofunctionalism, European Identity, and the Puzzles of European Integration." *Journal of European Public Policy* 12 (2): 291–309.

Rommetvedt, H. 2008. "Beliefs in Culture as an Instrument for Regional Development: The Case of Stavanger, European Capital of Culture 2008." In *Regional and Urban Regeneration in European Peripheries: What Role for Culture?*, edited by L. Malíková and M. Sirák, 59–63. Bratislava: Institute of Public Policy.

Rosamond, B. 2000. *Theories of European Integration*. Basingstoke: Palgrave.

Sassatelli, M. 2002. "Imagined Europe." *European Journal of Social Theory* 5 (4): 435–451.

Sassatelli, M. 2006. "The Logic of Europeanizing Cultural Policy." In *Transcultural Europe. Cultural Policy in a Changing Europe*, edited by U. H. Meinhof and A. Triandafyllidou, 24–42. Basingstoke: Palgrave Macmillan.

Sassatelli, M. 2009. *Becoming Europeans. Cultural Identity and Cultural Policies*. New York: Palgrave Macmillan.

Sassatelli, M. 2013. "Europe's Several Capitals of Culture: From Celebration to Regeneration, to Polycentric Capitalization." In *The Cultural Politics of Europe. European Capitals of Culture and European Union Since the 1980s*, edited by K. K. Patel, 55–71. London: Routledge.

Schuman, R. 1963. *Pour l'Europe*. Paris: Nagel.

Schmidt-Gleim, M. 2014. "Europe and the Spectre of the Barbarian." In *The Meanings of Europe. Changes and Exchanges of a Contested Concept*, edited by C. Wiesner, and M. Schmidt-Gleim, 33–46. London: Routledge.

Shore, C. 1993. "Inventing the 'People's Europe': Critical Approaches to European Community 'Cultural Policy.'" *Man* 28 (4): 779–800.

Shore, C., 2000. *Building Europe: The Cultural Politics of European Integration*. London: Routledge.

Shore, C. 2006 "Government without Statehood? Anthropological Perspectives on Governance and Sovereignty in the European Union." *European Law Journal* 12 (6): 709–724.

Staiger, U. 2013. "The European Capitals of Culture in Context: Cultural Policy and the European Integration Process." In *The Cultural Politics of Europe. European Capitals of Culture and European Union Since the 1980s*, edited by K. K. Patel, 19–38. London: Routledge.

Straczuk, J. 2012. "Local Practices of European Identity on the New Eastern Borders of the EU." In *A Companion to the Anthropology of Europe*, edited by U. Kockel, M. Nic Craith, and J. Frykman, 199–211. Oxford: Blackwell Publishing.

Stone, D. 2014. *Goodbye to All That? The Story of Europe since 1945*. Oxford: Oxford University Press.

Stråth, B. ed. 2000a. *Europe and the Other and Europe as the Other*. Brussels: PIE-Peter Lang.

Stråth, B. ed. 2000b. *Myth and Memory on the Construction of Community. Historical Patterns in Europe and Beyond.* Brussels: PIE-Peter Lang.

Suárez C., and M. Luz. 2018. "Bridging the Competing Views of European Cultural Integration: The Transformative View of Culture as a Means to Promote Growth, Employment and Social Cohesion." *Romanian Review of Social Sciences* 8 (14): 28–41.

Treaty of Paris 1951. Treaty Constituting the European Coal and Steel Community. Luxembourg: Publishing Services of the European Communities.

Triandafyllidou, A., and R. Gropas. 2015. *What is Europe?* New York: Palgrave.

Turunen, J. 2020. "Decolonising European Minds through Heritage." *International Journal of Heritage Studies* 26 (10): 1013–1028. doi:10.1080/13527258.2019.1678051.

Turunen. J., V. L. A Čeginskas, S. Kaasik-Krogerus, T. Lähdesmäki, and K. Mäkinen. forthcoming 2020. "Poly-Space: Creating New Concepts through Reflexive Team Ethnography." In *Challenges and Solutions in Ethnographic Research: Ethnography with a Twist*, edited by T. Lähdesmäki, E. Koskinen-Koivisto, V. L. A. Čeginskas, and A.-K. Koistinen, 3–20. London: Routledge.

Vos, C. 2017. "European Integration through 'Soft Conditionality'. The Contribution of Culture to EU Enlargement in Southeast Europe." *International Journal of Cultural Policy* 23 (6): 675–689.

Waechter, N. 2019. *The Construction of European Identity among Ethnic Minorities: 'Euro-minorities' in Generational Perspective.* London: Routledge.

Wiesner, C., and M. Schmidt-Gleim. 2014. "The Meanings of Europe: Introduction." In *The Meanings of Europe. Changes and Exchanges of a Contested Concept*, edited by C. Wiesner, and M. Schmidt-Gleim, 1–15. London: Routledge.

Wilken, L. 2012. "Anthropological Studies of European Identity Construction." In *A Companion to the Anthropology of Europe*, edited by U. Kockel, M. Nic Craith, and J. Frykman, 125–144. Oxford: Blackwell Publishing.

Yuval-Davis, N. 2006. "Belonging and the Politics of Belonging." *Patterns of Prejudice* 40 (3): 197–214.

Yuval-Davis, N. 2011. *The Politics of Belonging. Intersectional Contestations.* London: Sage.

Žilič-Fišer, S., and K. Erjavec. 2017. "The Political Impact of the European Capital of Culture: 'Maribor 2012 Gave Us the Power to Change the Regime'." *International Journal of Cultural Policy* 23 (5): 581–596.

Zito, A., S. Eckersley, and S. Turner. 2019. "The instruments of European heritage." In *Dimensions of Heritage and Memory. Multiple Europes and the Politics of Crisis*, edited by C. Whitehead, S. Eckersley, M. Daugbjerg, and G. Bozoğlu, 50–71. London: Routledge.

CHAPTER 2

Politics of Belonging: Concepts and Method

1   Politics of Belonging as an Intersectional Approach

We focus on studying citizens' subjective sense of belonging as well as how their construction of belonging interacts with agendas to enhance it in and through EU cultural initiatives, which we consider as politics of belonging. We understand politics of belonging in EU cultural policy as constructing and conveying notions about Europe and the 'European' to a wider public through diverse discursive, narrative, and cultural resources, which help to justify the Union's specific policies of European integration. In these processes, belonging functions as a discursive resource, which constructs, claims, justifies, or resists forms of socio-spatial inclusion and exclusion (see Antonsich 2010).

In our book, politics of belonging in the context of EU cultural policy is conceptualized through competing interpretations in the meaning-making processes of diverse actors. Our focus on audiences of the European Capital of Culture (ECOC) events, participants in the European Citizen Campus (ECC) project, and visitors of heritage sites awarded the European Heritage Label (EHL) helps us to explore the plurality of positions and formulations of belonging to Europe *from below*. We investigate how the production of meaning and creation of narrative attachments to Europe and the 'European' take place among citizens who participate in the EU cultural initiatives as well as whether and how these initiatives contribute to the citizens' sense of belonging. Instead of analyzing the reception of top-down EU narratives and their impacts on European citizens in different EU initiatives and their settings, we scrutinize how citizens' attachment or non-attachment to Europe manifests *from below* by analyzing their participation, agency, and co-construction of Europe in various discourses and narratives. We view these acts and manifestations as part of Europeanization, which we explore as a process that creates a new form of social organization through producing a distinctive discursive field (Sassatelli 2010, 68). Our analysis tries to identify aspects of Europeanization common to our diverse sets of data as well as to explore the interaction between top-down and bottom-up processes included in these aspects.

Our approach to understanding belonging to Europe goes beyond a rigid division between macro-, meso-, and micro-level actors, since we understand notions and politics of belonging to be formed by a fluid interaction between manifold interpretations and circulation of ideas at different levels. According to Yuval-Davis (2006, 197), the politics of belonging comprise "specific political projects aimed at constructing belonging in particular ways to particular collectivities that are, at the same time, themselves being constructed by these projects in very particular ways". Politics of belonging pertains to contestations to individual participation, membership, citizenship, social status, and specific narratives of identification (see Yuval-Davis 2006, 205). As Yuval-Davis (2006, 211) points out, the "[p]olitical project of belonging is primarily based on the identificatory and emotional level, it also assumes adherence to specific political and ethical values that are seen as inherent to good democratic citizenship".

As such, the politics of belonging shares several aspects with identity politics. Identity politics is commonly associated with activism claiming recognition, collective rights, or cultural rights (e.g. Taylor 1994; Young 1995; Isin and Wood 1999; Stevenson 2001; Parekh 2008), and may be related to the micro-level activities of minorities, for instance. It can, however, also refer to identity-building efforts by macro-level organizations in dominant power positions, such as a state or the EU. Similarly, both micro- and macro-level actors can use politics of belonging to draw boundaries of belonging. Both politics of belonging and identity politics are based on constructions of social categories and divisions but the former is more useful for our approach. In this book, instead of identity politics, we prefer to use the term of politics of belonging, as it offers a broader, intersectional framework for exploring the interrelation and power relations between social locations, variables, and phenomena that influence people and policies of identity building and participation.

Cultural and political processes and practices of politics of belonging can be viewed as an "arena of contestation", which can tell us about "social locations and constructions of individual and collective identities and attachments but also about the ways these are valued and judged" (Yuval-Davis 2006, 203). As Yuval-Davis argues, politics of belonging involve struggles related to membership and status, and reveal contestations "around ethical and ideological issues and the ways they utilize social locations and narratives of identities" (Yuval-Davis 2006, 203–204, 205; see also Yuval-Davis 2011, 118). We argue that in the context of EU cultural policy, politics of belonging are constructed through discourses that aim to situate people and, at the same, are shaped by specific social actors and through everyday practices. We explore how the politics of belonging to Europe is co-constructed, or imagined, from below, beyond the emphasis of institutional positions and interests from above. We understand the notions of Europe and the 'European' as fluid, contextual, and changing narrative constructions, discourses, and practices aimed at creating a certain order and meaning. In analyzing this, we are interested in the range of positions and analytical levels in citizens' notions of belonging and non-belonging to Europe that relate to "social locations; identifications and emotional attachments; and ethical and political values" (Yuval-Davis 2006, 199), as well as how they interrelate and connect to EU cultural policy.

In the following, we discuss the core concepts framing our analysis of the politics of belonging and our discussion of how Europe, the 'European', and belonging to Europe is understood by European citizens. We then present our understanding of how the core concepts interrelate and connect to the EU's politics of belonging. We move on to introducing our method, ethnography of Europeanization, and show how this enabled us to explore the variety of notions of and meanings attributed to the idea of Europe and the 'European' in our data.

2 Interrelation between Belonging, Identity, Culture, Citizenship, and Participation

Cultural policy with its identity-building and participatory agendas (see Chapter 3) is the EU's means of promoting cultural Europeanization. Based on parallel reading of the EU cultural policy documents, ethnographic data of our three cases, and prior research, we understand the politics of belonging in the EU cultural policy as formed by the entwinement and intersection of five core concepts: belonging, identity, culture, participation, and citizenship. The choice of these concepts shapes our framework for interpreting and contextualizing notions of belonging to Europe both from above, by the EU cultural policy initiatives, and from below, by the people participating in them. Notions of the 'European' and belonging (or non-belonging) to Europe are created by simultaneously strengthening certain narratives and perspectives on the one hand and negotiating social and communal meanings and boundaries of belonging on the other. The five concepts reflect the EU's attempts to build and deepen the relationship with its citizens by creating Europe as a common cultural space (see Calhoun 2007, 296). Even though these concepts can be theoretically distinguished, our empirical analysis (Chapters 4–7) indicates how in practice these five concepts interrelate in multiple ways.

2.1 *Belonging*
The concept of belonging differs from politics of belonging although they are closely linked (Yuval-Davis 2006, 2011). As Calhoun (2007, 286) writes:

> Everyone belongs, though some people belong to some groups with more intensity and often less choice than others belong to any. Such belonging

matters not only as a subjective state of mind – not insofar as it feels either good or bad to individuals. It matters also as a feature of social organization. It joins people together in social relations and informs their action.

Belonging to and identification with a particular entity is constructed through contested narrative and discursive processes of cultural distinction, social demarcation, and political border-making between identities and representations through time and geographical space (see Hall 1990, 1992; Bauman 1992; Massey 2005; Antonsich 2010; Yuval-Davis 2006, 204, 2011). In our approach, belonging is interpreted as forming a place-space, practice, resource, and biography that is created and (con)tested in terms of producing a feeling of home and alienation at the same time (see Antonsich 2010; Yuval-Davis et al. 2017). Thus, the concept of belonging encompasses both personal feelings of belonging to a certain group, place, or social location and the understanding of belonging as a resource that has affective dimensions (Yuval-Davis 2006, 2011, 6; see also Anthias 2013). Therefore, the construction of diverse narratives of belonging can be investigated along multiple social categories and (non-) identifications. In our view, the concept of belonging allows us to understand diverse social processes that shape the individual's sense of belonging and relationship to a specific entity, such as Europe, also based on the ideas of citizenship, participation, and membership (see Yuval-Davis 2011). Thus, belonging relates to the creation of boundaries and borders affected by different historical trajectories and social realities, which are not only bound by ancestry, 'authenticity', and places of origin (Anthias 2013; Yuval-Davis et al. 2017).

Belonging refers to the individual's dynamic processes of constructing conformity with specific political value systems and social locations at multiple levels that determine the individual's relationships with groups, communities, institutions, and entities and equally enable a personal experience of involvement (see Baumeister and Leary 1995, 498; Yuval-Davis 2006, 2011; Čeginskas 2015, 18). Yuval-Davis (2006, 199) describes belonging as encompassing processes of

> self-identification or identification by others, in a stable, contested or transient way. Even in its most stable 'primordial' forms, however, belonging is always a dynamic process, not a reified fixity, which is only a naturalized construction of a particular hegemonic form of power relations.

Scholars commonly define belonging as a fundamental human need that includes spatial and temporal meanings and relates to emotional attachments and constructions of home and safety shaped by everyday practices and experiences, social relations, and memories (e.g. Medved 2000, 76; Blunt 2005, 506; Antonsich 2010; Yuval-Davis et al. 2017). Theories of spaces of places and flows (Castells 1996, 1997) or scapes of cultural global flows (Appadurai 1990) help to understand the complex dynamics in processes of belonging that intersect people's social practices within territorial boundaries and their exposure to multi-directional and transnational cultural flows. While places play a role in people's spatial and social forms of organization, new cultural flows and technological processes transform such spaces and produce hubs of interaction and connection "at the interface between places and flows and between cultures and social interests, both in the space of flows and in the space of places" (Castells 1999, 302). Appadurai's concept of scapes stress the interrelation between the local and global in and through distinct dimensions that result from global and transnational processes and emphasize their relevance for the "situatedness of different sorts of actors" (Appadurai 1990, 50).

The emphasis on the dynamic interrelation and connection between distinct spaces or scapes in these models help to conceptualize the construction of belonging not as closed systems but as open processes. Accordingly, we understand belonging to be formed by contemporary logics of social organization and manifold cultural flows, which affect people's participation and membership, including diverse political and social identifications – such as citizenship, ethnicity, and religion – as well as individual agency, and practice. Our concept of belonging emphasizes the social features and structures that shape people's personal meaning-making in the world, in relation to communities and society and to social and cultural practices of the everyday (Block 2006, 28). However, belonging tends to be 'naturalized' and invisible in everyday practices, and only becomes articulated and politicized when under threat (Yuval-Davis et al. 2017, 230).

Belonging is often used interchangeably with identity, and both concepts can be understood as dynamic, fluid, and multidimensional processes of creating attachments and establishing boundaries at individual and collective levels (Antonsich 2010). Lately, however, the concept of identity has been criticized by several scholars for lacking analytical power (Brubaker and Cooper 2000, 2; Kendall and Wickham 2001, 156; Yuval-Davis 2006; Lähdesmäki et al. 2016). Instead, the concept of belonging has been perceived as a more accurate depiction of the individual desire for and processes of creating attachment to people, places, or modes of being, which implies a process of becoming rather than a stable social or cultural status, or identity (Probyn 1996, 19; see also Bell, 1999; Skrbiš et al. 2007, 262; Antonsich 2010). Thus, belonging is an active relation between individuals and communities that point to people's active participation in such processes. In our book, while acknowledging the analytical distinction between belonging and identity, we find both concepts equally important for exploring politics of belonging through people's personal meaning-making.

2.2   *Identity*

Questions of identity are central to political debates in Europe, and the EU has actively participated in the construction of a European identity in the context of its integration politics, not least through EU cultural policy, as further elaborated in Chapter 3 (e.g. Sassatelli 2002; Bruter 2003; Lähdesmäki et al. 2020a). EU cultural initiatives, including those studied in this book, use culture strategically, in an attempt to transmit specific positions and values to the wider European public (Sassatelli 2009; Lähdesmäki 2014a, 2014b; Niklasson 2017; Lähdesmäki et al. 2020a). In this context, various studies on EU cultural policy (e.g. Shore 2000; Sassatelli 2009; Patel 2013) and on European identity (e.g. Delanty 1995, 2005; Risse 2003, 2006; Bruter 2003, 2004, 2005; Beck and Grande 2007; Antonsich 2008; Pichler 2008, 2009) have highlighted the complexity and controversial notions embedded in the idea of 'Europe' and the 'European'. Depending on the discursive situations in which they are produced and defined, their meanings vary, and they can be used to include or exclude people, whether intentionally or not, and thereby create divisions between 'us' and 'them'.

Researchers commonly understand identity in the plural, i.e. identities, and emphasize the dynamic nature of their constructions, which are not stable but fragmented, contested and continuously in process (see Hall 1996, 4; Hermann and Brewer 2004). Identifications and social locations, in terms of ethnicity, nationality, race, gender, social background, education, language, religion, and so forth, while not fixed for life, provide significant orientation for people and root them in their everyday social and cultural practices (see May 2001, 39; see Block 2006, 28; Yuval-Davis 2006, 2017). They help to determine a person's self-identifications as well as identifications ascribed externally by others. Through their identities, people are able to position themselves, position others, and actively engage in processes of constructing belonging (see Block 2006, 29). Frequently, identity is explored in terms of its psychological dimension and personal meaning for the individual or a collective entity but this poses the danger of viewing descent and cultural and social identifications in an exclusionary way that connect to specific political agendas of inclusion and exclusion (see Eriksen 2007, 4). Social locations and identifications do not need to explain people's everyday practices of constructing belonging, as studies on transnational families and migration reveal (e.g. Fail et al. 2004; Bryceson and

Vuorela 2002; Gouldbourne et al. 2010; Čeginskas 2015). As Yuval-Davis (2006, 201) points out:

> Without specific social agents who construct and point to certain ana-
> lytical and political features, the other members of society would not be
> able to identify them. Rainbows include the whole spectrum of different
> colours, but how many colours we distinguish depends on our specific
> social and linguistic milieu.

It is important to recognize that identities are not constructed "along one power axis of difference" but in plural power relations in society (Yuval-Davis 2006, 200). Therefore, we use both concepts, belonging and identity, to look for the intersection and interrelation of various agendas and practices regarding identity building and participation. In addition, the concepts enable us to explore identity and belonging from below, showing how they condition and are conditioned by social interactions and social structures, in the context of social justice and equality.

2.3   Culture

The concept of belonging plays a central role in the EU's cultural policy (see Chapter 3). The EU attempts to construct belonging to the Union as not only in terms of political and economic integration, but also as a social and cultural community formed by European citizens (see also Shore 1993, 2000, 25). Hence, culture in this project can be perceived as an instrument of politics of belonging as Yuval-Davis (2006, 197) defines it: a particular way of constructing a certain kind of belonging to a collectivity and, at the same time, construct-ing that very collectivity (see also Block 2006, 28). In the context of Europe, politics of belonging and culture intertwine in discourses and practices, both in processes of official policy-making and in competing individual and group interpretations of meanings, in which various actors participate in creating social relations and a certain political order in society (Mouffe 2005).

Thus, culture is a crucial element in the EU's politics of belonging and com-plements the European politics of institutionalization and integration. As it has a strong symbolic potential for the construction and reproduction of nar-ratives of belonging, culture (including cultural heritage) creates the images and memories of a society. In our book, we understand culture predominantly from an ethnological and anthropological point of view, rather than solely in terms of so-called high culture (e.g. literature, art, music, and so forth), which often becomes associated with an underlying exclusionary and racist conno-tation of a 'progressive civilization'. In our understanding, culture refers to

diverse practices, traditions, and rituals that are inextricably linked with people's everyday way of life and meaning-making in the world. Memory plays a
central role in these processes by shaping narratives of the past and affecting
agency. Hence, the concept of culture intersects with the notion of belonging
and identity by evoking meaningful cultural and social relationships and networks in the everyday that affect an individual's relationship to a specific entity
(Lawler 2002, 252; see also Smith 2006; Antonsich 2010; Kisić 2017; Yuval-Davis
2017, 231). We understand culture as providing a space for constructing, sharing, and contesting multiple discourses of identity, belonging, non-belonging,
inclusion, and exclusion that produce the social and political contexts for discussing Europe and performing belonging to it (see also Chapter 3). Culture
can provide spaces of negotiations that break with essentialized categories
of 'us' and 'them', enabling the formation of fluid conceptions and complex
meanings of Europe and the 'European' (Sassatelli 2009, 14; see also Anthias
2006, 2009). Nevertheless, using culture to legitimize the idea of a European
community can also enforce exclusion and foster boundaries. Our focus on visitors to heritage sites and participants of cultural initiatives helps us to investigate the construction of belonging from below that shape their notions and
their subjective attachments to Europe and to research cultural phenomena
connected with processes of Europeanization.

2.4   *Participation*

The concepts of belonging, identity, and culture are crucial to constructing
and imagining community (Anderson 1991) and intersect with the concepts of
participation and citizenship that define membership in a (political) community. In the EU, both citizenship and participation are used to create belonging
to the EU and Europe. Citizens' participation in public decision-making and
civil society activities crucially contributes to the development of democracy
and social justice. In the context of the Union's cultural policy, the involvement of EU citizens in cultural initiatives is considered central for creating
a sense of belonging to Europe and rendering the 'European' a tangible reality that at the same time helps to legitimize the EU as a political community
(see Mäkinen 2018, 193, 194). The EU's cultural initiatives and programmes are
examples of how Europeanization intermingles top-down-governed politics
of belonging with EU citizens' individual conceptualizations from below. In
practice, people participate through a wide range of cultural activities, such
as by taking part in cultural events (ECOC) and workshops (ECC) or visiting a
heritage site (EHL). People's experiences and meanings encounter and intersect with narratives of belonging to Europe produced by macro and meso level
actors related to cultural initiatives. Through these EU cultural initiatives, the

visitors and participants engage in forming, transmitting and contesting cultural narratives and discourses used to construct belonging and identity in the European context, thereby affirming or limiting the EU's politics of belonging.

The understanding that in the EU cultural policy initiatives, participation is embedded in the EU's participatory governance, helps to interpret the role and space of visitors and participants in relation to the EU's politics of belonging. In participatory governance, citizens' participation is seen as part of good governance and as a partnership between citizens and the administration that lends legitimacy to decision-making (e.g. Cruikshank 1999; Dean 2010, 192–204, 263–264; Newman et al. 2004). As such, it is characterized by governmentality, typical of liberal and neoliberal governance, which through its technologies of agency seeks to produce subjectivities and guide conduct so that the objects of governance themselves participate in fulfilling the objectives of governance (Cruikshank 1999; Dean 2010; Foucault 1991). The participatory practices on the border between governance and citizens, as in the EU's cultural initiatives investigated here, can both promote and limit citizens' participation and democracy. Their complex implications for the agencies, modes, and effects of participation as well as for the relation between citizens and governance are hotly debated in academia (Michels 2011; Moini 2011; Mäkinen 2018; Nousiainen and Mäkinen 2015; Newman 2005; Newman and Clarke 2009; Papadopoulos and Warn 2007). In our book, we explore participation and agency of citizens in terms of their constructions of Europe and belonging that connect to issues of such as citizenship, inclusion, and exclusion, through their subjective meaning-making of Europe and the 'European'.

2.5   Citizenship

Participation is closely associated with citizenship. In our approach, citizenship intertwines with subjective feelings of membership and belonging, in terms of "a politically engaged and critical conceptualization; one that engages with social relationships in all their messiness, taking account of action, process, power and change" (Waterton and Smith 2009, 5). While our three case studies reveal plural conceptions and meanings of belonging to Europe among the respondents and interviewees, belonging as EU membership is still determined by concrete political and legal aspects of citizenship. Citizenship defines the relationship between an individual and a political entity, such as the EU, by providing access to membership, setting rights and duties, and entitling citizens to participate in a specific societal entity (see Wiesner et al. 2018, 8). By shaping people's roles and belonging, citizenship is ingrained in different modes of power struggles that take place through performed and negotiated positions and 'banal' practices in the everyday (see Billig 1995). While citizenship is a necessary element in democratic societies that facilitates belonging through practices in all political, social, and cultural dimensions of society, it may not only include, but also exclude and form boundaries. In the rhetoric of the EU's policy documents, citizenship is frequently associated with the notion of 'European identity' and connotes with a vaguely defined feeling of 'Europeanness' as well as membership in the EU, whereas its democratic and transformative potential as a channel for citizens to use power and make claims is not emphasized (Mäkinen 2018).

In the case study chapters of this book, the discussion of the politics of belonging is constituted by the five core concepts introduced above. Each of these concepts serves to connect the theoretical framework to the empirical data, helping to contextualize and approach Europe and the 'European' from different perspectives, in the specific context of ethnography of Europeanization. In essence, they enable understanding the complex and constructed processes of belonging(-making), identity projects, and politics of belonging from below. As our case study chapters deal with EU cultural initiatives with different thematic emphases, the core concepts emphasize their entwined nature and show how belonging is composed through them. The case studies share a critical stance on power relations in processes of producing narratives and meanings. Through our core concepts, we can examine the multiple, multilayered, and contested nature of the narratives and meanings produced in our empirical data – such as European identity, European cultural heritage, or European citizenship – as well as the dynamics of their production processes.

3   Ethnography of Europeanization

Following our understanding of the politics of belonging, we believe that a multifaceted and multi-sited ethnographic approach is needed to research and understand the numerous discursive and narrative ways in which the notion of Europe and the 'European' become voiced and manifested from below. Although our three distinct case studies exemplify different cultural initiatives implemented through the EU's top-down politics of belonging, all three are connected by our multi-sited and holistic exploration of processes, connections, and associations of belonging to Europe. Due to the nature of Europeanization and the transforming cultural mobilities that have broadened and changed the locations of cultural production (Marcus 1995, 97), the EU's politics of belonging manifests simultaneously at multiple sites and levels. This requires immersion in multiple locales and attention to interconnected processes of Europeanization.

The EU's cultural activities, such as the ECOC, ECC, and EHL, create the opportunity and space for encountering a wide range of discourses that reflect people's subjective thoughts, notions, and understandings. At the same time, these sites of contact and encounter are themselves situated in different geographical locations, so they hold and transmit multidimensional and multilayered understandings and discourses about Europe and the 'European'. Rather than producing "thick descriptions" (Geertz 1973) of the objectives and effects of the various cultural activities in question, we try to explore Europe and the 'European' in terms of ongoing processes and narratives produced and governed by social actors at different levels and places. To investigate a wide range of diverse conceptions of Europe and belonging and how they are generated in these processes, we require a versatile methodology.

Our core methodology can be described as an *ethnography of Europeanization* (for more details see Lähdesmäki et al. 2020a; Turunen et al. 2020). Ethnography of Europeanization refers to both the process of conducting research by ethnographic means and the written output of our research (see Koskinen-Koivisto, Lähdesmäki, and Čeginskas 2020). Thus, it helps to both examine and describe societal processes, practices, and transformations in Europe – but equally, as a written product, our research participates in establishing patterns of Europeanization. Traditionally, ethnographic methods refer to longitudinal observation and participation that allow researchers to immerse in social environments for a considerable amount of time. However, depending on the scope, time resource and field of research, ethnography can be conducted in a shorter time period and through experimental modes of approaching the data collection and interpreting findings (see Lähdesmäki et al. 2020b).

Processes of cultural Europeanization are part of politics of belonging and integrate a multitude of meanings, interpretations, and positions that circulate between and affect multiple actors at different levels along horizontal and vertical axes. We use ethnography of Europeanization as a methodology to research the processes of cultural Europeanization in dealing with the construction of 'Europe' and the 'European'. This multi-sited ethnography facilitates scrutinizing politics of belonging to Europe as a complex, multi-layered, and transnational cultural phenomenon that is constructed in both collective and individual processes at different levels: the micro (e.g. European citizens participating in cultural initiatives and actions), meso (e.g. heritage practitioners, project managers), and macro (e.g. EU cultural policy makers) levels. Studies on the EU's cultural policy predominantly focus on the meso- and macrolevel actors for analyzing their roles in the context of Europeanization (see Chapter 1). Our research offers a novel approach to cultural Europeanization by focusing on European citizens who do *not* deal with EU initiatives and policies in their everyday professional life but are the intended addressees of these initiatives and their actions. While participants of the ECC workshops were aware of the European dimension of the project, visitors to ECOC events were already less aware of these events representing part of the EU policy, and the majority of the EHL visitors, with only a few exceptions, did not know that their visited heritage sites belonged to a specific EU action.

Our ethnography of Europeanization scrutinizes the meanings that visitors and participants in the EU's cultural activities give to the idea of Europe, and how their constructions correlate with the objectives of the EU's cultural policy to form 'a community of Europeans'. We use ethnography of Europeanization to investigate discourses from below about belonging to Europe in terms of cultural phenomena and social and cultural practices that relate to processes of meaning-making, human interaction, and everyday experience (see Clifford and Marcus 1986). Our approach enables us to analyze not only multiple layers of meanings attributed to the notion of Europe from below but to explore processes of producing narratives and discourses in the context of power differences, inclusion, and exclusion in Europe that involve different people and multiple locales (see also Marcus 1995; Falzon 2009, 1). Our analysis of the citizens' narratives and responses about communities and belonging in Europe sheds light on the ways, in which citizens participate and co-construct Europeanization. Thus, it helps to understand the larger framework of Europeanization by exploring how participants and visitors share and support– or resist and reject – certain conceptualizations of Europe as well as how their conceptualizations interrelate with the EU's politics of belonging.

The participants and visitors to EU cultural initiatives and actions, who our book focuses on, represent a predominantly privileged share of population among European citizens. Our ECOC data included some respondents belonging to the non-privileged minority of Roma but we did not identify other vulnerable or marginalized people or groups in our data, such as refugees. This can be interpreted not only as a limitation of our study but also of the explored EU initiatives and their implementation. Despite this significant limitation, we believe that our approach and specific focus on participants from three different EU cultural initiatives offer a deeper qualitative interpretation of meanings of Europe and the 'European' from below– in contrast to some other larger quantitative data collections, such as the Eurobarometer.

Our ethnography of Europeanization is field-based and in our empirical Chapters 4–6 we cite the rich ethnographic data from our field research, which manifests the plural, complex, multidimensional, and contested processes of constructing belonging. The quotes reveal different views and perceptions people hold about Europe and the 'European'. The data-driven approach helps us to make visible meaning-making processes from below by giving people a voice, which in turn may trigger new interpretations and understandings of how Europe can be perceived as a changing, contested, and contextual construction. Our ethnography of Europeanization also reveals how interviewees and participants in our case studies engage with core concepts of politics of belonging: culture, identity, belonging, participation, and citizenship.

We combine several traditional ethnographic methods for our data collection (see Clifford and Marcus 1986; Culhane and Elliot 2016), including questionnaire surveys (ECOC), qualitative, semi-structured interviews (ECC and EHL), and participant observation (in all three case studies). The case study of the ECOC (Chapter 4) uses the responses to questionnaires (n = 893) distributed among the audiences of different cultural events in Pécs (April, May, October 2010), Tallinn (May 2011), and Turku (August 2011). In addition, responses from a pilot online study (n = 532) conducted in Pécs (2010) prior to the fieldwork on the ECOC are included. The data allows both for quantitative and qualitative analysis of the ECOC audiences' responses.

The data for the case study of the ECC project (Chapter 5) was collected in two art laboratories held in Strasbourg and Freiburg in the summer of 2014. These laboratories were organized for exploring the topic of European citizenship, focusing on the themes of 'roots' and 'home'. The data consists of qualitative semi-structured interviews with participants in the art laboratories (n = 15). Additional data included thematic writings and motivation letters by the project participants and an extended participant observation at the closing conference of the ECC project and in the exhibition of the art works from the laboratories in Antwerp in June 2015. In our qualitative analysis, the meso- and micro-level constructions of Europe in the project are juxtaposed with macro-level discourses in the official EU documents related to the EU programme that was funding the project.

The case study of the EHL (Chapter 6) draws on qualitative and semi-structured interviews with visitors (n = 271) that were conducted between August 2017 and February 2018 at eleven selected EHL sites in ten countries. These interviews were part of a broader research project, which also included qualitative interviews with key EU heritage officials for the EHL, members of the selection panel appointed by the EU, and heritage practitioners working at the selected sites. For this case study, we focus on interviews with the visitors, which include a variety of national backgrounds, both EU- and non-EU citizens (see Annex 1). In the interviews, we asked visitors about their perceptions of the site and its exhibition and the notions of European cultural heritage and European identity to explore their personal constructions of Europe and belonging to Europe. Finally, Chapter 7 offers a synthesis of our findings from the three case studies and provides a more detailed reflection on who was involved in the interviews, projects, and surveys by discussing background information.

Our emphasis on participants and visitors in EU cultural policy activities connects to the view that experiential and everyday narratives play a key role in the complex and fluid constructions of (non-)belonging. The focus on such qualitative data also helps to reveal how people utilize and appropriate concepts and notions from macro- and meso-level discourses as well as to scrutinize potential contradictions in these concepts and notions. For instance, it became evident in our EHL data that many people contest the use of the term 'identity', which in their view stresses divisions and boundaries more than creating a sense of community (see Chapters 6 and 7). Consequently, these interviewees rejected the notion of a 'European identity' but this did not automatically mean they did not feel a sense of belonging to Europe or had a negative attitude towards the EU. Rather, our data revealed the interviewees' negotiated attitude towards the complex term of identity and gave insights into their understanding of belonging as well as of how belonging to Europe and support for European integration are interrelated but not necessarily the same.

Our qualitative content analysis is based on hermeneutic close and repeated readings of the interview and survey data from the respective case studies. Through our analysis of the vocabulary, expressions, concepts, and metaphors in the data, we have formed thematic categories to demonstrate how the meanings of Europe and the 'European' are negotiated in each case. Our analysis was enriched by reflecting jointly on our various fieldwork observations (see Turunen et al. 2020 for details of this collaborative methodology). Co-production of data usually refers to the interdependent relationships between researcher, the researched, and the audiences towards whom the research is directed. In this book, we take co-production further, with a collaborative approach to understanding how Europe and the 'European' are constructed from below. This collaborative approach includes intensive discussions, which enabled us to analyze data together.

Producing, collecting and analyzing data together highlights the reciprocity in the process of research, making it a dialogic and multi-sided enterprise. For instance, the field context, social surroundings, time, and place may influence the roles of researcher and participants (see also Narayan 1993; Vasenkari and Pekkala 2000; De Laine 2000; Ellis et al. 2011). Similarly, discussions between research colleagues may reveal new ways in which a specific topic is approached, discussed, and understood. Joint analysis is a new methodological approach by which researchers are able to compare notes and ideas, and also to communicate and compare impressions, atmospheres, and affective experiences (see also Turunen et al. 2020; Lähdesmäki et al. 2020a). In our collaboration on the analysis and theoretical conceptualization, we were able to test different strategies and carry out small interventions that changed our perceptions and triggered a joint process of shared conceptual work.

The following case study chapters demonstrate our ethnography of Europeanization in practice. In them, we discuss in detail what kind of politics of belonging was implemented in the ECOC, ECC, and EHL initiatives, and how their visitors and participants engaged with this politics by adapting to, ignoring, or occasionally even objecting to it through their own constructions of Europe and the European. Our analysis is guided by respect for our interviewees' and respondents' notions of Europe and the 'European' in Chapters 4–6, we seek to illustrate the variety of conceptions of Europe and understand their premises. This variety manifests the richness of Europe and is a challenge for understanding Europe, as the analysis in Chapters 4–7 shows.

References

Anderson, B. 1991 [1983]. *Imagined Communities: Reflections on the Origin and Spread of Nationalism.* London and New York: Verso.

Anthias, F. 2006. "Belongings in a Globalizing and Unequal World: Rethinking Translocations." In *The Situated Politics of Belonging*, edited by N. Yuval-Davis, K. Kannabiran, and U. Vieten, 17–31. London: Sage.

Anthias, F. 2009 "Intersectionality, Belonging and Translocal Positionality: Thinking about Transnational Identities." In *Ethnicity, Belonging and Biography: Ethnographical and Biographical Perspectives*, edited by G. Rosenthal and A. Bogner, 229–249. Münster, Westfalen: Lit Verlag.

Anthias, F. 2013 "Moving Beyond the Janus Face of Integration and Diversity Discourses: Towards an Intersectional Framing." *The Sociological Review* 61: 323–343.

Antonsich, M. 2008. "The Narration of Europe in 'National' and 'Post-national' Terms: Gauging the Gap between Normative Discourses and People's Views." *European Journal of Social Theory* 11 (4): 505–522.

Antonsich, M. 2010. "Searching for Belonging – an Analytical Framework." *Geography Compass* 4 (6): 644–659.

Appadurai, A. 1990. "Disjuncture and Difference in the Global Cultural Economy." *Theory, Culture and Society* 7: 295–310.

Bauman, Z. 1992. *Intimations of Postmodernity.* Oxford: Routledge.

Baumeister, R. F., and M. R. Leary. 1995. "Need to Belong: Desire for Interpersonal Attachments as Fundamental Human Motivation." *Psychological Bulletin* 117 (3): 497–529.

Beck, U., and E. Grande. 2007. *Cosmopolitan Europe*. Cambridge: Polity Press.

Bell, V. 1999. *Performativity and Belonging*. London: Sage.

Billig, M. 1995. *Banal Nationalism*. London and Thousand Oaks: Sage.

Block, D. 2005. *Multilingual Identities in a Global City. London Stories*. Language and Globalization Series. Houndsmill: Palgrave Macmillan

Blunt, A. 2005. "Cultural Geography: Cultural Geographies of Home." *Progress in Human Geography* 29 (4): 505–515. doi: 10.1191/0309132505ph564pr.

Brubaker, R., and F. Cooper. 2000 "Beyond Identity." *Theory and Society* 29: 1–47.

Bruter, M. 2003. "Winning Hearts and Minds for Europe. The Impact of News and Symbols on Civic and Cultural European Identity." *Comparative Political Studies* 36 (10): 1148–1179.

Bruter, M. 2004. "Civic and Cultural Components of a European Identity: A Pilot Model of Measurement of Citizens' Levels." In *Transnational Identities. Becoming European in the EU*, edited by R. K. Herrmann, T. Risse, and M. B. Brewer, 186–213. Oxford: Rowman & Battlefield.

Bruter, M. 2005. *Citizens of Europe? The Emergence of a Mass European Identity*. New York: Palgrave Macmillan.

Bryceson, D., and U. Vuorela, eds. 2002. *The Transnational Family. New European Frontiers and Global Networks*. Oxford, New York: Berg.

Calhoun, C. 2007. "Social Solidarity as a Problem for Cosmopolitan Democracy." In *Identities, Affiliations, and Allegiances*, edited by S. Benhabib, I. Shapiro, and D. Petranović, 285–302. Cambridge: Cambridge University Press.

Castells, M. 1996. *The Rise of the Network Society*. Oxford: Blackwell.

Castells, M. 1997. *The Power of Identity*. Oxford: Blackwell.

Castells, M. 1999. "Grassrooting the Space of Flows." *Urban Geography* 20 (4): 294–302. doi: 10.2747/0272-3638.20.4.294.

Čeginskas, V. L. A. 2015. *Exploring Multicultural Belonging. Individuals across Cultures, Languages and Places*. Annales Universitatis Turkuensis 411. Turku: University of Turku.

Clifford, J., and G. E. Marcus, eds. 1986. *Writing Culture. The Poetics and Politics of Ethnography*. Berkeley: University of California Press.

Cruikshank, B. 1999. *The Will to Empower*. Ithaca: Cornell University.

Culhane, D., and D. Elliott, eds. 2016. *A Different Kind of Ethnography: Imaginative Practices and Creative Methodologies*. Toronto: University of Toronto Press.

Dean, M. 2010 *Governmentality: Power and Rule in Modern Society*. London: Sage.

De Laine, M. 2000. *Fieldwork, Participation and Practice. Ethics and Dilemmas in Qualitative Research*. London and Thousand Oaks: Sage.

Delanty, G. 1995. *Inventing Europe. Idea, Identity, Reality*. Basingstoke: Macmillan.

Delanty, G. 2005. "The Cosmopolitan Imagination: Critical Cosmopolitanism and Social Theory." *The British Journal of Sociology* 57 (1): 25–47.

Ellis, C., T. E. Adams, and A. P. Bochner. 2011. "Autoethnography: An Overview." *Forum Qualitative Sozialforschung / Forum Qualitative Social Research* 12:1. Accessed 20 March 2020. http://dx.doi.org/10.17169/fqs-12.1.1589

Eriksen, T. H. 2007. *Globalization. The Key Concepts*. Oxford, New York: Berg.

Fail, H., J. Thompson, and G. Walker. 2004. "Belonging, Identity and Third Culture Kids. Life Histories of Former International School Students." *Journal of Research in International Education* 3 (3): 319–338. doi: 10.1177/1475240904047358

Falzon, M.-A. 2009. *Multi-Sited Ethnography. Theory, Praxis and Locality in Contemporary Social Research*. Farnham: Ashgate Publishing.

Foucault, M. 1991. "Governmentality." In *The Foucault Effect: Studies in Governmentality*, edited by G. Burchell, C. Gordon, and P. Miller, 87–104. London: Harvester Wheatsheaf.

Geertz, C. 1973. *The Interpretation of Cultures. Selected Essays*. London: Hutchinson.

Gouldbourne, H., T. Reynolds, J. Solomos, and E. Zontini 2010. *Transnational Families. Ethnicities, Identities and Social Capital*. London and New York: Routledge.

Hall, S. 1990. "Cultural Identity and Diaspora." In *Identity, Community, Culture, Difference*, edited by J. Rutherford, 222–237. London: Lawrence & Wishart.

Hall, S. 1992. "The Question of Cultural Identity." In *Modernity and Its Futures*, edited by S. Hall, D. Held, and T. McGrew, 274–316. Cambridge: Polity Press.

Hall, S. 1996. "Introduction: Who Needs 'Identity'?" In *Questions of Cultural Identity*, edited by S. Hall and P. du Gay, 1–17. London: Sage.

Hermann, R. K., and M. L. Brewer. 2004. "Identities and Institutions: Becoming European in the EU." In *Transnational Identities. Becoming European in the EU*, edited by Hermann, R. K., T. Risse, and M. B. Brewer, 1–22. Lanham, Boulder: Rowman & Littlefield Publishers.

Isin, E. F., and P. K. Wood. 1999. *Citizenship and Identity*. London: Sage.

Kendall, G., and G. Wickham 2001. *Understanding Culture. Cultural Studies – Order – Ordering*. London and Thousand Oaks: Sage.

Kisić, V. 2017. *Governing Heritage Dissonance: Promises and Realities of Selected Cultural Policies*. Amsterdam: European Cultural Foundation.

Koskinen-Koivisto, E., Lähdesmäki, T., and V. L. A. Čeginskas. 2020. "Introduction: Ethnography with a Twist." In *Challenges and Solutions in Ethnographic Research. Ethnography with a Twist*, edited by T. Lähdesmäki, E. Koskinen-Koivisto, V. L. A. Čeginskas, and A.-K. Koistinen, xx–xxix. London, New York: Routledge.

Lähdesmäki, T. 2014a. *Identity Politics in the European Capital of Culture Initiative*. Joensuu: University of Eastern Finland.

Lähdesmäki, T. 2014b. "The Influence on Cultural Competence on the Interpretations of Territorial Identities in European Capitals of Culture." *Baltic Journal of European Studies* 4 (1): 69–96.

Lähdesmäki, T., T. Saresma, K. Hiltunen, S. Jäntti, N. Sääskilahti, A. Vallius, and K. Ahvenjärvi. 2016. "Fluidity and Flexibility of 'Belonging'. Uses of the Concept in Contemporary Research." *Acta Sociologica* 59 (3):233–247. doi:10.1177/0001699316633099.

Lähdesmäki, T., V. L. A. Čeginskas, S. Kaasik-Krogerus, K. Mäkinen, and J. Turunen 2020a. *Creating and Governing Cultural Heritage in the European Union: The European Heritage Label.* London: Routledge.

Lähdesmäki, T., E. Koskinen-Koivisto, V. L. A. Čeginskas, and A.-K. Koistinen (eds.). 2020b. *Challenges and Solutions in Ethnographic Research. Ethnography with a Twist.* London, New York: Routledge.

Lawler, S. 2002. "Narrative in Social Research." In *Qualitative Research in Action,* edited by T. May, 242–258. London: Sage.

Mäkinen, K. 2018. "'All about Doing Democracy'? Participation and Citizenship in EU Projects". In *Shaping Citizenship: A Political Concept in Theory, Debate and Practice,* edited by C. Wiesner, A. Björk, H.-M. Kivistö, and K. Mäkinen, 190–205. New York and London: Routledge.

Massey, D. 2005. *For Space.* London: Sage.

Marcus, G. E. 1995. "Ethnography in/of the World System: The Emergence of Multi-Sited Ethnography." *Annual Review of Anthropology* 24: 95–117. Accessed 23 April 2020. https://doi.org/10.1146/annurev.an.24.100195.000523.

May, S. 2001. *Language and Minority Rights.* London: Longman.

Medved, F. 2000. "The Concept of Homeland." In *Migrants and the Homeland. Images, Symbols and Realities,* edited by H. Runblom, 74–96. Uppsala Multiethnic Papers 44. Uppsala: Uppsala University Press.

Michels, A. 2011. "Innovations in Democratic Governance: How Does Citizen Participation Contribute to a Better Democracy?" *International Review of Administrative Sciences* 77 (2): 275–293.

Moini, G. 2011. "How Participation Has Become a Hegemonic Discursive Resource: Towards an Interpretivist Research Agenda." *Critical Policy Studies* 5 (2): 149–168.

Mouffe, C. 2005. *The Return of the Political.* London and New York: Verso.

Narayan, K. 1993. "How Native is a 'Native' Anthropologist?" *American Anthropologist* 95 (3): 671–686.

Newman, J., M. Barnes, H. Sullivan, and A. Knops 2004. "Public Participation and Collaborative Governance." *Journal of Social Policy* 33 (2): 203–223. doi: 10.1017/S0047279403007499

Newman, J. 2005. "Participative Governance and the Remaking of the Public Sphere." In *Remaking Governance,* edited by J. Newman, 119–139. Bristol: Policy Press.

Newman, J., and J. Clarke. 2009. *Publics, Politics and Power: Remaking the Public in Public Services.* London: Sage.

Niklasson, E. 2017 "The Janus-face of European Heritage: Revisiting the Rhetoric of Europe-making in EU Cultural Policies." *Journal of Social Archaeology* 17 (2): 138–162. doi: 10.1177/1469605317712122

Nousiainen, M., and K. Mäkinen. 2015. "Multilevel Governance and Participation: Interpreting Democracy in EU-Programmes." *European Politics and Society* 14 (2): 208–223.

Papadopoulos, Y., and P. Warn 2007. "Are Innovative, Participatory and Deliberative Procedures in Policy Making Democratic and Effective?" *European Journal of Political Research* 46: 445–472.

Parekh, B. 2008. *A New Politics of Identity. Political Principles for an Interdependent World*. Hampshire: Palgrave Macmillan.

Patel, K. K. 2013. "Introduction." In *The Cultural Politics of Europe. European Capitals of Culture and European Union Since the 1980s*, edited by K. K. Patel, 1–15. London: Routledge.

Pichler, F. 2008. "European Identities from Below: Meanings of Identification with Europe." *Perspectives on European Politics and Society* 9 (4): 411–430.

Pichler, F. 2009. "Cosmopolitan Europe. Views and Identity." *European Societies* 11 (1): 3–24.

Probyn, E. 1996. *Outside Belonging*. London: Routledge.

Risse, T. 2003. "European Identity and the Heritage of National Culture." In *Rethinking Heritage. Cultures and Politics in Europe*, edited by R. S. Peckham, 74–89. London: I. B. Tauris,

Risse, T. 2006. "Neofunctionalism, European Identity, and the Puzzles of European Integration." *Journal of European Public Policy* 12 (2): 291–309.

Sassatelli, M. 2002. "Imagined Europe: The Shaping of a European Cultural Identity Through EU Cultural Policy." *European Journal of Social Theory* 5 (4): 435–451. doi: 10.1177/136843102760513848

Sassatelli, M. 2009. *Becoming Europeans. Cultural Identity and Cultural Policies*. New York: Palgrave Macmillan.

Sassatelli, M. 2010. "European Identity between Flows and Places: Insights from Emerging European Landscape Policies." *Sociology* 44 (1): 67–83. doi: 10.1177/0038038509351625

Shore, C. 1993. "Inventing the 'People's Europe': Critical Approaches to European Community Cultural Policy." *Man* 28 (4): 779–800.

Shore, C. 2000. *Building Europe: The Cultural Politics of European Integration*. London: Routledge.

Skrbiš, Z., Baldessar, L., and S. Poynting 2007. "Introduction – Negotiating Belonging: Migration and Generations." *Journal of Intercultural Studies* 28 (3): 261–269. doi: 10.1080/07256860701429691

Smith, L. 2006. *Uses of Heritage*. London: Routledge.

Stevenson, N., ed. 2001. *Culture and Citizenship*. London: Sage.

Taylor, C. 1994. "The Politics of Recognition." In *Multiculturalism. Examining the Politics of Recognition*, edited by A. Gutman, 25–74. Princeton: Princeton University Press.

Turunen, J., V. L. A. Čeginskas, S. Kaasik-Krogerus, T. Lähdesmäki, and K. Mäkinen. 2020. "Poly-Space: Creating New Concepts through Reflexive Team Ethnography." In *Challenges and Solutions in Ethnographic Research. Ethnography with a Twist*, edited by T. Lähdesmäki, E. Koskinen-Koivisto, V. L. A. Čeginskas and A.-K. Koistinen, 3–20. London: Routledge.

Vasenkari, M., and A. Pekkala 2000. "Dialogic Methodology." In *Thick Corpus, Organic Variation and Textuality in Oral Tradition*, edited by L. Honko, 243–254. Studia Fennica, Folkloristica 7. Helsinki: Finnish Literature Society.

Waterton, E., and L. Smith. 2009. "There Is No Such Thing As Heritage." In *Taking Archaeology out of Heritage*, edited by E. Waterton, and L. Smith, 10–27. Cambridge: Cambridge Scholars Publishing.

Wiesner, C., A. Björk, H.-M. Kivistö, and K. Mäkinen. 2018. "Introduction: Shaping Citizenship as a Political Concept". In *Shaping Citizenship: A Political Concept in Theory, Debate and Practice*, edited by C. Wiesner, A. Björk, H.-M. Kivistö, and K. Mäkinen, 1–16. New York and London: Routledge.

Young, I. M. 1995. "Polity and Group Difference: A Critique of the Ideal of Universal Citizenship" In *Theorizing Citizenship*, edited by R. Beiner, 175–207. Albany: State University of New York Press.

Yuval-Davis, N. 2006. "Belonging and the Politics of Belonging." *Patterns of Prejudice* 40 (3): 197–214. doi: 10.1080/00313220600769331

Yuval-Davis, N. 2011. *The Politics of Belonging. Intersectional Contestations*. London: Sage.

Yuval-Davis, N., G. Wemyss, and K. Cassidy 2017. "Everyday Bordering, Belonging and the Reorientation of British Immigration Legislation." *Sociology* 52 (2): 228–244. doi: 10.1177/0038038517702599

CHAPTER 3

EU Cultural Policy: Europe from Above

1   Focus on Two Agendas

The potential of cultural policy for promoting and bringing together integration processes in several policy fields is generally acknowledged (see Chapter 8). In this chapter, we provide an overview of the EU cultural policy, interpreting it as an instrument for forming Union citizens and bridging the gap between them and the EU, as well as a means of constructing the EU community and legitimizing the EU integration processes. In other words, EU cultural policy aims at advancing the EU's politics of belonging by using culture to promote these objectives. In addition to culture, the notions of identity, participation, and citizenship have a key role in EU's politics of belonging, and all of them are entwined in the rhetoric of EU cultural policy. Here we separate them analytically into two clusters that we name 'identity-building agenda' and 'participatory agenda'. Under the 'identity-building agenda', we analyze discussions in the EU cultural policy in which factors that can be called cultural are referred to as elements of identity – such as cultural heritage, traditions, languages, religions, everyday practices, arts, values, symbols, and cultural institutions and activities. Under 'participatory agenda', we examine discussions in which citizens' participation and citizenship are regarded as a means of creating citizens' belonging to the EU and Europe. Our discussion is based on close reading of key policy documents on issues such as the Creative Europe programme, a critical reading of earlier academic studies on EU cultural policy, and the authors' previous empirical analysis of EU cultural policy discourse.

We start this chapter with an overview of the development of EU cultural policy and its main initiatives. In particular, we introduce the Creative Europe programme, together with its predecessors Culture and Culture 2000, which have been the EU's core culture programmes and form the umbrella for the three cases in our book – the European Capital of Culture (ECOC), European Citizen Campus (ECC), and European Heritage Label (EHL). Then we discuss how the EU's politics of belonging has developed in the context of cultural policy around two key ideas – European identity and participation. First, we consider how EU cultural policy connects to the concept of identity and the strengthening of its European dimension since its inception. After this, we discuss the participatory approach of EU cultural policy as well as its links to citizenship of the Union. These two sections start with a more general outline on

© TUULI LÄHDESMÄKI ET AL., 2021 | DOI: 10.1163/9789004449800_003

the identity-building agenda and participatory agenda, respectively, followed by a review specifying the role of the EU projects as well as the ECOC and the EHL actions in these agendas.

2   Development of the EU's Cultural Policy and Initiatives

The idea that integration covers not only economics, but also culture has been present in the action of the European Community from its early years. Long before its explicit official cultural policy, the European Community had given culture multifaceted instrumental value, using it as a channel of power to promote integration and to build its image and identity (e.g. Shore 1993; 2000; Shore and Black 1996). On the other hand, scholars (e.g. Rosamond 2000; Herrmann and Brewer 2004; Sassatelli 2006, 2009; Näss 2009) have pointed out how political actors in the European Community anticipated that cultural and social integration would emerge as a spill-over effect of cooperation in other sectors or policy fields, such as the economy and trade. According to this understanding, increasing cultural integration would, in turn, strengthen institutional integration (Herrmann and Brewer 2004, 1–2). Integration in different fields would hence be mutually reinforcing. To support this, the European Community and the EU have created various policies and practices to promote and govern matters related to culture.

From its earlier incarnation as the European Community, the Union has cooperated with other transnational actors in the field of culture, such as the Council of Europe and UNESCO. Culture has been at the core of the activities of the Council of Europe since the beginning, as is indicated by its initiation of the European Cultural Convention, signed in 1954. The Council of Europe has a major influence on the EU's political discourses. Its rhetorical formulations and areas of interest have been absorbed into the EU's political discourses and goals, particularly in questions related to culture (Sassatelli 2009, 43; Patel 2013, 6). For example, the Framework Convention on the Value of Cultural Heritage for Society (Council of Europe 2005) has impacted on the EU's cultural heritage policy. The Council of Europe's European Heritage Days have been organized in cooperation with the European Commission since 1999. Collaboration with Europa Nostra, in turn, is manifested by the Europa Nostra Awards for Cultural Heritage, which have been awarded in cooperation with the Commission since 2002. These were later renamed as the European Union Prize for Cultural Heritage and then as the European Heritage Awards in 2018.

The first steps in the cultural policy arena of the European Community were taken in the 1970s. Since 1977, the European Commission has published cultural communications, setting guidelines for the cultural activity of the European Community (e.g. EC 1977, 1982, 1987, 1992, and 1994). These early communications raise issues of free trade and discuss how to apply the treaty establishing the European Economic Community to the cultural sector. As early as these documents, culture was considered "as a means of arousing a greater feeling of belonging and solidarity amongst Europeans" (EC 1977, 5; see also EC 1987, 5, 7). These communications increasingly took up issues such as values, reaching wider audiences for cultural productions in Europe, or creating a European cultural area, which have become core points of the EU's cultural policy.

In the 1980s, the European Community launched cultural initiatives more actively, and the European Council adopted several resolutions dealing with cultural matters, such as films, the mobility of artists, and networking libraries. In 1987, the European Community officially established the Council of Ministers of Culture and the ad hoc Commission of Cultural Issues. Through its structural funds, the European Community provided funding for culture well before it had established culture as an official policy sector. Between the early 1980s and mid-1990s, the funding instruments for cultural heritage included the European Historical Monuments and Sites Fund, initiated by the European Parliament, which provided financial support for restoring and conserving archaeological and heritage sites (Niklasson 2016, 82–91).

The Maastricht Treaty – the founding agreement of the EU adopted in 1992 – made culture an official sector of EU action, as it introduced an article explicitly focusing on culture. Since then, the EU's interest in culture and the development of its cultural policy has been increasing. During the 1990s and 2000s, the EU implemented various new cultural programmes and actions offering economic support for inter-European collaboration in the field of culture. Kaleidoscope, a Community support programme for artistic and cultural projects with a European dimension, ran from 1996 to 2001. It aimed at enhancing artistic and cultural creation and fostering dissemination and knowledge about culture by focusing mainly on performing arts, visual and spatial arts as well as multimedia and applied arts. A Community support programme in the field of books and reading called Ariane sought to promote dissemination and translation of literature in the five-year period from 1996. The third Community action programme for the same period, Raphael, focused on cultural heritage, with the objective of promoting, conserving, and restoring cultural heritage "of European importance" (EP&C 1997, 33), improving transnational cooperation, and encouraging the general public to participate in preserving and developing cultural heritage.

Cultural policy gained prominence in the EU during the 2000s (e.g. Sassatelli 2009; Näss 2010; O'Callaghan 2011; Lähdesmäki 2012a) when several new cultural initiatives were launched. The ECOC (see Chapter 1) had already been turned from an intergovernmental initiative to an EU action in 1999. Europeana – a European digital library, archive, and museum – was initiated by the Commission in 2005, focusing on digital heritage, the digitalization of (non-digital) heritage, and open access. The EHL was launched as an intergovernmental scheme in 2006 and turned into an EU action in 2011 (see Chapter 1). In addition, the European Parliament became active in cultural matters during the 2000s. For instance, the Parliament made a decision on establishing a visitors' center in 2005 due to which the Parlamentarium, an exhibition space of 3,000 square meters, was opened in the administrative block of the Parliament in Brussels in 2011. The decision to establish a House of European History was made in 2008 by the European Parliament, and this history museum was opened in Brussels in 2017. The role of culture in the EU's international relations was highlighted in the Commission's communication on international cultural relations (EC 2016a), which emphasized cultural diversity as an important asset both within the EU and in its international relations. This communication connected culture to sustainable social and economic development and sought to promote cooperation on cultural heritage, as well as intercultural dialogue for peaceful inter-community relations.

The first European Community framework programme in support of culture, Culture 2000, was established for the period from 2000 to 2004, and subsequently extended to the end of 2006. The programme merged the fields of the previous three Community action programmes into one single instrument financing and regulating cultural cooperation. Its activities were continued in the Culture programme (2007–2013) and in the Creative Europe programme (2014–2020). These programmes sought to further artistic and cultural creation and their competitiveness, as well as to enhance knowledge and dissemination of culture. The main objective was to advance mobility and cooperation between member states in the field of culture (EP&C 1996; EP&C 2000, 2–3; EP&C 2006b, 4; EP&C 2013, 226). The Creative Europe programme consisted of Media and Culture sub-programmes and a cross-sectoral strand. The Culture sub-programme comprised five support measures, including "transnational cooperative projects", through which funding was allocated to projects such as the ECC, and "special actions", such as the ECOC and the EHL. All our case studies in this book are thus part of this core programme in EU cultural policy, but in its successive generations. The ECOC has been included in the actions of the Kaleidoscope, Culture 2000, Culture, and Creative Europe programmes. The ECC project was funded from the Culture programme from 2013 to 2015. Finally, the EHL falls under the Creative Europe programme.

3   The Identity-Building Agenda in EU Cultural Policy

Since its formative phases, cultural policy has been closely entangled with the EU's interest in identity building and its subsequent politics of creating and fostering a European identity and thereby fortifying (economic, political and cultural) unification in Europe (e.g. Shore 2000, 2006; Littoz-Monnet 2004, 2007, 2012; Sassatelli 2006, 2009; Tzaliki 2007; Näss 2009, 2010; Dewey 2010; Patel 2013; Calligaro 2014; Mattocks 2017; Lähdesmäki et al. 2020). While the rhetoric and objectives of this identity-building agenda have transformed over the decades, its core focus has been on creating belonging so that the citizens of member states would perceive the EU as a cultural and social entity close to them and their concerns, rather than a distant economic and intergovernmental organization.

In the years directly following World War II, European institutions regulating the economy and trade were established to develop an identity surpassing the exclusive national chauvinistic appeals of the past (Herrmann and Brewer 2004, 1–2). The actual emergence of the identity discourse of the European Community can be located in the 1970s. Due to the recession in this decade, the legitimacy of the European Community could no longer be based on economic prosperity. Simultaneously, the post-war consensus that the Community was a provider of stability had started to erode, not least because of the first enlargement of the Community (e.g. Calligaro 2014, 65). In this context the Declaration on European Identity, signed in Copenhagen in 1973 by the then nine member states, can be perceived as the starting point of the official discourse on the idea of European identity.

In the 1980s, the role of cultural issues in creating a sense of belonging was highlighted in the reports of the Committee on a People's Europe (1985). These reports became influential milestones in the process of increasing the importance of cultural factors in integration, and many of their proposals were later implemented. Furthermore, the cultural article of the Treaty of Maastricht (1992, Article 128) as well as the subsequent founding treaties (Amsterdam 1997, Article 151, and Lisbon 2007, Article 167) implicitly referred to promoting a common identity by aiming at "bringing the common cultural heritage to the fore" while respecting national and regional diversity.

In the 2000s, several interrelated challenges influenced European societies and politics, the EU included (see Chapter 1). The Union has sought to respond to these by advancing the idea of unity in Europe – together with respect and tolerance for diversity – and by enhancing both symbolic and concrete European integration. As in earlier decades, culture and heritage served as political tools in this process (Lähdesmäki 2016; 2020; Lähdesmäki et al. 2020). High-lighting the human dimension of the EU – by appealing to common cultural roots, identity, and shared values – is a means to restore the legitimacy of the EU and integration (Shore 1993, 785–786).

The Union's official slogan 'United in diversity' shapes EU's current identity discourse, which combines the collective and individual dimensions of belonging and different territorial scales – particularly the local and regional – as central elements of constructing a shared European identity. Recent cultural policy documents follow the earlier discourses on culture as a vector of identity building. In 2007, the Commission presented a 'European Agenda for Culture in the Globalizing World'. In it, the Commission described Europe as diverse in terms of history, languages, and cultures, and at the same time united through shared values and principles (EC 2007, 2). In its communication titled 'Strengthening European Identity through Education and Culture', the Commission repeated the importance of culture and education in producing European identity as well as "strengthening the sense of belonging together and being part of a cultural community" (EC 2017, 2). Values, cultural heritage, and diversity were seen as prerequisites of "our cultural community, our common values and identity" (EC 2017, 3), and mobility and transnational cooperation were understood as enhancing European identity and belonging. Furthermore, according to 'A New European Cultural Agenda', adopted by the European Commission in 2018, "Europe's rich cultural heritage and dynamic cultural and creative sectors strengthen European identity, creating a sense of belonging" (EC 2018a, 1). In a Commission communication on the subject, cultural heritage was seen as "a major factor in defining Europe's place in the world" and as a way of creating belonging among European citizens (EC 2014a, 2). According to the communication, several territorial scales are involved in the narrating of the past: "heritage is always both local and European", as it is "made up of local stories that together make the history of Europe" (EC 2014a, 2–3). In another communication, the Commission perceived cultural heritage as a way of "raising awareness of common history and values, and reinforcing a sense of belonging to a common European cultural and political space" (EC 2018b, 1). These central policy documents from the first two decades of the 2000s exemplify the consolidation of the concept of belonging in the EU's official vocabulary alongside the concept of identity and the rhetoric of "common" culture, history, and values.

Cultural programmes play a key role in the EU's identity-building agenda. In the programmes, culture is an instrument of integration for defining Europe and the EU as a community, for producing identity for this community and its members, and for attaching European citizens to this community. Identity comes to mean belonging and sharing 'European culture' as defined in the programme documents. Thus, the cultural programmes continue the trajectory paved by the Committee on a People's Europe (1985) emphasizing cultural identity as a core element in the integration process.

The three first cultural programmes highlighted the idea of Europe as a cultural community. They referred to culture and cultural activity as central elements for conceptualizing and accomplishing the idea of a shared European identity. According to the Kaleidoscope programme documents (EP&C 1996, 20), culture is a defining element of this identity:

> in reality, the most tangible and influential aspect of Europe as a whole is not merely its geographical, political, economic and social features but also its culture; whereas the perception of Europe in the world is largely determined by the position and strength of its cultural values.

The Culture 2000 and Culture programmes continued to highlight the role of culture in building identity and legitimizing EU integration (EP&C 2000, 1; EP&C 2006b, 1). Both programmes sought to support such cultural activity that helps "to increase their [i.e. the "people of Europe's"] sense of belonging to the same community" (EP&C 2000, 6; EP&C 2006b, 8), to raise awareness of cultural diversity in the member states, and to contribute to intercultural and international dialogue. Emphasizing the goal of enhancing belonging, the Creative Europe programme mentioned ECOC and EHL as particularly useful for stimulating this kind of activities (EP&C 2013, 223).

In the three most recent cultural programmes, the idea of Europe as a cultural community was conceptualized as "a cultural area common to the European people" (EP&C 2000, 1–2; EP&C 2006b, 2–4; EP&C 2013, 222–223). The concept of a common cultural area was not only a way of producing the EU as a cultural community but also exemplifies how EU's cultural policy initiatives are used to create identity and belonging to this imagined community and its members. As the decision on Creative Europe (EP&C 2013, 3) stated:

> Funding should also be provided for the European Capitals of Culture action and for the administration of the European Heritage Label action, as they contribute to the strengthening of the feeling of belonging to a common cultural area, to the stimulation of intercultural dialogue and mutual understanding and to the enhancement of the value of cultural heritage.

ECOC and EHL are here explicitly identified as instruments of the EU's politics of belonging. Moreover, the decisions on these programmes linked the
"common cultural area" to ideas of a "common cultural heritage" in Europe,
"intercultural dialogue", "transnational mobility", "cultural exchanges", and "the
emergence of European citizenship", as can be seen in the following quotations from the Culture Programme (EP&C 2006b, 2, 4):

> The Council, in its abovementioned resolutions, has stressed the need
> to adopt a more coherent approach at Community level with regard to
> culture, and that European added value is an essential and determining
> concept in the context of European cultural cooperation, and a general
> condition for Community measures in the field of culture. [...]

> In order to make this common cultural area for the peoples of Europe a
> reality, it is important to promote the transnational mobility of cultural
> players and the transnational circulation of artistic and cultural works
> and products, and to encourage dialogue and cultural exchanges. [...]

> The general objective of the Programme shall be to enhance the cultural
> area shared by Europeans and based on a common cultural heritage
> through the development of cultural cooperation between the creators,
> cultural players and cultural institutions of the countries taking part in
> the Programme, with a view to encouraging the emergence of European
> citizenship.

Cultural activities and transnational cooperation were presented as both the
basis and a means for establishing this cultural area (EP&C 2000, 1–2; EP&C
2006b, 2–4; EP&C 2013, 222). Transnational mobility was regarded as equally
important for constructing a European area in terms of culture as it is for economics (EC 2004, 11; EP&C 2006b, 2–3). The mobility of cultural actors and
cross-border dissemination of art and cultural products were core purposes of
the programmes.

The cultural programmes mention values, history, cultural heritage, way of
life, symbols, cultural events, and cultural cooperation as important and dis-
tinctively 'European' elements of identity. In the Culture 2000 and Culture programmes, citizens' common values and roots were seen as central factors in
their identity and "their membership of a society founded on freedom, equity,
democracy, respect for human dignity and integrity, tolerance and solidarity"
(EP&C 2006b, 1; see also EP&C 2000, 1). The importance given to values in the
context of identity and belonging echoes the value discourses of the early

phases of European integration, which became repeated in the later EU treaties and were adopted by the Charter of Fundamental Rights in 2000 (EP&C&COM 2000). In these initial and subsequent steps towards integration, the cultural sphere has been tightly linked with the goal of promoting values perceived as European (Calligaro 2014, 61). The central values emphasized in the discourse over the years include solidarity, peace, and reconciliation in the initial phase; representative democracy, the rule of law, social justice, and respect for human rights in the Copenhagen Declaration on the European Identity (CofEC 1973, 119); and liberty, democracy, respect for human rights and fundamental freedoms, the rule of law, and equality as core principles of the Union (Treaty of Amsterdam 1997, 8; Treaty of Lisbon 2007, 10). Throughout the value discourse, Europe is presented as something sublime, and as the cradle and protector of these values.

The identity-building aspect of EU cultural policy is thus clearly present in the Creative Europe programme and its predecessors, which form the umbrella for the three cases examined in this book. Cultural programmes will "contribute actively to the development of a European identity from the grass roots", as the Commission argued in its programme proposal for 2007–2013. It saw "theatres, museums, professional associations, research centers, universities, cultural institutes, the authorities, etc." as intermediaries in reaching citizens and offering them "cultural actions with a European dimension" (EC 2004, 4).

However, culture is a problematic tool for building identity and belonging to Europe. While the EU seeks to overcome national and cultural divisions within Europe by furthering a sense of communality and constructing a positive feeling of belonging to Europe among its citizens, the emphasis on a common European identity may create explicit and implicit boundaries. Moreover, the narrative of Europe as a unique cultural area with its distinctive cultural heritage and history is also (mis)used by nationalist parties and extreme right-wing movements to justify political attitudes and actions that are often based on explicit xenophobic, Islamophobic, anti-Semitic, sexist, misogynist, and anti-immigration positions. Thus, culture serves as an argument to simultaneously include some and exclude (many) others and to construct Europe as a precious fortress that needs to be defended against 'non-European others' in particular migrants from the Middle East, Africa, and Asia (see Vejvodová 2014; Lähdesmäki 2015, 2019; Brubaker 2017; De Cesari and Kaya 2019).

Despite its controversiality, the EU's identity-building discourse functions as a reference point for the rhetoric, programmes, and initiatives of EU cultural policy and for the actors at its different levels. EU cultural policy documents and other discourses contribute to identity discussions by both producing and reproducing conceptions of Europe and Europeanness. Furthermore, the actors at national and local levels need to position themselves in relation to the EU's identity-building endeavors. Whether cities applying to become the European Capitals of Culture, or projects, such as the ECC, applying for funding from the Creative Europe programme, or heritage sites applying for the EHL, they all need to use the same rhetoric in one way or another to become accepted, funded, or awarded by the EU.

4   The Role of the Projects, ECOC, and EHL in the Identity-Building Agenda

The EU's cultural programmes explicitly seek to raise awareness of Europe through various measures, such as citizens' cooperation within programme activities. The projects funded through the programmes, such as the ECC, serve this aim by producing and distributing knowledge about Europe, presenting Europe as an entity that can be an object of knowing and a meaningful framework for manifold matters. Moreover, the projects contribute to the programme objective of constructing EUrope as a lived and experienced place that is visible in citizens' everyday lives, thereby making it easier for them to identify with it. Practices such as encounters with other project participants may guide the participants' conceptions of Europe and offer elements of their identity. For example, through personal experiences of speaking and hearing several languages in the project, participants may come to regard multilingualism as a feature of a European identity. However, in many cases, EU funding and contact with participants from other member states may be perceived as the only defining link to the EUrope. Nevertheless, this may be enough to strengthen the symbolic or practical presence of the EU or Europe.

In the most recent guidelines for cooperation projects funded through the Creative Europe programme, the Commission defined five priorities for the projects. One of them was to "raise awareness of common history and values, and reinforce a sense of belonging to a common European space" (EC 2019, 4). This priority indicates that the EU's politics of belonging is explicit in its project funding. The Commission stated that funding would be available through Creative Europe for projects that enable "cultural heritage organisations [to give] a European dimension to their activities" (EC 2019, 9). This means that the purpose of the programme is not to support all cultural (heritage) activities for their own sake, but only those with an explicit "European dimension".

As one of the EU's best known and longest running cultural initiatives, the ECOC plays a relevant role in the EU's politics of belonging. Focusing on urbanity and urban cultural matters, the initiative resonates with the idea of European cities as significant sites of governing the process of Europeanization

(Le Galès 2002; Sassatelli 2009, 79). Constructing a common European cultural area and strengthening citizens' feeling of belonging to it have been both implicit and recently also explicitly stated aims of the ECOC since its launch as an intergovernmental event in 1985 (EP&C 2006b, 2; EP&C 2013, 223). When the initiative became an EU action in 1999, its European focus was sharpened by introducing the criterion of "European dimension" into the decision (EP&C 1999, 2). This criterion was characterized as "based principally on cultural cooperation" (ibid.). The discourse emphasizing the 'European' was heightened in the second decision of the ECOC action in 2006. In this decision, the required criteria for the local cultural programme was divided into two categories, "the European Dimension" and "City and Citizens". The first category aimed to "foster cooperation between cultural operators, artists and cities from the relevant Member States", "highlight the richness of cultural diversity in Europe", and "bring common aspects of European cultures to the fore" (EP&C 2006a, 2). The European Commission's guide for ECOC applicants advised cities to find their "European dimension" by linking their local culture to the "European culture", thereby indicating "their sense of belonging" (EC 2009, 11):

> In other words, candidate cities must present the role they have played in European culture, their links with Europe, their place in it and their sense of belonging. They must also demonstrate their current participation in European artistic and cultural life, alongside their own specific features. This European dimension may also be designed and perceived by the cities through the dialogue and exchange which they establish with other cultures and artists from other continents, so as to foster intercultural dialogue.

The Commission's proposal for the third decision of the ECOC action emphasized the European dimension as the core discourse of the action (EC 2012). The new decision, made in 2014, again highlighted the idea of belonging to a common cultural area, as its first general objective was "to safeguard and promote the diversity of cultures in Europe and to highlight the common features they share as well as to increase citizens' sense of belonging to a common cultural area" (EP&C 2014, 4). The decision continued to emphasize that the ECOC's cultural programmes must have "a strong European dimension" (EP&C 2014, 2, 5). The meanings of this European dimension were specified by connecting them to cultural diversity, intercultural dialogue, and mutual understanding between European citizens; common aspects of European cultures, heritage, and history, including European integration and current European themes; European artists and transnational cooperation; as well as attracting broad European and international public (EP&C 2014, 5).

The Commission's latest guide for the applicant cities went on to underline how "the European dimension is at the heart of an ECOC's programme" (EC n.d., 18) and how it can be manifested by linking the local culture to the 'European' (ibid., 19). The ECOC policy discourse intertwines cultural elements from the local and European levels and thus produces the 'European' as a multi-layered construction. This discourse avoids addressing the national layer that has been sometimes perceived in the EU cultural policy discourse as a challenge to the construction of the 'European' (Lähdesmäki et al. 2020). The frequent bypassing of the national in the official EU discourses indicates how nations can be interpreted as one of the EU's 'others', even though, simultaneously, 'Europe of nations' is one of the images included in the EU's identity building.

Several consultations and evaluation reports of the ECOC action have criticized the designated cities for giving the European dimension only a minor role in their plans and events (e.g. ECOTEC 2009; Ecorys 2011, 24; EC 2012, 3). Hence, the strengthening of the discourse of the European dimension in the ECOC policy documents can be interpreted as a response to the perceived lack of this dimension in both ECOC applications and the designated cities' cultural programmes. Several scholars have also noted how the 'European' is difficult to perceive from the ECOC's programmes and events (e.g. Myerschough 1994; Sassatelli 2002, 444; Palmer 2004, 85–86; Richards and Wilson 2004, 1945). The cities' diverse interpretations of the European dimension and varying emphases between the notions of European and local identities indicate the complexity of the idea of Europe, which can be understood and manifested in myriad ways.

The ECOC action has, nevertheless, contributed to the Europeanization of cities around Europe through requiring them to find ways to narrate and present themselves as European (see e.g. Sassatelli 2006, 2008; Mittag, 2013). The action played a strong role in the cultural Europeanization of former socialist states during the Eastern enlargement of the Union and soon after it (see for instance Habit 2013; Lähdesmäki 2014). Since 2009, the EU has annually designated at least two ECOCs – one in an 'old' member state and one in the 'new' states that joined the EU in 2004 or 2007 (EC 2005). Since then, the ECOC title has been used to brand cities as European in the new member states and, more broadly, in rethinking and remapping the cities and their host countries in the geography of Europe (Lähdesmäki 2014). This mode of selecting the ECOCs will continue until 2032 (EC 2012).

The role of the ECOC action as a policy instrument for cultural Europeanization and integration in Europe was further bolstered by a decision that enabled cities beyond the EU member states to apply for the ECOC title for the years 2021, 2024, 2028, 2030, and 2033 (EP&C 2017a). Applications were opened to cities in EU candidate countries, potential candidate countries, or members of the European Free Trade Association party to the Agreement on the European Economic Area (called EFTA/EEA countries). Even though some non-EU cities had been designated as ECOCs already before this decision, the official broadening of the ECOC action blurs the boundaries between the EU and non-EU and enlarges the perception of a 'common European cultural area'.

The EHL, finally, is a good example of how the EU seeks to respond to its identity crisis and tackle the unwanted effects of the recent political, economic, and social challenges in Europe by constructing a European identity through focusing on the past. The past has been important in the identity-building efforts of the European Community and the EU since European integration began, but since the 1970s, the amount and scope of EU heritage policy documents has increased enormously (Delanty 2005; Sassatelli 2008; Lähdesmäki and Mäkinen 2019, 36–37; see also Kaasik-Krogerus 2019). In the 2010s, political interest in creating and promoting a common European narrative of the past and an idea of shared cultural heritage has increased among EU actors and cultural policy-makers. In the EU's "move to history" (Prutsch 2013, 36), the narrations of the past and attempts to foster common cultural heritage in Europe function as building blocks for a future Europe and to educate a new generation of European citizens.

Even though the EHL can be seen as the EU's response to the various recent challenges in Europe, it can also be interpreted as a reaction to a very specific identity crisis inside the EU and its institutions: the shock rejection of the Treaty establishing a Constitution for Europe in the referenda of the Netherlands and France in 2005. At the time, this was commonly referred to as a constitutional crisis in the political and academic debates. The European Council quickly launched a period of reflection on the EU's future, aiming to improve connections with citizens. In its proposal on establishing the EHL as an EU action, the Commission noted that as an intergovernmental scheme, the EHL "emerged in 2005 as one of the responses to the gap between the European Union and its citizens" (EC 2010a, 2; see also EC 2010b, 15). According to the Commission, the gap is due to a lack of knowledge of both the history of Europe and the role of the EU, its institutions, and values (EC 2010a, 2; EC 2010b, 15). According to the impact assessment accompanying the EHL proposal, the low turnout in the European Parliament elections in June 2009 and the relatively negative perception of the image of the EU in the Eurobarometer survey indicated that the gap between citizens and the EU had not closed (EC 2010b, 16–17). Neither of these documents mentioned the 'constitutional crisis' but the impact assessment explained that repairing the EU's connections to citizens was an aim of both the EHL and other EU instruments, such as "Plan D for Democracy, Dialogue and Debate" (EC 2010b, 15), which was launched precisely during the period of reflection. Hence, it can be interpreted that the EHL continues the mode of action adopted in prior phases of integration: in the face of (identity) crises, new cultural policy tools are developed to highlight identity building, thereby promoting and legitimizing integration.

The core motive for the initiative stems from the EU's politics of belonging. Its objective is to turn cultural heritage, hitherto framed mainly in national and/or local terms, into a shared transnational basis for evoking a notion of "our" (European) identity and feeling of belonging. The intergovernmental declaration on the EHL proclaimed that "our heritage in all its diversity is one of the most significant elements of our identity, our shared values and our principles" (Declaration on the initiative for a European Heritage Label 2007). A Commission press release on the forthcoming EHL action announced that in order "[t]o give Europeans a greater sense of belonging, the Commission has decided to sponsor the European Heritage Label, a registry of historical sites whose significance transcends national borders" (EC 2010c). Another example of using the EHL in the EU's politics of belonging is provided by the Commission's communication on cultural heritage, in which the EHL sites were described as "concrete examples of European values and identity, explained directly to citizens and thus made tangible" (EC 2018b, 12).

The politics of belonging is visible in the goals of the EHL action. The action has two general objectives: "strengthening European citizens' sense of belonging to the Union, in particular that of young people, based on shared values and elements of European history and cultural heritage, as well as an appreciation of national and regional diversity" and "strengthening intercultural dialogue" (EP&C 2011, 3, Article 3). The aims for the EHL sites follow these general objectives and include "highlighting their European significance [and] raising European citizens' awareness of their common cultural heritage" (EP&C 2011, 3, Article 3). Consequently, the criteria for awarding sites a Label emphasize the sites' "symbolic European value" and "significant role in the history and culture of Europe and/or the building of the Union" (EP&C 2011, 4). Narratives related to crossing borders between member states are underlined as a means of demonstrating this (EP&C 2011, 4).

The policy documents directly dealing with the EHL indicate conceptual changes in the EU's politics of belonging. In the intergovernmental phase, the concept of European identity was frequently used, but in the proposal and decision of the EHL as an EU action, the concept of belonging replaced it. In the documents of the international selection panel (see Chapter 1), which are core texts in the implementation of the EHL as an EU action, neither of the concepts was used. Instead, these documents conceptualized belonging as "European significance", which is the key criterion of the EHL award.

5 The Participatory Agenda in the EU Cultural Policy

Similarly to identity, participation is perceived in the EU documents as a way of deepening citizens' belonging to the EU. Cultural programmes are the instruments proposed for enhancing citizens' participation in the Union and thereby strengthening their support for EU integration. As such, the programmes are embedded in the EU's participatory governance (see Chapter 2). The White Paper on European Governance (EC 2001) has had a significant role in distributing the idea of participation as a central principle of good governance, although it has been criticized for a narrow understanding of participation (Magnette 2003; Bevir 2006). Participatory governance is increasingly popular in various contexts (Bache 2010; Saurugger 2010; Lindgren and Persson 2011; Kohler-Koch and Quittkat 2013; Wolff 2013), and the EU programmes, with their emphasis on multilevel cooperation, can be seen as part of this participation boom. Participatory governance requires the involvement of actors from multiple levels as partners in making, supporting, and implementing policy. Utilizing local actors and their projects and networks is typical for EU cultural policy, as the ECOC and EHL exemplify (see also Sassatelli 2009, 68–73).

The cultural articles in the EU founding treaties did not discuss participation in culture. Similarly, the Commission's cultural agendas, presented in 2007 and 2018, made little mention of participation. However, the European Agenda for Culture in the Globalizing World noted the need for dialogue, including civil society actors, which was supposed to create "a renewed sense of partnership and ownership of EU action to achieve these objectives" (EC 2007, 8). The idea of seeking to involve various partners in implementing the EU's policy goals exemplifies participatory governance. Typically of participatory governance, the agenda did not specify how people would participate, in what, and whether they could influence the processes and outcomes – that is, whether their "ownership of EU action" was real or illusory. In the New European Cultural Agenda, citizens' participation in culture was connected to well-being and social cohesion, and particularly to the idea of European belonging: "there is clear scope to increase cultural participation, and bring Europeans together to experience what connects us rather than what divides us" (EC 2018a, 1).

Participation has been addressed increasingly in some recent EU cultural policy discourses. In its communication on cultural heritage, the Commission called for a "more participative interpretation and governance models [of cultural heritage] that are better suited to contemporary Europe, through greater involvement of the private sector and civil society" (EC 2014a, 7). It also underlined the importance of diversifying audiences and saw digitization as a way to enable citizen access and engagement with cultural heritage (EC 2014a, 8). Another communication continued to highlight a "participatory approach to cultural heritage" (EC 2018b, 1). The first of its five pillars concerned participation and access to cultural heritage, which was connected to constructing an "inclusive Europe" (EC 2018b, 5). The communication did not only emphasize "citizens' participation and engagement with Europe's shared heritage" (EC 2018b, 13) but wished to "foster cultural heritage as a key enabler of citizen participation and a vehicle of shared values such as dialogue and diversity" (ibid.). The notion of participation in cultural heritage was closely connected to the idea of constructing a European community and belonging: "engagement with cultural heritage also fosters a sense of belonging to a European community, based on common cultural legacies, historical experiences and shared values" (EC 2018b, 6).

The notion of participation is present in the cultural programmes of the EU, improving access to culture being one of their central goals. The very first cultural programmes, Kaleidoscope, Ariane, and Raphael, emphasized participation in terms of access to culture. For example, one programme objective stated in the decision on Raphael was "to improve access to the cultural heritage in its European dimension and encourage the active participation of the general public, in particular children, young people, the underprivileged and those living in the outlying and rural areas of the Community, in the safeguarding and development of the European cultural heritage" (EP&C 1997, 33). This objective acknowledges that different groups do not have equal access to and opportunity to participate in cultural heritage.

Similar objectives about furthering access to and participation in culture were set in the following programmes, Culture 2000 (EP&C 2000, 3) and Culture (EP&C 2006b, 1). The most recent cultural programme, Creative Europe, sought to "support [...] audience development as a means of stimulating interest in, and improving access to, European cultural and creative works and tangible and intangible cultural heritage" (EP&C 2013, 229). These documents also recognized that citizens' opportunities to engage in cultural activities differ due to age, economic situation, or social background (e.g. EP&C 1996, 20; EP&C 1997, 33). For example, the authors of the Culture 2000 programme conceived culture as an instrument of social integration and emphasized access to and participation in culture by young or underprivileged people from various social, regional, and cultural backgrounds (EP&C 2000, 1, 5). Similarly, Creative Europe aimed "to reach new and enlarged audiences and improve access to cultural and creative works in the Union and beyond, with a particular focus on children, young people, people with disabilities and under-represented groups" (EP&C 2013, 226).

In this context, citizens' participation in culture primarily referred to cultural cooperation within the programmes themselves, consuming cultural goods, and receiving cultural services provided by various private, public, third-sector, formal, and non-formal cultural actors. Other forms of participation in culture – such as involvement in knowledge production or public decision-making regarding culture or producing and experiencing culture through citizen-driven grass-roots activities – did not receive equal attention.

The cultural programmes also emphasized citizens' participation in the process of European integration. In particular, culture and participation in it were seen as developing and concretizing the citizenship of the Union that was adopted in the Maastricht Treaty in 1992. In the EU's politics of belonging, culture, citizenship, and identity are tightly intertwined and used to co-create each other (see also Steiger 2009). Improving access to culture, cultural and linguistic cooperation, diversity, and "knowledge of Europe's cultural roots" (EC 1995a, 10) contributes to this end, according to the programmes (e.g. EC 1995b, 10; EP&C 1996, 20; EC 2004, 10; EP&C 2006b, 1). For instance, the Culture 2000 programme specifically aimed at "explicit recognition of culture as an economic factor and as a factor in social integration and citizenship" (EP&C 2000, 3). The "emergence of European citizenship" was part of the general objective of the Culture programme to enhance the cultural area (EP&C 2006b, 4). In the EU documents, rather than referring to political agency, the concept of citizenship – like the concept of identity – is used to legitimize EU integration (Mäkinen 2012).

The programme documents demonstrate how participation and identity are often entwined and mutually reinforced in the EU's politics of belonging. For example, the Culture 2000 and Culture programmes (EP&C 2006b, 1; see also EP&C 2000, 1) included an almost identical formulation on this:

> For citizens to give their full support to, and participate fully in, European integration, greater emphasis should be placed on their common cultural values and roots as a key element of their identity and their membership of a society founded on freedom, equity, democracy, respect for human dignity and integrity, tolerance and solidarity, in full compliance with the Charter of Fundamental Rights of the European Union.

According to this formulation, citizens' participation in and support for European integration requires attention to cultural identity. Related to this, citizens' membership in the EU community was emphasized. This community was described as a society based on values such as freedom, equity, democracy, human rights, and solidarity – frequently listed in EU discourses as the core principles of the EU and central elements of its identity, as noted above. In a nutshell the quote states the idea common to the EU's cultural programmes that both culture and participation are tools for creating identity, belonging, and bringing citizens closer to the EU and to each other. These building blocks construct the EU community as a cultural or people's union, which is more than an economic union. The programme text cited above continued by referring to the need for this construction to work as a whole: "a better balance should be achieved between the economic and cultural aspects of the Community, so that these aspects can complement and sustain each other" (EP&C 2000, 1).

In these culture programmes, Europe and an idea of Europeanness are not only to be constructed from above through symbols and rhetoric but also from below through citizens and their participation. The aspiration is to build an EU community and European identity founded on personal relations and interaction through citizens' participation in the EU programmes and in the EU integration project. Therefore, in the programmes, citizens are encouraged to engage in different forms of cooperation and dialogue, in order to advance integration in practice by raising awareness of their own culture as well as improving knowledge of other cultures and mutual understanding between Europeans. For instance, the Culture programme assumed that "intercultural dialogue leads to mutual enrichment and a common search for shared values and interpretations" (EC 2004, 6). These goals can be seen as attempts to legitimate European integration, based on the assumption that it is easier for citizens to accept an organization in which they feel involved. In sum, participation is assigned a similar function to identity in EU cultural policy.

6   The Role of the Projects, ECOC, and EHL in the Participatory Agenda

The projects funded through EU cultural programmes provide an example of the EU's participatory governance in practice. Often involving civil society actors as organizers and participants, the projects themselves can be understood as participation and civil society activity. However, the projects funded through the programmes are not primarily about participation in decision-making but rather about creating networks and advancing transnational cooperation in various cultural fields. Nevertheless, this type of project participation allows participants from different countries to encounter each other and can create a sense of engagement, European identity, and a sense belonging to the EU.

In the EU documents, projects funded through the EU programmes are seen as channels that enable citizens' participation in EU integration (e.g. EC 2018b, 13). The project examined in this book, the ECC, sought to encourage debate on the citizenship of the Union through art (see Chapter 5). Indeed, the EU projects can make citizenship of the Union more tangible – but in the EU programme documents, citizenship is depicted primarily as mobility across member state borders and as European identity rather than as political agency (Mäkinen 2012). Even though the importance of culture and the EU's cultural activity in developing the citizenship of the Union is explicitly underlined in several policy documents, this is not backed up by specific discussion of how funded projects promote citizen participation in society or in European integration.

Instead, participation is commonly discussed in the programmes in terms of access to culture, and the funded projects play a key role in facilitating this access. Already the first Kaleidoscope programme was to fund projects promoting access to culture (EP&C 1996, 24). While the notions of access and audience participation were not discussed any further in the programme decisions, this was done in the Commission's guidelines for cooperation projects funded through the Creative Europe programme. Audience development was one of the four main objectives for these projects (EC 2019, 4). According to the guidelines, the projects were to "follow an inclusive and participatory approach, putting the audience and the project beneficiaries at the center of activities, and involving them in their design and/or implementation" (EC 2019, 8) and specifically focus on young people and other groups that are hard to reach. The guidelines advised that "[a]udience development should be an integral part of the project" (EC 2019, 6), and that this could mean both broadening and diversifying audiences and deepening the relationship with existing audiences. The aim was to engage audiences "in the programming, production, participatory art, physical dialogue, social media interaction, volunteering or creative partnerships with other sectors" (EC 2019, 6). Furthermore, mobility of artists and cultural operators was to include interaction with local communities and audiences (EC 2019, 6). These guidelines thus explained the ways in which the projects were to promote citizens' participation in culture.

Participation has an established role in the ECOC action. In the programme period 2007–2019, the second criterion for local cultural programmes, "City and Citizens", focused on participation of those living in the city and its surroundings (EP&C 2006a, 2–3). In the programme period 2020–2033, widening access to and participation in culture was one of four specific objectives set for the action, and citizens' participation was one of the six categories of assessing applications. According to the decision, the local population and civil society should participate in preparing and implementing the ECOC programme (EP&C 2014, 6). Specific groups to involve included young and elderly people, volunteers, marginalized, disadvantaged, and minority populations, as well as persons with disabilities (ibid.). In a guide for potential applicant cities, the

Commission underlined an "active participation and not just participation as audiences" (EC n.d. 20).

Since 2005, more and more ECOC programmes have had elements of community engagement, including community-led projects (EP 2013, 76). They often use rhetoric of social inclusion and have utilized the ECOC year to improve public participation in the cultural activity (EP 2013, 91). This "citizenship dimension", as it is sometimes called, has even been interpreted as a key success factor of the ECOCs (EP 2013, 91). However, approaches to public engagement vary greatly from one city to another, and involving local people remains a challenge (e.g. Lähdesmäki 2013; EP 2013, 91, 171).

Participation in processes and practices concerning cultural heritage and the interaction between heritage institutions and communities is commonly emphasized in cultural heritage policies at local, regional, national, European, and global levels (e.g. Vergo 1989; Sandell 2003; Council of Europe 2005; Macdonald 2005; 2007; Applegate Krouse 2006; Hooper-Greenhill 2006; Watson and Waterton 2010; Adell et al. 2015; Murawska-Muthesius and Piotrowski 2015; Bidault 2018). While a participatory approach to the past is increasingly emphasized in the EU's cultural heritage policy (EC 2014a, 7; CofEU 2014; EC 2018b; EC 2018c; EP&C 2017b, 5), participation in cultural heritage is not further discussed in the EHL policy documents (e.g. EP&C 2011; EC 2013; 2014b; 2015; 2016b).

As in many other EU initiatives, networking is a key goal and core mode of action in the EHL, as the decision of the action emphasizes (EP&C 2011, 2, 4, 7). This mode can be interpreted as a type of participatory approach that seeks to involve heritage practitioners in advancing the EHL objectives through furthering their mobility and cooperation (see Lähdesmäki et al. 2020). Another mode of action is micro-level participation at the EHL sites and in EHL governance. The sites already encourage people living in the vicinity of the sites to participate in their activities, but based on our previous research, so far citizen-driven engagement does not have ongoing effects on the governance of cultural heritage in the EHL context (see Lähdesmäki et al. 2020).

In sum, cultural initiatives have long had a central role in the EU's politics of belonging. They continue to serve as political instruments to advance cultural Europeanization and reinforce the legitimacy of European integration. In this chapter, we have shown how identity building and citizen participation are important elements in the EU's politics of belonging as articulated in its cultural policy. Both elements are closely entwined with the notions of culture and citizenship but these relations are not clearly defined in the EU policy rhetoric. Thus, identity, participation, citizenship, and culture are intertwined instruments of creating belonging in the EU cultural policy.

References

Adell, N., R. F. Bendix, C. Bortolotto, and M. Tauschek, eds. 2015. *Between Imagined Communities and Communities of Practice: Participation, Territory and the Making of Heritage.* Universitätsverlag Göttingen.

Applegate Krouse, S. 2006. "Anthropology and the New Museology." *Reviews in Anthropology* 35 (2): 169–182.

Bache, I. 2010. "Partnership as an EU Policy Instrument: A Political History." *West European Politics* 33 (1): 58–74.

Bevir, M. 2006. "Democratic Governance: Systems and Radical Perspectives." *Public Administration Review* 66 (3): 426–436.

Bidault, M. 2018. "Heritage and Participation as Matters of Human Rights." In *Heritage is Ours: Citizens Participating in Decision Making*, edited by A.-M. Halme, T. Mustonen, J.-P. Taavitsainen, S. Thomas, and A. Weij, 74–85. Helsinki: Europa Nostra Finland.

Brubaker, R. 2017. "Between Nationalism and Civilizationism: the European Populist Moment in Comparative Perspective." *Ethnic and Racial Studies*, 40 (8): 1191–1226.

Calligaro, O. 2014. "From 'European Cultural Heritage' to 'Cultural Diversity'? The Changing Core Values of European Cultural Policy." *Politique Européenne* 45 (3): 60–85. Accessed 17 April 2020. https://www.cairn.info/revue-politique-europeenne -2014-3-page-60.htm

Committee on a People's Europe. 1985. "A People's Europe: Reports from the ad hoc Committee." *Bulletin of the European Communities*, Supplement 7.

CofEU (Council of the European Union). 2014. "Council Conclusions on Participatory Governance of Cultural Heritage." *Official Journal of the European Union* C 463: 1–3.

CofEC (Council of the European Communities). 1973. "Declaration on the European Identity. Meeting of the Heads of State of Government, Copenhagen, 9 December 1973." *Bulletin of the European Communities*, Supplement 12-1973, 118–122.

Council of Europe. 2005. "Framework Convention on the Value of Cultural Heritage for Society. Faro, 27.10.2005." *Council of Europe Treaty Series No. 199.* Accessed 22 April 2020. https://www.coe.int/en/web/conventions/search-on-treaties/-/conventions/ rms/0900001680083746

De Cesari, C., and A. Kaya. eds. 2019. *European Memory in Populism. (Mis)Representations of Self and Other.* London: Routledge.

Declaration on the Initiative for a European Heritage Label. 2007. Madrid: Ministry of Education, Culture and Sport. Accessed 12 April 2013. http://en.www.mcu.es/ patrimonio/MC/PatrimonioEur/docs/en_declaracionMinistrosPatEu.pdf

Delanty, G. 2005. "The Idea of a Cosmopolitan Europe: On the Cultural Significance of Europeanization." *International Review of Sociology* 15 (3): 405–21.

Dewey, P. 2010. "Power in European Union Cultural Policy." In *International Cultural Policies and Power*, edited by J. P. Singh, 113–126. New York: Palgrave Macmillan.

Ecorys. 2011. Ex-post Evaluation of 2010 European Capitals of Culture. Final Report for the European Commission DG Education and Culture. Birmingham: Ecorys.

ECOTEC. 2009. Ex-Post Evaluation of 2007 and 2008 European Capitals of Culture. Birmingham: Ecotec.

EC (Commission of the European Communities). 1977. "Community Action in the Cultural Sector. Commission Communication to the Council." *Bulletin of the European Communities*, Supplement 6.

EC (Commission of the European Communities). 1982. "Stronger Community Action in the Cultural Sector. Communication from the Commission to the Council and Parliament." *Bulletin of the European Communities*, Supplement 6.

EC (Commission of the European Communities). 1987. "A Fresh Boost for Culture in the European Community. Commission Communication to the Council and Parliament. COM(87)603 final." *Bulletin of the European Communities*, Supplement 6.

EC (Commission of the European Communities). 1992. New Prospects for Community Cultural Action. Communication from the Commission to the Council and Parliament and the Economic and Social Committee. COM(92)149 final. Brussels: European Commission.

EC (Commission of the European Communities). 1994. European Community Action in Support of Culture. Communication from the Commission to the Council and Parliament. COM(94)356 final. Brussels: European Commission.

EC (European Commission). 1995a. "Amended Proposal for a European Parliament and Council Decision Establishing a Programme to Support Artistic and Cultural Activities Having a European Dimension (Kaleidoscope 2000) COM(95) 373 final." *Official Journal of the European Communities* C 278: 9–22.

EC (European Commission). 1995b. "Amended Proposal for a European Parliament and Council Decision Establishing a Support Programme in the Field of Books and Reading through Translation (Ariane) COM(95) 374 final." *Official Journal of the European Communities* C 279: 7–22.

EC (European Commission). 2001. "European Governance – A White Paper. COM(2001)428." *Official Journal of the European Union* C 287: 1–29.

EC (European Commission). 2004. Proposal for a Decision of the European Parliament and of the Council Establishing the Culture 2007 Programme (2007–2013). COM(2004) 469 final. 14.7.2004. Accessed 10 January 2020. http://www.europarl.europa.eu/registre/docs_autres_institutions/commission_europeenne/com/2004/0469/COM_COM(2004)0469_EN.pdf

EC (European Commission). 2007. European Agenda for Culture in a Globalizing World. Communication from the Commission to the European Parliament, the European Council, the European Economic and Social Committee and the Committee of the Regions. 10.5.2007. COM(2007) 242 final. Accessed 22 April 2020. https://eur-lex.europa.eu/legal-content/EN/TXT/?uri=CELEX:52007DC0242

EC (European Commission). 2009. Guide for Cities Applying for the Title of European Capital of Culture. Brussels: European Commission.

EC (European Commission). 2010a. Proposal for a Decision of the European Parliament and of the Council Establishing a European Union Action for the European Heritage Label. COM(2010) 76 final. Brussels: European Commission.

EC (European Commission). 2010b. Commission Staff Working Document. Impact Assessment. Accompanying document to the Proposal for a Decision of the European Parliament and of the Council establishing a European Union action for the European Heritage Label. COM (2010) 76 final. Brussels: European Commission.

EC (European Commission). 2010c. "Monuments to Europe", Official website of the European Commission, 9 March. Accessed 16 December 2010. http://ec.europa.eu/news/culture/100309_en.htm

EC (European Commission). 2012. Proposal for a Decision of the European Parliament and of the Council Establishing a Union Action for the European Capitals of Culture for the Years 2020 to 2033. COM(2012) 407 final. Brussels: European Commission.

EC (European Commission). 2013. European Heritage Label 2013. Panel Report. Brussels: European Commission.

EC (European Commission). 2014a. Communication from the Commission to the European Parliament, the Council, the European Economic and Social Committee and the Committee of the Regions: Towards an Integrated approach to Cultural Heritage for Europe. COM(2014) 477 final. Brussels: European Commission.

EC (European Commission). 2014b. European Heritage Label 2014. Panel Report. Brussels: European Commission.

EC (European Commission). 2015. European Heritage Label 2015. Panel Report. Brussels: European Commission.

EC (European Commission). 2016a. Towards an EU Strategy for International Cultural Relations. Joint Communication to the European Parliament and the Council. JOIN(2016) 29 final. Brussels: European Commission.

EC (European Commission). 2016b. European Heritage Label: Panel Report on Monitoring. Brussels: European Commission.

EC (European Commission). 2017. Strengthening European Identity through Education and Culture. Communication from the Commission to the European Parliament, the Council, the European Economic and Social Committee and the Committee of the Regions. COM(2017) 673 final. Brussels: European Commission.

EC (European Commission). 2018a. A New European Agenda for Culture. Communication from the Commission to the European Parliament, the European Council, the European Economic and Social Committee and the Committee of the Regions. COM(2018) 267 final. Brussels: European Commission.

EC (European Commission). 2018b. Commission Staff Working Document. European Framework for Action on Cultural Heritage. SWD(2018) 491 final. Brussels: European Commission.

EC (European Commission). 2018c. Participatory Governance of Cultural Heritage: Report of THE OMC (Open Method of Coordination) Working Group of Member States' Experts. Brussels: European Commission.

EC (European Commission). 2019. Creative Europe. Culture Sub-programme. Support for European Cooperation Projects 2020. Call for Proposals EACEA 32/2019. Guidelines. Accessed 9 January 2020. https://eacea.ec.europa.eu/sites/eacea-site/files/2._guidelines_eacea_29-209_coop_2020_1.pdf

EC (European Commission). n.d. European Capitals of Culture 2020 to 2033. A Guide for Cities Preparing to Bid. Accessed 8 February 2020. https://ec.europa.eu/programmes/creative-europe/sites/creative-europe/files/capitals-culture-candidates-guide_en_vdec17.pdf

EP (European Parliament). 2013. European Capitals of Culture. Success Strategies and Long-term Effects. Study. Accessed 7 February 2020. https://www.europarl.europa.eu/RegData/etudes/etudes/join/2013/513985/IPOL-CULT_ET(2013)513985_EN.pdf

EP&C (European Parliament and the Council). 1996. "Decision No 719/96/EC of the European Parliament and of the Council of 29 March 1996 Establishing a Programme to Support Artistic and Cultural Activities Having a European Dimension (Kaleidoscope)." *Official Journal of the European Communities* L 99: 20–26.

EP&C (European Parliament and the Council). 1997. "Decision No 2228/97 /EC of the European Parliament and of the Council of 13 October 1997 Establishing a Community Action Programme in the Field of Cultural Heritage (the Raphael Programme)." *Official Journal of the European Communities* L 305: 31–41.

EP&C (European Parliament and the Council). 1999. "Decision 1419/1999/EC of the European Parliament and of the Council of 25 May 1999 Establishing a Community Action for the European Capital of Culture Event for the Years 2005 to 2019." *Official Journal of the European Communities* L 166: 1–5.

EP&C (European Parliament and the Council). 2000. "Decision No 508/2000/EC of the European Parliament and of the Council of 14 February 2000 Establishing the Culture 2000 Programme." *Official Journal of the European Communities* L 63: 1–9.

EP&C (European Parliament and the Council). 2006a. "Decision No 1622/2006/EC of the European Parliament and of the Council of 24 October 2006 Establishing a Community Action for the European Capital of Culture Event for the Years 2007 to 2019." *Official Journal of the European Union* L 304: 1–6.

EP&C (European Parliament and the Council). 2006b. "Decision No 1855/2006/EC of the European Parliament and of the Council of 12 December 2006 Establishing the Culture Programme (2007 to 2013)." *Official Journal of the European Union* L 372: 1–11.

EP&C (European Parliament and the Council). 2011. "Decision no 1194/2011/EU of the European Parliament and of the Council of 16 November 2011 Establishing a European Union Action for the European Heritage Label." *Official Journal of the European Union* L 303: 1–9.

EP&C (European Parliament and the Council). 2013. "Regulation (EU) No 1295/2013 of the European Parliament and of the Council of 11 December 2013 Establishing the Creative Europe Programme (2014 to 2020)." *Official Journal of the European Union* L 347: 221–237.

EP&C (European Parliament and the Council). 2014. "Decision No 445/2014/EU of the European Parliament and of the Council of 16 April 2014 Establishing a Union action for the European Capitals of Culture for the Years 2020 to 2033." *Official Journal of the European Union* L 132: 1–12.

EP&C (European Parliament and the Council). 2017a. "Decision (EU) 2017/1545 Amending Decision No 445/2014/EU Establishing a Union Action for the European Capitals of Culture for the Years 2020 to 2033." *Official Journal of the European Union* L 237: 1–4.

EP&C (European Parliament and the Council). 2017b. "Decision (EU) 2017/864 on a European Year of Cultural Heritage (2018)." *Official Journal of the European Union* L 131: 1–9.

EP&C&COM (European Parliament, the Council and the Commission). 2000. "The Charter of Fundamental Rights." *Official Journal of the European Communities* C 364: 1–22.

Habit, D. 2013. "Peripheral ECOCs between Cultural Policy and Cultural Governance: The Case of Sibiu 2007." In *The Cultural Politics of Europe. European Capitals of Culture and European Union Since the 1980s*, edited by K. K. Patel, 127–140. London: Routledge.

Herrmann, R., and M. B. Brewer. 2004. "Identities and Institutions: Becoming European in the EU." In *Transnational Identities*, edited by R. K. Herrmann, T. Risse, and M. B. Brewer, 1 – 22. New York: Rowman & Littlefield.

Hooper-Greenhill, E. 2006. "Studying Visitors." In *Companion to Museum Studies*, edited by S. Macdonald, 362–376. New York: Blackwell.

Kaasik-Krogerus, S. 2019. "Identity Politics of the Promotional Videos of the European Heritage Label." *Contemporary Politics*. doi:10.1080/13569775.2019.1611207

Kohler-Koch, B., and C. Quittkat. 2013. *De-Mystification of participatory democracy*. Oxford University Press.

Le Galès, P. 2002. *European Cities. Social Conflicts and Governance*. Oxford: Oxford University Press.

Lindgren, K.-O., and T. Persson. 2011. *Participatory Governance in the EU*. Basingstoke: Palgrave Macmillan.

Littoz-Monnet, A. 2004. *The Construction Process of EU Cultural Policy: Explaining Europeanisation and EU Policy Formation*. Oxford: University of Oxford.

Littoz-Monnet, A. 2007. *The European Union and Culture: Between Economic Regulation and Cultural Policy*. Manchester: Manchester University Press.

Littoz-Monnet, A. 2012. "The EU Politics of Remembrance: Can Europeans Remember Together?" *West European Politics* 35 (5): 1182–1202.

Lähdesmäki, T. 2012a. "Rhetoric of Unity and Cultural Diversity in the Making of European Cultural Identity." *International Journal of Cultural Policy* 18 (1): 59–75.

Lähdesmäki, T. 2013. "Contention on the Meanings and Uses of Urban Space in Turku as the European Capital of Culture 2011." In *Space and Place: Exploring Critical Issues,* edited by D, Kılıçkıran, C, Alegria and C. Haddrell 153–164. Oxfordshire: Inter-Disciplinary Press.

Lähdesmäki, T. 2014. "European Capital of Culture Designation as an Initiator of Urban Transformation in the Post-socialist Countries." *European Planning Studies* 22 (3): 481–497.

Lähdesmäki, T. 2015. "The Ambiguity of Europe and European Identity in Finnish Populist Political Discourse." *Identities: Global Studies in Culture and Power* 22 (1): 71–87.

Lähdesmäki, T. 2016. "Politics of Tangibility, Intangibility, and Place in the Making of European Cultural Heritage in EU Heritage Policy." *International Journal of Heritage Studies* 22 (10): 766–780.

Lähdesmäki, T. 2019. "European Culture, History, and Heritage as Political Tools in the Rhetoric of the Finns Party." In *European Memory in Populism. (Mis)Representations of Self and Other* edited by C. de Cesari and A. Kaya, 191–209. London: Routledge.

Lähdesmäki, T. 2020. "Politics of Belonging in Brussels' European Quarter." *International Journal of Heritage Studies* 26 (10): 979–997. doi:10.1080/13527258.2019.1663237

Lähdesmäki, T., and K. Mäkinen. 2019. "The 'European Significance' of Heritage: Politics of Scale in EU Heritage Policy Discourse." In *Politics of Scale. New Directions in Critical Heritage Studies* edited by T. Lähdesmäki, S. Thomas, and Y. Zhu, 36–49. New York: Berghahn's Books.

Lähdesmäki, T., V. L. A. Čeginskas, S. Kaasik-Krogerus, K. Mäkinen, and J. Turunen. forthcoming in 2020. *Creating and Governing Cultural Heritage in the European Union: The European Heritage Label.* London: Routledge.

Macdonald, S. 2005. "Accessing Audiences: Visiting Visitor Books." *Museum and Society* 3 (3): 119–136.

Macdonald, S. 2007. "Interconnecting: Museum Visiting and Exhibition Design." *CoDesign* 3 (1): 149–162.

Magnette, P. 2003. "European Governance and Civic participation: Beyond Elitist Citizenship?" *Political Studies* 51 (1): 144–160.

Mattocks, K. 2017. "Uniting the Nations of Europe? Exploring the European Union's Cultural Policy Agenda." In *The Routledge Handbook of Global Cultural Policy,* edited by V. Durrer, T. Miller, and D. O'Brian, 397–413. London: Routledge.

Mittag, J. 2013. "The Changing Concept of the European Capitals of Culture. Between the Endorsement of European Identity and City Advertising." In *The Cultural Politics of Europe. European Capitals of Culture and European Union Since the 1980s,* edited by K. K. Patel, 39–54. London: Routledge.

Murawska-Muthesius, K., and P. Piotrowski. 2015. *From Museum Critique to the Critical Museum.* London: Routledge.

Myerscough, J. 1994. *European Cities of Culture and Cultural Months*. Glasgow: The Network of Cultural Cities of Europe.

Mäkinen, K. 2012. *Ohjelmoidut eurooppalaiset. Kansalaisuus ja kulttuuri EU-asiakirjoissa* [Programmed Europeans. Citizenship and Culture in EU Documents]. Jyväskylä: University of Jyväskylä.

Näss, H. E. 2009. *A New Agenda? The European Union and Cultural Policy*. London: Alliance Publishing Trust.

Näss, H. E. 2010. "The Ambiguities of Intercultural Dialogue: Critical Perspectives on the European Union's New Agenda for Culture." *Journal of Intercultural Communication* 23. Accessed 22 April 2020. http://immi.se/intercultural/nr23/nass.htm

Niklasson, E. 2016. Funding Matters: Archaeology and the Political Economy of the Past in the EU. PhD Thesis, Stockholm University.

O'Callaghan, C. 2011. "Urban Anxieties and Creative Tensions in the European Capital of Culture 2005: 'It Couldn't Just Be about Cork, Like'." *International Journal of Cultural Policy* 18 (2): 185–204.

Palmer, R. 2004. *European Cities and Capitals of Culture. Part I*. Brussels: European Commission & Palmer/Rae Associates.

Patel, K. K. 2013. "Introduction." In *The Cultural Politics of Europe: European Capitals of Culture and European Union Since the 1980s*, edited by K. K. Patel, 1–15. London: Routledge.

Prutsch, M. J. 2013. *European Historical Memory: Policies, Challenges and Perspectives*. Directorate-General for Internal Policies. Policy Department B: Structural and Cohesion Policies. Culture and Education. Brussels: European Parliament.

Richards, G., and J. Wilson. 2004. "The Impact of Cultural Events on City Image: Rotterdam, Cultural Capital of Europe 2001." *Urban Studies* 41 (10): 1931–1951.

Rosamond, B. 2000. *Theories of European Integration*. Basingstoke: Palgrave.

Sandell, R. ed. 2003. *Museums, Society, Inequality*. Reprint, London: Routledge.

Sassatelli, M. 2002. "Imagined Europe. The Shaping of European Cultural Identity through EU Cultural Policy." *European Journal of Social Theory* 5 (4): 435–451.

Sassatelli, M. 2006. "The Logic of Europeanizing Cultural Policy." In *Transcultural Europe. Cultural Policy in a Changing Europe*, edited by U. H. Meinhof and A. Triandafyllidou, 24–42. Basingstoke: Palgrave Macmillan.

Sassatelli M., 2008. "European Cultural Space in the European Cities of Culture." *European Societies* 10 (2): 225–245.

Sassatelli, M. 2009. *Becoming Europeans. Cultural Identity and Cultural Policies*. New York: Palgrave Macmillan.

Saurugger, S. 2010. "The Social Construction of the Participatory Turn: The Emergence of a Norm in the European Union." *European Journal of Political Research* 49 (4): 471–495.

Shore, C. 1993. "Inventing the 'People's Europe': Critical Approaches to European Community 'Cultural Policy.'" *Man* 28 (4): 779–800.

Shore, C. 2000. *Building Europe: The Cultural Politics of European Integration*. London: Routledge.

Shore, C. 2006. "'In Uno Plures' (?) EU Cultural Policy and the Governance of Europe." *Cultural Analysis* 5: 7–26.

Shore, C., and A. Black. 1996. "Citizens' Europe and the Construction of European Identity." In *The Anthropology of Europe. Identities and Boundaries in Conflict*, edited by V. A. Goddard, J. R. Llobera, and C. Shore, 275–298. Oxford and Washington D.C.: Berg.

Staiger, U. 2009. "New Agendas? Culture and Citizenship in EU Policy." *International Journal of Cultural Policy* 15 (1): 1–16.

Treaty of Maastricht. 1992. "Treaty on European Union." *Official Journal of the European Communities* C 191, 1–112.

Treaty of Amsterdam. 1997. "Treaty of Amsterdam Amending the Treaty on European Union, the Treaties establishing the European Communities and Certain Related Acts." *Official Journal of the European Communities* C 340, 1–144.

Treaty of Lisbon. 2007. "Treaty of Lisbon Amending the Treaty on European Union and the Treaty establishing the European Community." *Official Journal of the European Union* C 306, 1–271.

Tzaliki, L., 2007. "The Construction of European Identity and Citizenship through Cultural Policy." *European Studies: A Journal of European Culture, History and Politics* 26: 157–182.

Watson, S., and E. Waterton, eds. 2010. Special Issue on Heritage and Community Engagement. *International Journal of Heritage Studies* 16 (1–2): 1–159.

Vejvodová, P. 2014. The Identitarian Movement – Renewed Idea of Alternative Europe. Paper in ECPR General Conference, Glasgow, UK, 3 – 6 September 2014. Accessed 22 April 2020. https://ecpr.eu/Filestore/PaperProposal/ff2ea4db-2b74-4479-8175-7e7e468608ba.pdf

Vergo, P. 1989. *The New Museology*. London: Reaktion Books.

Wolff, C. 2013. *Functional Representation and Democracy in the EU*. Colchester: ECPR Press.

CHAPTER 4

Case 1: The European Capital of Culture

1 From the Policy Discourse to the Implementation and Reception

The European Capital of Culture (ECOC) is the longest running EU cultural initiative with a strong emphasis on foregrounding common culture in Europe, promoting European cultural narratives, supporting the cooperation of European cultural actors, and activating Europeans to participate in cultural creation and reception. This action forms our first case study. As discussed in Chapter 3, the macro-level policy discourse of the action seeks to construct Europe as a cultural entity and thus advance cultural Europeanization. The EU's interest in strengthening the discourse of the 'European dimension' in the ECOC action responds to the European Commission's view that this dimension was lacking in both ECOC applications and the cultural programmes of designated cities. This view was based on various *ex-post* evaluations of the action that noted how the European dimension has often been only modestly dealt with in the ECOC applications and cultural programmes (see Chapter 3). Indeed, the European dimension may be challenging to measure and therefore to perceive in the ECOC applications and programmes because Europe and the 'European' can be understood and manifested in various ways.

In this chapter, we first briefly outline how the 'European' was discussed and framed in the applications, commonly referred to as bid books, of three case ECOCS – Pécs2010 in Hungary, Tallinn2011 in Estonia, and Turku2011 in Finland – and how the European Commission's *ex-post* evaluations of them considered their European dimension. After this, these macro- and meso-level discussions are broadened by discussing field research observations from these cities. The observations offer first-hand information about how the 'European' was manifested in ECOC events themselves, in their marketing and information signs in the cities, and in diverse cultural regeneration practices in their urban space. We then analyze the results of a questionnaire study conducted with audiences in these ECOCS, focusing on how the respondents understood the 'European' in the context of the ECOC events. We conclude that for the three cities, the European dimension was indeed included in their ECOC bid books, the implementation of their ECOC year, and their audiences' perception of the events organized during it. While their understandings of the 'European' vary greatly in both form and content, some elements of understanding the 'European' recur in our data.

In 2006 Pécs, a city in Southern Hungary with 157,000 inhabitants, was designated as the ECOC for 2010 along with two other cities: Essen, including the broader Ruhr region, in Germany, and Istanbul in Turkey. Tallinn, the capital of Estonia with a population of 426,000, and Turku, a city with 180,000 inhabitants located in South-West Finland, were selected in 2007 as the ECOCs for 2011. The three cities differ in terms of their social, cultural, economic, and political history. Their host countries – Hungary, Estonia, and Finland – are geographically located in the eastern and northern borders of the EU (Pécs is even located at the EU's southern border) and have joined the Union in different phases – Finland in 1995 and Hungary and Estonia in 2004. Two of the cities, Tallinn and Pécs, are in former socialist countries. The three cities have several characteristics in common. In all of them, contemporary art and culture have been developed together with old urban layers through public art, artistic events, new museums and other cultural institutions, and new or renewed architecture. All three cities have been multicultural and multilingual players of their regions since the Middle Ages. These similarities and differences can be perceived from the cities' ECOC bid books and programmes.

2 Manifestations of the 'European' in the Official Discourse of Pécs2010, Tallinn2011, and Turku2011

> People living along borders enjoy an experience of Europe which is very different from that seen by people living in the Western European centre. (Takáts 2005, 22)

> As a candidate for the European Capital of Culture 2011, Tallinn and Estonia have the potential to return to the European Cultural map as full members, forming a new European identity. (Tarand 2006, 26)

> Through encounter, interaction and internationality, our children become open-minded European citizens who reinforce the European multicultural community. (Helander et al. 2006, 9)

These three quotations from the ECOC bid books of Pécs, Tallinn, and Turku indicate different ways of dealing with the 'European' in the framework of this EU action. The quotations reflect the different historical and societal contexts of the cities, which impact on how the 'European' was approached and utilized in their ECOC programmes. At the same time, these quotations indicate a common interest in being or becoming European.

The ECOC programmes in the three case cities followed the same EU policy guidelines. Thus, the programmes had several similar emphases, aims, and interests. During their ECOC year, the cities aimed to promote the cultural characteristics of the city, its surrounding region, host country, and Europe. The main themes of Pécs2010 followed the slogan 'Pécs – The Borderless City'. The city's bid book named several pillars of its ECOC year: lively public spaces, cultural heritage and innovation, multiculturalism, regionalism, and the city as a cultural gateway to the Balkans (Takáts 2005, 17). Europe and a common European cultural identity were important concepts in the promotional rhetoric of Pécs2010. The objectives of the city included celebrating "artistic achievements of European standard" (Takáts 2005, 11), "diversity of European and world culture" (Toller 2005, 7), and invoking in visitors "aspects of culture which contribute to the heritage of Pan-European culture" (Takáts 2005, 21).

In the *ex-post* evaluation for the EU, the Pécs cultural programme was considered as strongly emphasizing its European dimension, through "the common cultural heritage and historical links between the city and neighboring countries in southeast Europe" (Ecorys 2011b, 86). Moreover, the evaluation report noted that the 'European' was manifested in Pécs2010 through activities whose content, delivery mechanism, and audiences were "European in essence" (Ecorys 2011b, 91). Content-wise, "the European theme promoted by Pécs focused on its potential as a 'Gateway to the Balkans', with many cultural activities focused on promoting a pan-Balkan culture" (Ecorys 2011b, 91). As delivery mechanisms, the report emphasized cooperation with cities in neighboring countries and noted that the city experienced a very substantial increase in European visitors (Ecorys 2011b, 92).

The main objectives of Tallinn's ECOC year were developing cultural participation, a creative economy, international cultural communication, and cultural tourism (Tarand 2006). Tallinn's bid book also emphasized the importance of introducing local culture to people beyond Estonia. The book stated: "Although home to many cultures, Tallinn firmly represents the character of the Estonian people and their land", and, thus, "it bares the responsibility of representing the republic and its culture to the world" (Tarand 2006, 11). The national emphasis was, however, intertwined with creating and strengthening European identity. The bid book stated: "Tallinn's leaders envisage the cultural capital as one part of a far-reaching process of transforming urban spaces into cultural centers and introducing Estonian culture to the rest of Europe while helping Estonians create a new European identity" (Tarand 2006, 17). The aim was to familiarize other Europeans with the Estonian culture and transform the notions of Europe among Estonians. This kind of two-way Europeanization has characterized other Estonian attempts to opening up the country to Europe and 'becoming' more European (see Kaasik-Krogerus 2019).

In both the selection documents and the *ex-post* evaluation, Tallinn received criticism for lacking a strong European dimension and focusing too much on celebrating local and national culture (on similar criticism in the EHL context, see Lähdesmäki et al. 2020). Due to the criticism from the selection panel, Tallinn changed the focus of its programme from folklore and fairytales to opening up the city to the sea. Still, the new focus was considered in the *ex-post* evaluation report as being "of local rather than European significance" (Ecorys 2012, 27). According to the report, which evaluated Tallinn2011 and Turku2011 simultaneously, in both cities the European dimension mostly related to efforts to support transnational cultural cooperation and to internationalize the cities' cultural sectors (Ecorys 2012, 65).

In Turku's bid book, the main goals for the ECOC year were to encourage well-being, internationalism, creative industries, and cultural export (Helander et al. 2006). The programme of Turku2011 was organized under five main themes: bringing culture into everyday life, offering cultural breaks from everyday life, introducing the maritime region surrounding the city, discussing issues related to identities and selfhood, and exploring the city through its history, memories, and stories (Määttänen 2010, 7). Besides the everyday, local, and regional aspects, Turku2011 sought to include the European dimension in its ECOC year. In the bid book, the European dimension was simply defined as a value penetrating each project in the city's ECOC programme (Helander et al. 2006, 37).

The panel monitoring its preparations recommended that Turku foreground the European dimension better (Ecorys 2012, 39). The *ex-post* evaluation of Turku's ECOC year recognized that the European dimension manifested for instance through "attracting cultural productions from other European countries", "highlighting environmental issues especially related to the Baltic Sea", and "developing two opera productions based on ancient and medieval history in Europe" (Ecorys 2012, viii). The evaluators came to the conclusion that Turku2011 "attempted to emphasize a local 'narrative' and yet articulate it in European context and to European audiences" (Ecorys 2012, 46–47) but European themes did not permeate the entire cultural programme (Ecorys 2012, 65).

To sum up, the European dimension was dealt with in the official discourse of all three case ECOCs, but only Pécs2010 managed to discuss and concretize it in a way that the external evaluators considered as sufficiently European.

3   Experiencing Europe during the Field Research in the Case ECOCs

Even though the *ex-post* evaluators thanked one city and criticized two of them for their approach to the European dimension, none of the cities can be reproached for lacking, ignoring, or misinterpreting it. The 'European' includes diverse interpretations and understandings of its contents, meanings, and contexts, and can be, thus, dealt with in various ways. The ethnographic research focusing on the micro level helps to understand how the European dimension was perceived and how, thus, the 'European' could be faced by ECOC audiences in the cities. One of the authors of this book explored how the European dimension was manifested and delivered to the audiences in the three cities through an observation during fieldwork in Pécs in April, May, and October in 2010, in Tallinn in May 2011, and in Turku in August 2011. The observation included participation in dozens of cultural events, gaining first-hand experiences of their contents, arrangement, and promotion practices. In addition, diverse regeneration, reparation, restoration, and construction projects were observed, considering their impacts on urban space and people's everyday lives. The observation was documented by taking notes and by photographing the transformation of public spaces and the cultural participation of the audiences in the ECOC events.

The ECOC title means a major endeavor for the host cities that both visitors to and inhabitants of the city cannot help noting. Celebration of the cultural year is linked in the ECOCs to the ideas of Europe and the EU through various discursive, visual, material, and spatial means. The most obvious means to manifest these is widespread use of the ECOC logos and slogans, combined with the EU flag, in promotional and information material and on signs and banners in the cities. This marks both urban space and various cultural events organized in it as 'European'. In addition, the signs and banners in the city connect efficiently the 'local', and the very spots where they are located, to the idea of Europe – 'Europe is here' in this city, in this park or building, and at this venue or work of art (see Figure 4.1 and 4.2).

In the brochures, leaflets, and other printed and online promotional material, ECOC events are typically described as European when they include performers, artists, and works of art from other European countries. This European character of the events was also often emphasized in their opening speeches or welcoming words in the three case ECOCs. Particularly in bigger festival-type events, this kind of European dimension, stemming from art 'imported from elsewhere in Europe', was easy to experience. During various festivals in the

FIGURE 4.1   Sign boards with the ECOC title in a Tallinn street scene in 2011. The text on the
board says 'More hospitable Tallinn'.
PHOTO: TUULI LÄHDESMÄKI

case ECOCs, the city centers were enlivened by foreign performers, performing
groups, and audiences from different countries. The multinational nature of
these events could be experienced through the multiplicity of languages used
in the performances, heard among the audiences, and printed in the communication materials. The use of national flags in the events or the texts in the

FIGURE 4.2   In Turku, the ECOC title was advertised in the city center through large sign
boards that played with the logo of Turku2011.
PHOTO: TUULI LÄHDESMÄKI

promotional material that listed the countries of origin of the performers or
artists also emphasized this multinationality (Figure 4.3). Some events in the
case ECOCs focused particularly on celebrating folk cultures in Europe, such as
folk dance or folk music. At these events, 'multinational Europe' could be perceived through different folk costumes, dances, and musical styles (Figure 4.4).

FIGURE 4.3   Outdoor performance by a Lithuanian group at the puppet theatre festival in
Tallinn2011. The flag indicates the home country of the group.
PHOTO: TUULI LÄHDESMÄKI

FIGURE 4.4   Finnish performers wearing folk costumes at the folk dance festival in Pécs2010.
PHOTO: TUULI LÄHDESMÄKI

Rather than folk traditions, the ECOC programmes more commonly focus on contemporary urban culture. Programme events seek to enliven cities through contemporary public art and community art projects, aiming at bringing people together and enabling them to participate in diverse creative activities. This kind of contemporary urban culture invokes associations with European metropoles from where the latest street art and 'cultural buzz' spread to other urban environments. In the case ECOCs, it was difficult to overlook the new artistic projects in urban space. These projects commonly included temporary public art in squares or parks (Figure 4.5) or smaller street art projects enlivening the urban space and its structures (Figure 4.6) in the city centers.

FIGURE 4.5   *Daisy* by Jani Rättyä and Antti Stöckell at the 'Flux Aura' environmental art
festival in Turku2011.
PHOTO: TUULI LÄHDESMÄKI

The ECOC year is usually combined with improving the respective city's (cultural) infrastructure. In many ECOCs, particularly in Central and Eastern Europe, the ECOC year has meant major regeneration plans, investments in diverse infrastructural projects, restoration of buildings and public spaces in city centers, and construction of new buildings for cultural uses (Lähdesmäki 2014b). In all the three case ECOCs, the city centers were transformed, polished, and enlivened in more or less permanent ways, and new cultural spaces were built to enrich the urban cultural scene. In Pécs (Figure 4.7), these changes were the most dramatic and could be perceived form the point

FIGURE 4.6   Painted water post with the ECOC logo in Pécs2010.
PHOTO: TUULI LÄHDESMÄKI

of view of the 'European'. The construction and renovation projects in the city were linked to Europe and the EU through signs indicating that the EU was a project funder. The renovations of buildings and public spaces in the center turned Pécs into a modern 'European city' like many others, with medieval and classical architectural layers and modern urban furniture. In general, the construction of (cultural) infrastructure, renovation of buildings, and transformation of urban spaces are probably the most influential components of the ECOC year. They not only change the city space but also impact on visitors' and inhabitants' notions of the city, as well as their movement, activities, and cultural behavior in the city.

The ECOC title has diverse influences on their host cities. Investing in cultural buildings, regenerating public spaces, hosting multinational cultural festivals, and implementing projects of contemporary urban culture create the ECOCs active, cultural atmosphere and groomed look. A researcher who has visited various ECOCs during the past decade can easily recognize similarities,

FIGURE 4.7   Renovating and constructing Széchenyi square in Pécs during its ECOC year.
PHOTO: TUULI LÄHDESMÄKI

repetitions, and reminders of other ECOCs. All cities seem to come up with very
similar ideas and seek to emphasize the same ideals in their promotion of the
European dimension. Some of the photos taken during the fieldwork are therefore so similar that their locations are difficult to tell based on the image alone.
This similarity can be perceived as stemming from the nature of the ECOC
action based on a competition and a set of selection criteria (Lähdesmäki
2014b). All the candidates seek to fit their applications, plans, and programmes
into this framework, as well as to find and utilize the most recent trends in participatory culture, cultural regeneration, and revitalization of urban space. As a
result, the ECOC action has succeeded in constructing a year-long urban event
that we find very 'European' in a sense that its European dimension is constantly discussed, negotiated, debated, manifested, and, thus, constructed in it.

4   Construction of Europeanness among ECOC Audiences

4.1   *Researching Europeanness: Data and Methods*
Audiences of the ECOC events have diverse views on Europe and how it is eventually manifested in the events they experience. Next, we examine these views

through a questionnaire issued during the fieldwork in Pécs, Tallinn, and Turku. The data comprises 1,425 responses: 200 from Pécs, 293 from Tallinn, and 400 from Turku collected through printed questionnaires, and 532 responses to a pilot online survey from Pécs. During the field research, the questionnaire data was collected at 23 events in Pécs, 17 events in Tallinn, and 21 events in Turku. The selected events differed greatly in their size, location, organization, target audience, and genre. Some were festivals or series of events including various types of performances. The aim was to include in the study an extensive range of events, which would represent the variety of the whole ECOC programme in the case cities. The respondents (aged 15 and older) were selected during or after the chosen events. The data collection was based on focal sampling (Mony and Heimlich 2008; Yocco et al. 2009): In advance, the data collectors divided the event venue (public space or foyer) into three to five imaginary parts and aimed to collect one to ten responses from the people who happened to be in the middle of the imagined areas. From three to thirty responses were collected from each event depending on its size.

The online pilot study in Pécs was based on a combination of convenience, purposeful, and snowball sampling (Patton 2002; Everett and Barrett 2009): Notice of the online questionnaire was sent to the contact persons of ten local cultural organizations or networks representing various cultural fields. Contact persons were advised to inform their staff and stakeholders about the questionnaire. The responses were collected online from February till May 2010.

The printed questionnaire was available in Pécs in Hungarian and English, in Tallinn in Estonian, Russian, English, Finnish and Swedish, and in Turku in Finnish, Swedish, and English. Those languages that the fieldwork researcher was not able to read were translated to English by local research assistants with experience of doing translations. Core information of the respondents is gathered to the Annex 1.

The questionnaire included 23 questions with a focus on respondents' notions of the 'local', 'regional', 'national', and 'European' and how they felt these dimensions were and should be represented in the ECOC events. Here, we focus only on the 'European' and how it was constructed in the closed and open responses. A more detailed qualitative analysis of the responses from each case city and a comparison of the results on the four scalar dimensions in the three cities have been presented elsewhere (Lähdesmäki 2011; 2013a; 2013b; 2014a; 2014c; 2014d).

One aim of the questionnaire study was to explore the ECOC audiences' notions of the 'European' through the concept of Europeanness. The concept was not explained or defined in the questionnaire: Respondents were instructed to concretize and describe it according to their own understanding. However, the ECOC events through which they were recruited probably guided respondents to perceive the concept in cultural and social terms. In the analysis, we first focus on the responses to closed questions on the 'European'. After this, we focus on open questions and explore the respondents' notions through qualitative thematic analysis. Here, we look at two questions: 'In your opinion, how is Europeanness represented in the European Capital of Culture events?' and 'In your opinion, how should Europeanness be represented in the European Capital of Culture events?'

In the analysis, we sought to identify expressions of themes recognized from the responses through careful reading and constant comparison between linguistic patterns. For us, a theme could be expressed in "a single word, a phrase, a sentence, a paragraph or an entire document", as Zhang and Wildemuth (2009, 310) have described the premises of qualitative thematic analysis. Our aim was to structure the 'polyphonic' nature of the responses in order to perceive how the 'European' was constructed in data. First, we identified a broad variety of different topics and linguistic expressions in the responses, and then we arranged and combined similar recurring topics and expressions under unifying themes, as systematically as possible. The most frequent themes – which inevitably overlap – are shown in Table 4.3. After this, the identified themes were quantified in order to get an idea of their frequency. In the quantification, each identified theme was given a code number and the responses to the open questions were coded with these numbers. The thematic quantification of the responses was content-based, not respondent-based. Thus, a response from one respondent might comprise several views of the 'European'.

4.2   *Quantifying Respondents' Views of Europeanness*
The analysis of the closed responses indicates that the EU's identity political aims for the ECOC action were fulfilled from the point of view of the ECOC audiences. Most of the respondents had very positive views of Europeanness and thought that it was and should be represented in the ECOC events. Of all respondents, 49% saw Europeanness as to some extent important and for 42% it meant a lot for their identity; 74% considered that for them, Europeanness invoked positive or very positive impressions; 62% thought that it was and 71% that it should be represented a lot or very much in the ECOC events. When comparing these figures for the case ECOCs, the respondents from Tallinn seemed to have the most positive attitude to Europeanness overall, while respondents from Turku emphasized it less (Table 4.1).

Despite these positive views, in all the case ECOCs, 'national culture' invoked even more positive impressions in the respondents and it was considered as the dimension that the ECOC events should represent the most. The open questions revealed, however, that views on Europeanness and national culture were nuanced and included some controversial meanings.

TABLE 4.1   Views of Europeanness among the respondents of the ECOC questionnaire study

	Respondents considering that Europeanness means 'a lot' for their identity	Respondents in whom Europeanness invokes 'positive' or 'very positive' impressions	Respondents for whom ECOC events represent Europeanness 'a lot' or 'very much'	Respondents for whom ECOC events should represent Europeanness 'a lot' or 'very much'
Pécs, paper	44%	64%	66%	73%
Pécs, online	45%	72%	60%	77%
Tallinn	46%	80%	67%	76%
Turku	33%	77%	55%	59%

In general, the results of the questionnaire study indicate that different scalar dimensions of culture – 'local', 'regional', 'national', and 'European' – are important and meaningful to the respondents, and international cultural events, such as the ECOC, are expected to represent scalar dimensions of culture both directly in their contents and indirectly in their organization and promotion. People structure their cultural perceptions and notions on cultural differences around these scalar dimensions.

In the policy discourse, the ECOC's key scalar focus is on Europe. Sassatelli (2009, 129–131) investigated the ECOC action's European dimension by interviewing key informants, such as programme directors, project managers, artists, curators, and local stakeholders, in nine ECOCs for the year 2000. The majority of her interviewees responded positively to the questions about the existence of European culture and identity: The idea that Europe should be the focus of the ECOC initiative and its implementation was never challenged (Sassatelli 2009, 135). Sassatelli notes, however, that the interviewees seemed to have difficulties verbalizing the idea of European culture or identity in a way that satisfied them. How did the ECOC audiences in Pécs, Tallinn, and Turku verbalize Europeanness? The open responses in the questionnaire study illustrate diverse ways of perceiving it and understanding its essence (Table 4.2).

4.3   Europeanness in Respondents' Words

The respondents in all the case cities most often approached Europeanness in the ECOC events by emphasizing the involvement of Europeans in them, such as European (or just foreign) artists and performers, European visitors to

TABLE 4.2 The most repeated themes in responses on how Europeanness was represented (A) in the ECOC events and how it should be represented (B) based on percentage of responses in which each theme in the table was mentioned in Pécs2010, Tallinn2011, and Turku2011.

Themes	Total		Pécs		Tallinn		Turku	
	A	B	A	B	A	B	A	B
European or foreign artists or performers	27%	16%	31%	17%	14%	12%	35%	18%
European or foreign works of art or performances	16%	12%	15%	12%	11%	11%	21%	12%
European visitors	10%	7%	11%	5%	12%	5%	9%	4%
diversity and plurality in general	7%	4%	11%	7%	3%	5%	7%	4%
displaying different national cultures in Europe	6%	8%	10%	13%	7%	9%	2%	5%
cooperation with other ECOCs or foreign partners	6%	6%	5%	7%	3%	3%	9%	9%
emphasizing the city as part of Europe	5%	8%	4%	4%	6%	11%	4%	11%
atmosphere, common mentality, or European values	5%	8%	2%	9%	8%	8%	4%	7%
ECOC title	5%	5%	2%	<1%	11%	4%	3%	2%
foreign languages	4%	3%	3%	4%	4%	5%	5%	1%
emphasizing various connections between the host country and Europe	3%	5%	6%	11%	3%	10%	2%	4%
special quality and scale of the events and reaching European standards	3%	3%	6%	7%	1%	2%	3%	2%
EU sponsorship, EU symbols, or other connections to the EU	3%	3%	5%	4%	5%	3%	<1%	<1%
emphasizing common European culture, heritage, history, or traditions	2%	4%	2%	4%	2%	4%	2%	5%
advertisement or promotion in media	2%	2%	2%	2%	3%	6%	<1%	<1%
university life and science	2%	1%	7%	3%	<1%	<1%	<1%	<1%
established international events or festivals in the ECOC programme	2%	<1%	<1%	<1%	<1%	<1%	4%	1%
renovation and improvement of architecture and public spaces	1%	1%	3%	2%	<1%	<1%	<1%	<1%

the cities, and European partners in diverse cooperation projects during the
ECOC year. In these responses, Europeanness was verbalized as being manifested for example in "joint projects that cross state borders" (Turku, male, b.
1950), "cooperation with other European countries" (Turku, female, b. 1971),
or "involving European friend and partner cities to the events" (Pécs, male, b.
1980). The respondents commonly mentioned the presence of people who
were considered as 'Europeanizing' the ECOC events. These "European personalities" (Pécs, male, b. 1985) were seen as having an influence on the 'European'
atmosphere of the city as "the artists from abroad bring a piece of Europe to us"
(Pécs, male, b. 1982). Besides European or foreign performers, the respondents
commonly stressed foreign visitors and tourists as indicators of Europeanness.
They noted for instance: "I see and hear a lot of foreign people" (Pécs, female,
b. 1965), "in the events, you can see and hear a plenty of different nationalities"
(Turku, male, b. 1982), and "hundreds of tourists in the squares of the city: it is
Europe to me" (Tallinn, female, b. 1935). In addition, the visitors from abroad
could be seen as Europeanizing the ECOCs and their host countries through
being informed by the cities' and countries' 'European essence', as one respondent (female, b. 1989) described Europeanness in Tallinn:

> First of all, it is represented in the form of the visitors to the Estonian
> state. I am sure that many people will notice that, after all, Estonia is not
> an unknown and a far-away country in Russia, but a beautiful and mod-
> ern country in Europe.

Besides artists and performers, the respondents also commonly emphasized
the exhibitions of European (or foreign) art and cultural performances from
abroad as indicators of Europeanness in the ECOC events. For most of these
respondents, the contents or topics of the exhibitions, performances, or artistic projects, were not crucial – the home country of their artists, performers, or
producers was more significant in perceiving the event as a representation of
Europeanness. Thus, notions of Europeanness were closely linked in the data
to the distinction between the 'national' and 'non-national': other nationalities
manifested Europe and Europeanness. The nationality of artists and performers from another European country determined the European character of the
events. These notions also indicate how mobility is perceived as fundamental
to the idea of Europe. Moving artists, the arts, and people as visitors, audiences,
and tourists characterize respondents' notions of Europe.

Reflecting clear categories of the 'national' and the 'foreign', many of the respondents connected Europeanness to the display of different national cultures in
the ECOC events. This notion of Europeanness emphasizes the uniqueness

and particularity of national cultures – and Europeanness as being composed of them and their differences rather than having a shared culture, heritage, or identity of its own. In these responses, Europeanness could be manifested through "thematic programmes on European countries" (Pécs, female, b. 1965), events in which "each national culture is represented" (Tallinn, female, b. 1992), and "[d]ifferent performances of European artists groups, who present the cultural traditions of just their own country" (Turku, female, b. 1951). As another respondent from Turku noted: "It would be fun to see more differences between different countries" (Turku, female, b. 1957). These responses indicate how Europe was often perceived as a 'Europe of nations'.

Europeanness was also quite often related to more general cultural diversity in the case cities, different languages heard and used in the ECOC events, and various other modes of cultural and social plurality. Thus, Europeanness could be explained as being manifested in "'multilingual events" (Pécs, female, b. 1977), displaying "the culture of European minorities" (Pécs, female, b. 1988), and "giving an opportunity to ethnicities and minorities to perform" (Pécs, female, b. 1987). Many of respondents equated Europeanness simply with diversity. As one respondent from Tallinn stated: "What do we now think that goes under Europeanness? Diversification, everything that is not mainstream? If so, then it is shown" (Tallinn, male, b. 1987). In contrast, a few respondents in Tallinn criticized the ECOC discourse for presenting the city more culturally diverse than it was considered to be. As one respondent noted: "Tallinn and to [a] lesser extent Estonia is tried to be shown as [more] European and multicultural and urban than it is in reality" (Tallinn, female, b. 1986).

The emphasis on the 'European' in the EU policy rhetoric, and hence in the ECOCs' promotional discourse, impacts inevitably on the reception of the ECOC events. In their open responses to the questionnaire, many respondents repeated the slogans and expressions used in the official promotional material of the case ECOCs. In general, the ECOC action was often considered European or typical of Europe: "The Cultural Capital initiative is already itself very European. At least, I have never heard anything like it from the United States or Asia, etc." (Turku, male, b. 1988). In Pécs and Tallinn, the ECOC links to the EU – such as the EU funding of the certain events and regeneration projects in the city and the presence of the EU flag in ECOC events and promotional material – were considered as indications of Europeanness. In many responses from these cities, the notions of Europeanness were intertwined with the EU, as these two respondents from Pécs noted: "The whole city is full of plaques about [the EU] support. In addition, every time (for example in the welcoming speeches) the question of Europeanness is addressed" (Pécs, female, b. 1965); "We are an EU member state, Pécs is the European Capital of Culture in 2010:

an integral part of the EU, and this is stressed in the events" (Pécs, female, b. 1987). Various links with the EU, as well as the ECOC title itself, could be seen as Europeanizing the host city, as one respondent (female, b. 1990) from Tallinn noted:

> Europe is already inside the title. Also because it is a question of the European Capital of Culture, we are now in a way totally taken as Europeans, which we have been afraid of. Afraid that we are not Europeans or that we are not taken as Europeans.

This quotation also reflects the respondent's view on Tallinn's and Estonia's liminal position in becoming European. In general, it was expected that Europeanness would be represented in the ECOC events as a rather 'thin' cultural identity (on thin and thick identities, see Delanty 2003; Axford 2006; Davidson 2008; Terlouw 2012): that is, an identity transmitted and represented through contemporary international cultural actors and their interaction and presence in the ECOCs and realized through the (sometimes forgotten or ignored) 'fact' that the ECOCs and their host countries are already part of Europe. This fact was often seen as proved by the EU membership of these countries or their other links to the EU. Respondents rarely discussed Europeanness as a 'thick' cultural identity based on common European culture, history, heritage, traditions, monuments, or historical sites. In Pécs, these latter views were often linked to major restorations and renovations of historical buildings, monuments, and squares in the city center. The Europeanness of the city was linked to its improved appearance. As one respondent from Pécs explained, the Europeanness was manifested "[a]bsolutely in the appearance of the renovated squares and the reconstructed buildings. In attempts to develop up to the standards of other European cities" (Pécs, female, b. 1989).

In general, the notions of Europeanness in the data were notably non-historical. The lack of history in the responses on Europeanness can be interpreted in several ways. First, Europeanness may be commonly perceived through contemporariness – as a cultural identity shaped through relations and interaction between people in the present time. Second, Europeanness may be easily associated with the EU, particularly in the context of EU cultural initiatives. Third, history is often related to identity formation at the national or local – not the European – level (see Mayer and Palmowski 2004). History and cultural traditions were indeed more often discussed in the questionnaire responses related to local, regional, and national culture. Fourth, the ECOC action celebrates contemporary culture, 'living' traditions, and intangible heritage, which does not guide the audiences to perceive Europe in historical terms.

While respondents typically related tangible culture to the 'local' or 'national', many of them characterized the 'European' by a particular atmosphere or mentality, emphasizing its intangible character. In all case cities, this atmosphere or mentality was described mostly in positive terms, such as being tolerant, open-minded, modern, civilized, and united. Thus, Europeanness was understood as a set of certain liberal values. These values included being cultural and civilized" (Turku, female, b. 1963), "inclusion of young people [and] elderly people (> very European!)" (Turku, female, b. 1982), "ability to act together" (Turku, male, b. 1945), "patience and paying attention" (Pécs, female, b. 1981), "tolerance, diversity, hospitality" (Tallinn, male, b. 1974), "positive thinking, inclusiveness, hospitality, solidarity, tolerance and openness" (Pécs, female, b. 1984), and "peaceful, helpful, and smiling mentality, which characterizes an established peaceful democracy and the well-being in Europe" (Pécs, female, b. 1965). Moreover, some of the respondents related the 'European' in the ECOC events to their manifoldness, experimentality, innovativeness, and "high standard, quality and professional arrangement" (Pécs, female, b. 1988). If the events were considered as lacking this expected quality, appealing to Europeanness could be used to argue for this. As one respondent from Turku stated: "Unfortunately the level of communication / organization [of the ECOC events] do not reach the common European standards" (Turku, male, b. 1978).

Besides liberal values and high quality, some respondents linked the intangible nature of Europeanness to the 'modern' in all case ECOCs, and, particularly in Pécs and Tallinn, to the idea of development. This idea meant the improvement and modernization of urban spaces in the city, developing better living standards, and a well-functioning and fair society. Responses on Europeanness mentioned for example, the "economy and development" (Pécs, female, b. 1986), "working conditions" (Pécs, female, b. 1990), and "reaching the standard of the European Union" (Pécs, male, b. 1987). The idea of the 'European' being sought after and needing to be 'reached' was included in several responses. As a respondent from Tallinn put it: "We want to be like other Europeans. That means that everything is fine and in good order and good condition" (Tallinn, male, b. 1955).

4.4   *The Relationship between the 'National' and the 'European'*

In the all case ECOCs, 'national culture' and 'Europeanness' formed a conceptual pair that could be considered as closely connected, even inseparable dimensions of culture and identity, but at the same time as contradictory elements. Indeed, 'national culture' was discussed in many of the responses as involving a positive patriotic ethos and, thus, crucial to strengthening the national feeling of belonging and maintaining national cultural particularity.

Some respondents, who strongly emphasized the importance of 'national culture' in the ECOC events, interpreted Europeanness as its rival opposite. In such
accounts, Europe was often closely linked to the EU. As one respondent noted:
"It [Europeanness] should be less important than our own identity. We should
not belong there [the EU] at all, it [the ECOC year in Pécs] should be about
what we are" (Pécs, male, b. 1986). In some responses (e.g. Pécs, female, b. 1989),
Europeanness was considered as a direct threat to a more important national
identity:

> Primarily, the interests of the city and the country should be kept in mind,
> and after that those of Europe. The lowest level of Europeanness should
> be addressed, even if we are members of the EU. We should be members
> of the Union in a way that we would still preserve our identity, and not
> merge with everyone.

In these views, Europeanness was interpreted as a homogenizing identity,
which flattens the particularity and originality of national cultures in Europe.
Thus the ECOC action with its emphasis on including the European dimen-
sion in events raised concerns. As one respondent noted regarding Tallinn's
ECOC programme, "Europe must not prevent Estonia from keeping its culture"
(Tallinn, female, b. 1988). The threat of the 'European' included negative views
on the unwanted blurring of (national) cultural characteristics and originality
of cultural phenomena. As one respondent from Turku stated: "The Capital of
Culture should emphasize the culture of the particular country instead of the
European muddle" (Turku, male, 1981).

In the responses emphasizing the importance of national culture, the
'national' and 'local' were commonly perceived as easily recognizable, clear,
and coherent entities, while Europeanness was interpreted as being more
diverse and incoherent, and thus blurred in a negative way. In these views, the
idea of multi-layered cultural identities did not reach the supranational level.
The local and national culture were often perceived as linked and their representations could be described as enmeshed, but the distinction between them
and Europeanness remained clear – probably because conceiving of Europeanness was difficult.

Moreover, some respondents from all three cities approached Europeanness,
again tightly entwined with the EU, as a bureaucratic force to which 'national
cultures' have to stand up. The rise of nationalist, populist, and radical right-
wing movements in all three case countries may have encouraged some respondents to stress the European dimension as a negative counter-discourse to the
'national'. During the data collection, debates on nationalism were particularly

timely in Hungary due to the parliamentary election in the spring of 2010. The election was preceded by active political campaigns in which right-wing parties with their conservative and nationalistic rhetoric received strong media attention. The tension caused by the election and the victory of the right-wing parties was also reflected in the reception of the ECOC events in Pécs: Party-political points of view and nationalist rhetoric were present in several responses (Lähdesmäki 2011). As one respondent stated: "Instead of the Union, present true Europeanness: Christian and Aryan traditions" (Pécs, male, b. 1984). The debates on nationalism are still very timely in Hungary, as indicated for instance by the parliamentary election in 2019. In it, national and Christian traditions were juxtaposed with internationalization (that was connected with anti-Semitism), the EU, and its interest in deeper political integration.

In pro-European responses, 'national culture' could be considered as including certain negative values and qualities, such as a narrow-minded national ethos, which many of these respondents wanted to overturn. Among these respondents, Europeanness was seen as a positive element that could renew the content of 'national culture' (Lähdesmäki 2013b; 2014a). In the responses that were positive about Europeanness, it was often contrasted with recent history and its impacts on the societal and political climate in the case countries. Particularly in Pécs and Tallinn, respondents often discussed being part of Europe and its economic, social, and cultural sphere in relation to societal changes in these countries.

After the collapse of the socialist regimes, Eastern and Central European countries commonly emphasized their cultural and historical links to Europe, their Europeanness, as the countries aimed to detach themselves from their socialist identities and image (Kolankiewicz 1993, 106–107). A similar discourse was used when Hungary and Estonia joined the EU in 2004 and when Estonia joined the Eurozone in 2011. These strengthened connections to the European polity, increased public debate on European issues, and positive expectations regarding the EU and Eurozone memberships might influence the respondents' positive views of Europeanness in Pécs and Tallinn. As discussed above, many respondents described Europeanness in relation to the EU with pride, feeling the importance of being part of the Union. In Tallinn, the Euro currency was presented in a positive light in several instances where respondents shared their views of Europeanness.

While many respondents contrasted the 'national' and the 'European', plenty of others stated that national culture and identity were important elements of Europeanness. In these instances, the notion of Europeanness was often seen as multi-layered: People have multiple identities, which are mobilized in particular circumstances. The same qualities and issues serve as markers of various identities in different situations or discourses (Lähdesmäki 2014a). Thus, many of the respondents emphasized – in their words – the "natural", "self-evident", and "taken-for-granted" links between the city, region, country, and Europe or the EU. To take one case from each city: "Culture of Pécs = Hungarian culture = A part of European culture" (Pécs, female, b. 1949), "Turku has always been a part of Europe, thus Europeanness is a natural part of Turku. Turku is the most European and international city in Finland" (Turku, female, b. 1969), and "I do not know how to separate the concepts of what is Europeanness and Estonian-ness. For me, Europeanness is a part of Estonia" (Tallinn, female, b. 1977).

5   Conclusions: Belonging to Europe through the Everyday

The analysis of the questionnaire data from Pécs2010, Tallinn2011, and Turku2011 reveals how the audiences of the ECOC events constructed the 'European' through what Billig (1995) calls "banal" forms of culture. These forms included well-known and repeated symbols of the EU, such as the EU flag, and easily recognized features of diversity and difference, such as people speaking and performing in foreign languages. The notions of the 'European' were commonly drawn from the respondents' everyday experiences of encountering 'European people' – artists, performers, and visitors from other European countries – and enjoying cultural events known to have been produced by or in cooperation with artists, performers, or cultural producers from other European countries. The 'European' in the responses mainly appeared in everyday life and a familiar environment. Besides in the events, the respondents encountered the 'European' in the atmosphere of the cities as well as, in Pécs, in the renovated, developed, and improved urban spaces in the city center.

Respondents commonly constructed the 'European' through their own participation in (European) culture. This participation ranged from enjoying (European) cultural events in the audience to communicating and cooperating in various ways with 'European people' during the ECOC year. It included physical movement in the urban space, engagement with the 'beat of the city', and sensing its atmosphere, transformation, and cultural peculiarities. This kind of experience of 'lived space' in the ECOCs, in Lefebvre's (1991) terms, produced 'lived' experiences of Europeanness (Lähdesmäki 2014e).

Such everyday experiences of the 'European' are likely to invoke everyday experiences of belonging to Europe. One EU aim for the ECOC action is to "increase citizens' sense of belonging to a common cultural area" (EC 2014, 4), as discussed Chapter 3. The EU officials have been concerned about how this EU politics of belonging is being implemented in the ECOC programmes: in their understanding, a strong European dimension is lacking. The analysis of the questionnaire responses from Pécs2010, Tallinn2011, and Turku2011 indicate the cities' cultural events did evoke a sense of the 'European', though this was less linked to the contents of the events or shared European culture or common heritage or history. The analysis reveals how many respondents experienced Europe and the 'European' through contemporary cultural practices in everyday environments and how the EU has become an internalized everyday actor in people's lives.

The analysis also shows how the respondents approached the different layers or dimensions of culture and cultural identity through relationships – either in terms of connectedness or distinctiveness. On the one hand, the respondents emphasized culture as multi-layered and cultural identities as 'thin' categories, which are intertwined and entangled in various ways. On the other hand, the respondents perceived cultural identities, especially local and national culture, as 'thick' and essentialist categories that were clearly distinguished and should not be meshed with the 'European'. The previous analysis of the data has revealed some differences in respondents' views of the multi-layered nature of culture and cultural identities in different case cities (Lähdesmäki 2013b). In Pécs, more respondents strongly emphasized distinction than integration of different scalar layers of culture, while in Turku the idea of integrating these layers was strongest. In Tallinn, the views on these scalar layers were more evenly balanced, however, integration was raised slightly more often than distinction.

The exploration of macro-, meso- and micro-level discourses within it reveals how the politics of belonging functions in the ECOC action. The macro-level policy aim of strengthening Europeans' feeling of belonging to Europe and the EU dovetails with the meso-level policy and promotional discourses and guides the implementation of ECOC cultural programmes. This macro-level politics of belonging is also diffused to the micro-level and is reflected in the views and notions of people who participate in ECOC events. However, this process is not only in one direction: Participants play a proactive role in the EU cultural initiatives. Like our other two case studies, our ECOC case study indicates that belonging to Europe and the EU is also initiated and constructed at the micro level and in 'lived space' through which people experience, grasp, and give meanings to Europe.

References

Axford, B. 2006. "The Dialectic of Borders and Networks in Europe: Reviewing 'Topological Presuppositions'." *Comparative European Politics* 4 (2): 160–182.

EC (European Commission). 2014. "Decision No 445/2014/EU of the European Parliament and of the Council of 16 April 2014 establishing a Union action for the European Capitals of Culture for the years 2020 to 2033 and repealing Decision No 1622/2006/EC." *Official Journal of the European Union* L 132: 1–12.

Ecorys 2011. Ex-post evaluation of 2010 European Capitals of Culture. Final Report for the European Commission DG Education and Culture. Birmingham: Ecorys.

Ecorys 2012. Ex-post Evaluation of 2011 European Capitals of Culture. Final Report for the European Commission DG Education and Culture. Birmingham: Ecorys.

Everett, M., and M. S. Barrett. 2009. "Investigating Sustained Visitor/Museum Relationships: Employing Narrative Research in the Field of Museum." *Visitor Studies* 12 (1): 2–15.

Davidson, A. C. 2008. "Through Thick and Thin: 'European Identification' for a Justified and Legitimate European Union." *Journal of Contemporary European Research* 4 (1): 32–47.

Delanty, G. 2003. "Is There a European Identity?" *Global Dialogue* 5 (3–4). Accessed 13 March 2020. http://www.worlddialogue.org/content.php?id=269

Helander, N., S. Innilä, M. Jokinen, and J. Talve, eds. 2006. *Turku on Fire. The Application of the City of Turku for the European Capital of Culture 2011*. Turku: City of Turku.

Kaasik-Krogerus, S. 2019. "Politics of Mobility and Stability in Authorizing European Heritage: Estonia's Great Guild Hall." In *Dissonant Heritages and Memories in Contemporary Europe*, edited by T. Lähdesmäki, L. Passerini, S. Kaasik-Krogerus, and I. van Huis, 157–181. New York: Palgrave Macmillan.

Kolankiewicz, G. 1993. "The Other Europe: Different Roads to Modernity in Eastern and Central Europe." In *European Identity and the Search for Legitimacy*, edited by S. García, 106–130. London: Pinter.

Lähdesmäki, T. 2011. "Contested Identity Politics: Analysis of the EU Policy Objectives and the Local Reception of the European Capital of Culture Programme." *Baltic Journal of European Studies* 1 (2): 134–166.

Lähdesmäki, T. 2013a. "Interpretations of Cultural Identities in the European Capital of Culture Events in Turku." *Ethnologia Fennica* 40: 66–88.

Lähdesmäki, T. 2013b. "Identity Politics of the European Capital of Culture Initiative and the Audience Reception of Cultural Events Compared." *The Nordic Journal of Cultural Policy* 16 (2): 340–365.

Lähdesmäki, T. 2014a. *Identity Politics in the European Capital of Culture Initiative*. Joensuu: University of Eastern Finland.

Lähdesmäki, T. 2014b. "European Capital of Culture Designation as an Initiator of Urban Transformation in the Post-socialist Countries." *European Planning Studies* 22 (3): 481–497.

Lähdesmäki, T. 2014c. "The Influence of Cultural Competence on the Interpretations of Territorial Identities in the European Capitals of Culture." *Baltic Journal of European Studies* 4 (1): 69–96.

Lähdesmäki, T. 2014d. "Area-based Identities and Their Audience Reception in the European Capital of Culture Events in Tallinn2011." In *Culture! Capital. Change? Effects of the European Capital of Culture Year on Tallinn´s Cultural Life*, edited by M. Hellrand, 109–131.Tallinn: Tallinn Creative Hub.

Lähdesmäki, T. 2014e. "Discourses of Europeanness in the Reception of the European Capital of Culture Events: The Case of Pécs 2010." *European Urban and Regional Studies* 21 (2): 191–205.

Lähdesmäki, T., V. L. A. Čeginskas, S. Kaasik-Krogerus, K. Mäkinen, and J. Turunen. 2020. *Creating and Governing Cultural Heritage in the European Union: The European Heritage Label*. London: Routledge.

Lefebvre, H. 1991. *The Production of Space*. Oxford: Blackwell.

Määttänen, S. ed. 2010. *Aivan kuten epäilinkin: kulttuuria! Turku Euroopan kulttuuripääkaupunki 2011. Ohjelmakirja* [*As I Expected: Culture! Turku – the European Capital of Culture. Programme Book*]. Turku: Turku 2011 Foundation.

Mayer, F. C., and J. Palmowski. 2004. "European Identities and the EU – The Ties That Bind the People of Europe." *Journal of Common Market Studies* 42 (3): 573–598.

Mony, P. R. S., and J. E. Heimlich. 2008. "Talking to Visitors about Conservation: Exploring Message Communication Through Docent-Visitor Interactions at Zoos. *Visitor Studies* 11 (2): 151–162.

Patton, M. Q. 2002. *Qualitative Research and Evaluation Methods*. Thousand Oaks, CA: Sage.

Sassatelli, M. 2009. *Becoming Europeans. Cultural Identity and Cultural Policies*. New York: Palgrave Macmillan.

Takáts, J. 2005. *Borderless City. European Capital of Culture – Pécs, 2010*. Pécs: Pécs2010 Application Centre.

Tarand, K. 2006. *Everlasting Fairytale, Tallinn...* Tallinn: Foundation for Tallinn as the Capital of Culture.

Terlouw, K. 2012. "From Thick to Thin Regional Identities?" *GeoJournal* 77 (5): 707–721.

Toller, L. 2005. "Foreword." In *Borderless City. European Capital of Culture – Pécs, 2010*, by J. Takáts, 7. Pécs: Pécs 2010 Application Centre.

Yocco, V. S., J. E. Heimlich, E. Meyer, and P. Edwards. 2009. "Measuring Public Value: An Instrument and an Art Museum Case Study." *Visitor Studies* 12 (2): 153–163.

CHAPTER 5

Case 2: The European Citizen Campus

1   Citizenship through Art

In this chapter, we focus on the implementation of the EU's cultural programmes and explore what kinds of conceptions of Europe are constructed
in the framework of an individual EU project. The European Citizen Campus
(ECC) received funding from the Culture programme between 2013 and 2015.
EU projects are used as channels to engage participants in the Union's activities, and as such, they can be seen as core elements of the EU's politics of
belonging. In the chapter, we examine the performative and discursive construction of Europe and the 'European' as well as the notions of European citizenship as a part of this construction at different levels of the project.

The ECC was a student exchange project whose main coordinator was a
Berlin-based organization that provides services for students in higher education. Other partners were similar organizations at local, regional, or national
levels in Belgium, France, Germany, Italy, Luxembourg, the Netherlands, and
Portugal, including two universities, eight organizations responsible for student services, two national umbrella organizations, and six regional or local
organizations. In the summer of 2014, the project organized six art laboratories
in universities or other institutions of higher education located in the partner
countries. Based on their applications, 114 students from the seven countries
were selected to participate in the laboratories. The core concept of the project was European citizenship, and the themes of the laboratories were viewed
as "thematic variations of European citizenship" (Detailed description n.d.,
4). The themes were addressed through various art genres in the laboratories,
which were led by 12 artists. These themes were identity (art genres used in the
laboratory: visual arts), roots (illustration, sculpture made from waste material), home (painting, crossover), conflict (visual arts, clay works, crossover),
freedom (photography, optic media), and dialogue (music, dance).

We begin by introducing the research material and methods. After this, we
explore the notions of Europe produced in the meso-level discourses related
to the ECC. These discourses are produced by the organizations involved in
coordinating the project before, during, and after it, and they concretize in the
materials created for the project and in the implementation practices. Next,
we analyze the micro-level ECC discourses – the project participants' notions
of Europe and the 'European'. This analysis is divided into three parts. First, we

© TUULI LÄHDESMÄKI ET AL., 2021 | DOI: 10.1163/9789004449800_005

explore the participants' perceptions of Europe defined by history, unity, diversity, geography, and borders. After that, we examine how the participants construct their own relation to Europe by referring to transnational mobility and interaction. Finally, we investigate how the participants understand citizenship in the context of Europe and the EU. The chapter concludes with remarks placing the meso- and micro-level discourses in the macro-level context, consisting of the EU documents on the Culture programme (see Chapter 3).

2   Collecting Data and Conducting Field Research in the ECC Project

Our analysis of the politics of belonging in the ECC context is based on an ethnographic study that includes interviews, observation, and research material consisting of texts and images created within the ECC project. The materials produced at the meso and micro levels of the project enable indicating the differences and similarities in the notions of Europe and exploring identifications with it constructed at these levels. The meso-level data includes texts produced by the organizers of the ECC project, regarding planning, presenting, and reporting on it. The most important of these is the Detailed Description (n.d.), which was attached to the project application; it is a text written by the organizers explaining their core ideas and forthcoming activities. This data also contains a catalogue of the art exhibition included in the project (Art Catalogue 2015) as well as a declaration (Antwerp Declaration 2015) made and published at the dissemination conference held at the end of the project. The micro-level data was mainly collected from participants in one of the aforementioned laboratories, the Roots lab in Strasbourg in July 2014. The fieldwork entailed observing two workshops and other activities at the laboratory over four days, writing a field diary, taking photos, and conducting nine interviews with 11 participants. In addition, the researcher had the opportunity to conduct informal discussions with the participants on various topics in the course of the laboratory.

The Roots lab programme consisted of workshops that ran daily from 10 am until 6 pm. On one day, there was a visit to the museum of the illustrator Tomi Ungerer with a film screening and presentation about him in the Strasbourg museum of modern and contemporary art. The participants were mostly in their early twenties and many of them studied art in some form but also other subjects. They came from Western Europe, because the project partner countries were located in this part of the continent. In general, more women than men participated: in the Roots lab, 20 of the participants were female and four male; in the other laboratories, slightly more than two thirds (17–18) of the participants were female, except in the Home lab, with a 1:1 ratio of male and female participants.

In the Roots lab, the participants were divided into two workshops; in both, participants eagerly volunteered to be interviewed once they had heard about the research. Three interviewees participated in the workshop making sculpture from waste material, held in the main building of the University of Strasbourg and led by a crossover artist. The other eight interviewees participated in the illustration workshop, led by an illustrator at the Strasbourg École supérieure des arts décoratifs, which is part of the Haute école des arts du Rhin. The interviews (ten female interviewees, one male) were conducted either during workshop breaks or in the evenings on public premises. They were held in English and lasted approximately 30 minutes. The interviews started with questions about the participants' initial expectations of the laboratory and what they had been doing in the project so far. After this, the questions focused on 'roots' as the topic of the laboratory and 'citizenship' as the topic of the project. The last question invited the interviewees to anticipate the effects of the project in their lives and whether they thought that participating would empower to act on issues important for them.

In addition, we were allowed to use research interviews that were conducted for a master's thesis by Janine Fleck (2015) with the participants of the Home lab in Freiburg in July 2014. Four participants, one woman and three men, gave their consent to use the interviews. The questions in these interviews explicitly addressed the idea of European identity in relation to home – the topic of the laboratory – intercultural exchange, and art. Interviews were conducted in French, English, and German.

Our ECC material additionally included thematic writings by eight project participants, four women and four men. Writing invitations were sent to all those participants who had agreed to give their e-mail addresses to the researcher. The participants were invited to write about their experiences in the project without giving any further instructions. One of the thematic writings related to participation in the Conflict lab, two to the Home lab, and the remainder to the Freedom lab.

The ECC data also includes motivation letters written by German applicants when they were applying to join the project. Eleven applicants (eight women, one man, and two anonymous) gave permission for us to use their motivation letters for research purposes, and their letters were forwarded via e-mail to the researcher by the project organizers. We do not know whether all of these applicants were accepted, but in this chapter, all the applicants are called participants because preparing and sending an application can be seen as a way of participating in the procedures of the project.

Additional ethnographic material was collected through participant observation in the dissemination conference of the ECC project in Antwerp in June 2015, at which one of the authors was invited to present research findings. The same researcher also observed the art exhibition organized as part of the conference and presenting a selection of the art works made in the laboratories. This material includes photos of the art exhibition and notes about the conference presentations.

In the following analysis, the interviews from the Roots lab are numbered 1–11 and the ones from the Home lab are numbered I–IV. The thematic writings are coded TW1–TW8 and the motivation letters are coded ML1–ML11. The interviews were transcribed and the quotes from the interviews and texts in French, German, and Italian translated by the authors. We take a conceptual approach (Wiesner et al. 2018) to the data, focusing on the meanings given to Europe (see Chapters 1 and 2). Our data-driven analysis is based on close reading that enabled clustering the variety of thematic categories interpreted in the research material.

3   "A Sense of European Identity": Constructions of Europe in the Meso-level ECC Discourse

A poster advertising the project illustrates the key idea of the ECC: European citizenship. The text of the poster invites the reader to "give your definition about European citizenship" (see Figure 5.1).

The purpose of the ECC project was "to raise general awareness and concern on the issue of European citizenship and to develop new visions to this concept from a student perspective (Detailed Description n.d., 8). Art had been chosen as the heart of the project, as a way to "create a new focus on the reality of citizenship" (ibid., 1). The project description envisaged that participants' debates on citizenship were to be stimulated through the simultaneous presence of two art genres in each of the laboratories (ibid.). According to the Antwerp Declaration (2015, 4) published by the project organizers at the dissemination conference, the "[artistic] engagement enriched the ongoing political discourse and created an emotionally-personal level, without it the EU citizenship would have remained an abstract construct". In the implementation of the project, citizenship was approached in different ways. For example, in the Roots lab, citizenship was not present in discussions or practices, whereas, according to the Art Catalogue (2015, 57), the artists directing the Conflict lab "accompanied and encouraged micro-conflicts among the participating students, in order to bring out the contradictions of living as citizens of Europe".

FIGURE 5.1   A poster (detail) that advertised the ECC in Strasbourg in 2014 on the wall of the
student canteen where meals for the Roots lab were served.
PHOTO: KATJA MÄKINEN

In the Conflict lab, citizenship was viewed as a contested condition that is not
the same for everyone, even though citizenship is often understood as a status
that presumably guarantees citizens' equality.

The locations of the laboratories were envisioned to support "reflection
on new European Citizenship visions" (Detailed Description n.d., 2). Cultural
heritage sites were deliberately selected, because "European citizenship and
European cultural heritage are considered to be complementary concepts as
both issues are related to questions about roots, past, provenance, identity etc."
(ibid., 6). The selected locations were university sites, since "[a] university site is
the best suited starting point for the promotion of active European citizenship"
(ibid., 3) and is "naturally predestined for an artistic reflection on the European
citizenship model" (ibid., 5). This is because universities are seen as meeting
places of "citizens of the world" (ibid., 3), supposedly enabling manifold debate
and providing opportunities for intercultural dialogue, sharing knowledge and
values, developing deeper understanding of diversity, and fostering equality.

In the ECC, developing the participants' European identity was an explicit
aim. The purpose of the laboratories was to stimulate "an awareness building
process on Europe's cultural richness based on its diversity and the development of a sense of European identity [...] amongst the project participants"

(ibid., 8). In the final conference of the project, the plan was to discuss, based on the experiences gained in the laboratories, "the essential components of this European identity" (ibid., 7). Moreover, identity was defined as one of the six dimensions of citizenship, and thus one laboratory was dedicated to it. In this laboratory, identity was understood as involving constant change, quest, dialogue, difference, and confrontation, and as becoming recognized "in the public space through forms of cultural mediation and (artistic) expression" (Art Catalogue 2015, 7).

European identity was understood in the meso-level ECC texts as a cultural identity reflecting the cultural richness and diversity of Europe. Because some of the project organizers were specialized in providing cultural services to students, it is understandable that the cultural dimension of identity was emphasized. Nevertheless, a project on European citizenship could focus on a myriad other questions: access to citizenship; fundamental, social, political, and cultural rights; or various forms of civic participation in different fields. Admittedly, identity is commonly understood as one dimension of citizenship. For democracy to function, we need a *demos*, a democratic collective subject that recognizes itself as such and is able to use power in democracy. This means that a sufficient part of the population identifies with their political community and each other. When defining citizenship, questions of both identity and difference need to be considered so that diverse voices can be heard in decision-making. In the ECC discourse at the meso level, the relations between citizenship and identity are not, however, elaborated on further.

In the meso-level materials produced by the ECC coordinators, Europe was seen as an entity in the making (see also Chapter 6). The central role of citizens in this making was emphasized, which is not surprising given that the topic of the project was European citizenship. The Detailed Description (n. d., 1) explicitly defined Europe as "an ongoing process of construction [that] should be shaped and defined by its citizens". According to the project description, "[y]oung people, in particular, have a special interest and concern about what kind of Europe they live in" (ibid.). Therefore, the project sought to explore questions around students' European identity and their engagement in the social and political life of the EU. It especially underlined the role of universities and student service organizations as the first objective of the project was to highlight "the vital role that universities and their partnering student service organization can play in the development of a European identity amongst young people" (ibid., 3). Above all, the project description emphasizes students' perspective on European citizenship. Because students are personally affected by the European integration process, both in their studies and as citizens, their contribution to "promotion of active European citizenship and the creation of an ever closer Europe" (ibid., 1) is seen as important. The wording "ever closer Union among the peoples of Europe" originates from the Treaty of Rome (1957) and is frequently used in the EU documents. This key phrase implies that Europe is understood as a continuous process of integration and community construction.

Europe and its construction were understood as objects of public debate in the meso-level ECC discourses. The ECC project was seen as a channel for the participants to contribute to the public debate on Union citizenship, as explained in the Detailed Description (n.d., 3): "ECC starts a creative process on different vision(s) of the European citizenship concept seen by student eyes with the purpose to stimulate debate on this issue with the wider audience". According to the Antwerp Declaration (2015, 6), "[s]tudents and their artistic potential should be recognized as a resource for political dialogue in Europe". Moreover, the declaration claims that "[s]tudents are very keen [...] to contribute to the general political discourse via their art work" (ibid., 3). This was also clearly stated in the Art Catalogue (2015, 2):

> With the ECC project we bring in the voice of European students in the political debate on the identity of the European Union. [...] the creative process of art production in which students from all academic disciplines took part will enrich the often abstract political discussion on European citizenship.

According to these quotes, the ECC sought to help make students' voices heard in debates on the identity of the EU and on European citizenship, which exemplifies the entwined relation between identity and citizenship. Moreover, in these texts, Europe is frequently equated with the EU.

The public dimension was manifested in the art exhibition, which presented some of the art works produced in the laboratories. The exhibition was circulated in the partner countries and at the final dissemination conference in Antwerp in June 2015. The aim of the exhibition was "to give an overall view and new visions on European citizenship as well as to stimulate a debate on this topic with the broader public" (Detailed Description n.d., 2) and to "enhance the European visibility of the project and to reach out to a wide public" (Detailed Description n.d., 6). Indeed, public debate is essential if citizenship is understood as political agency. Politics is done in the public sphere through acting together and sharing acts and speech (Arendt 1998, 180–183, 198). In the research data on the ECC implementation, however, the notion of citizens' public activity remained invisible, as our analysis will show.

The analysis of the meso-level ECC discourses shows that the project organizers practiced three types of politics of belonging. First, they explicitly aimed to develop participants' European identity and, second, to involve participants in one of the key institutions of the Union: citizenship. Third, the project as such can be understood as a platform for engagement at the European level. The ECC can therefore be interpreted as a technology of agency (Walters and Haahr 2005, 124) embedded in the EU's participatory governance. The students were invited to become active collaborators in the process of 'European construction' and simultaneously to feel partnership with and belonging to Europe and the EU.

4 "That Would Really Be Europe": Europe Perceived by Project Participants

The notion of Europe was central in the participants' interviews and motivation letters, and to a lesser extent in the thematic writings. This can be explained by the obvious fact that the participants were involved in a project funded by the EU. Particularly in the motivation letters, the centrality of Europe was not surprising: one would suppose that in an application for an EU project about European citizenship, it is a good idea to discuss Europe. The thematic writings focused mostly on the participants' experiences of encounters with other participants, visiting a new place, and making art. In three thematic writings (TW 1, 4, 7), Europe was discussed more extensively.

In the interviews in the Roots lab, Europe was one of the main themes the interviewees raised, besides art, themselves as participants, and other participants. The role of Europe was central to their experiences of this laboratory, even though the interviews did not include any questions about Europe, nor was it explicitly present in the practices of the two workshops. The interviewees mentioned Europe mostly when answering questions about roots and citizenship, that is, when pondering the core topics of the ECC project and the laboratory. This is partly explained by the fact that the researcher conducting the interviews mentioned European citizenship in this context. The participants did not proactively mention citizenship and found the question about it confusing. When the interviewees asked for clarification, the interviewer explained that because the topic of the project is European citizenship, this study explores their conceptions of citizenship. The questions in the interviews with the participants in the Home lab deliberately focused on Europe and European identity. Hence, Europe was frequently discussed in these interviews.

Participants discussed Europe in close connection to the EU and sometimes the two terms were used as synonyms, which is common in political, media, and everyday discourses. For many participants, the EU appeared as something taken for granted, and one of the factors contributing to this, mentioned by several participants, is the Euro currency as an everyday practice. Some of them constructed their relation to Europe through the EU membership of their own home country: Europe feels like home because their homeland is an EU member state.

When defining Europe, some participants drew from history. In their view, Europe was also characterized by both diversity and unity. Geography and borders were other central elements in interviewees' notions of Europe. The roles of these three interrelated themes in the participants' constructions of Europe are analyzed in the following.

4.1   *History*

The venue of the sculpture workshop in the Roots lab was the main building of the University of Strasbourg, where the initial steps of the European integration were taken, as the Assembly of the Council of Europe had its first meeting there in 1949. According to the founding narrative repeated in the EU discourse, European integration was started in order to prevent new wars between countries in Europe, most notably France and Germany (see Mäkinen 2019). It is thus fitting that the assembly met in the Franco-German border area: the city of Strasbourg itself had faced several wars but also represented the potential for peaceful relations across national, cultural, and linguistic borders.

The role of Alsace in World War II and the initial phase of post-war integration was not discussed in the laboratory, apart from a very brief remark by the leader of the sculpture workshop, placing the topic of the laboratory "in the European context". He referred to "our roots [that] are broken because of the war" (Artist 1) and conceptualized the workshop as a revisit to that past. He connected roots as a topic to the history of Europe, that is, to World War II and the post-war cooperation. "We", the laboratory participants in the present moment, were linked to those past processes.

Two participants (7 and 9) in the sculpture workshop indicated that the teacher's remark helped them to link their art-making to the roots topic and the European context. Both participants referred to reconstruction and repairing the connections that the war had broken. Some of the art works made in the sculpture workshop indeed reflected the idea of Europe and its roots (Art Catalogue 2015, 52–55), whereas in the ethnographic data, there were no signs of connecting the roots topic with Europe in the illustration workshop.

A visit to the Tomi Ungerer museum and a film about him, included in the programme of the Roots lab, illuminated these aspects. In the personal history of the illustrator Tomi Ungerer, several layers of identity overlap: he was Strasbourgeois, Alsacien, and French. Alsace as both a battlefield and a multilingual

FIGURE 5.2 The plaque in the hall of the main building of the University of Strasbourg commemorates the first session of the Assembly of the Council of Europe.
PHOTO: KATJA MÄKINEN

and multicultural border region between France and Germany played a significant role in the life and art of Ungerer, and he strove to improve Franco-German relations. Hence, the museum and the film offered opportunities to reflect on both roots and citizenship and their context embedded in Europe and its history. There was no time scheduled for discussing the museum and the film in the laboratory programme. Despite this, one of the participants connected the topic of roots and Tomi Ungerer in a comment published in the catalogue

FIGURE 5.3   Roots of Europeans crisscross in an art work being made in the sculpture workshop.
PHOTO: KATJA MÄKINEN

presenting the project and the art exhibition based on it (Art Catalogue 2015, 53):

> My strongest experience in the ECC lab was watching the Tomi Ungerer movie. He had to change his life and language several times due to war...

he has difficult roots and you can see this in his art. The movie made me understand why Strasbourg, where Tomi Ungerer was born, chose the topic 'roots'.

She also linked the roots topic and the personal history of Tomi Ungerer to Strasbourg as a place. In general, the interviews, thematic writings, and motivation letters dealt with history relatively little. One participant (ML7) pondered the idea of roots when living in Europe during the Euro crisis and related it to questions asking what is special about these roots and how they become a means of distinguishing from others. This participant wondered if roots could grow together in an intercultural sense to approach peace and solidarity, and how the next generation would perceive them. The reference to the next generation implies that the current moment is history for the next generation and that roots are not only about the past but also about the future and about relationships between people. The metaphor of growing refers to the conception of Europe in transformation. Furthermore, various participants (ML1; Interview 11) referred to the integration of European states after the two world wars and the collapse of the Iron Curtain and the Warsaw Pact, which indicates the importance of borders and their changes in the history of Europe. The participants connected their conceptions of Europe to the transformation processes in its history and the relations between states in it, acknowledging that there are factors that can both unite and separate different people and regions in Europe.

4.2   Unity and Diversity

Within the ECC project, the diversity of languages was an everyday experience for the participants, as one of them described (Interview IV):

> one sees, however, a unity, even though they speak a different language [...] Although there are different languages, they are almost the same persons. The persons, they are not different. One cannot say: she is French, she is Italian, and he is Belgian.

A spontaneous collective practice manifested this cross-linguistic 'we feeling' in the Home lab: "at the end of the day, the idea came [that] we say: 'we are Europe', in all our different languages [...] We had our flags of our countries painted on our hands" (Interview VI). Another participant confirmed that in the Home lab, besides small mentality differences, there were no differences between participants, which to him illustrated that particularly the younger Europeans are already "rather well adjusted to each other" (Interview 11).

According to the same participant, media, the internet, music, films, and art provide a "relatively broad common cultural basis" (ibid.) for European people in the younger generations. Indeed, as stated by a participant in the Roots lab, "we all come from different countries but I feel that we have much in common when we meet" (Interview 8).

For one of the participants, to be a European citizen meant a "strive for inter-culturality" and the ability to speak several languages. According to her, "every culture has a different feeling [...] people are different", and she finds "this kind of diversity" positive and interesting (Interview 10). Another participant – who wrote in this context that he speaks five languages – described himself as "a young European, who together with other young Europeans would like to discuss and form the future of our continent, aware of our diverse nations and our several commonalities" (ML1). He acknowledged both diversity and unity in Europe and, moreover, understood himself as an active agent in shaping Europe.

These experiences in the ECC project and other contexts illustrate that the participants often depicted Europe as an entity consisting of different countries and languages, yet sharing a lot in common – as "a big country made up of small countries" (Interview VI). The plurality of languages spoken in Europe was not viewed as something that separates people but as a source of diversity that can create a sense of unity: "I see it like a big country where we speak other languages, but we are all together" (Interview 2).

The unity of Europe was considered more visible when perceived "from another continent" (Interview 11), as the same interviewee went on to show.

> I think if you are from another continent, you think Europe is quite close. The countries may be quite similar but I think even if France and Germany are quite close, there are huge differences. You can feel them but that doesn't mean that you can't cooperate, that doesn't mean that you can't get along with each other. [...] Sometimes the differences are good, and you have to keep them up because they belong to culture and identity.

Nevertheless, this participant pointed out that there are 'feelable' differences within Europe. In her view, these differences do not prevent cooperation, but are an integral part of culture and identity. Other participants agreed that when taking a closer look, the cultures in Europe are not similar – on the contrary, "many different peoples with their own languages and cultures are squeezed on our continent making it so diverse" (ML5). In addition, diverse ethnicities and religions were seen as part of Europe (ML9). Referring to countries beyond

Western Europe, one participant underlined "how people from different places are something very different" (Interview V).

Identities are often constructed in relation to 'others' and by drawing distinctions. Thus, European identity is commonly approached by contrasting Europe to the rest of the world. In comparison with cultures outside Europe, such as in the United States, Asia, or Africa, the others appear "different" (Interviews 1, 2, IV) to some participants (see also Chapter 6). One of them thought that for a long time Europe has been more developed than the rest of the world, although other places are increasingly catching up. She said: "In other sections of the world, they have to learn so much. They live so different, they think different" (Interview 1). In contrast, this interviewee connected "our vision of the world" to principles such as equality, rights, and freedoms, which she said still makes Europe a popular immigration destination. The tremendously problematic perception of Europe as a higher form of civilization has been very influential but in the ECC data there were no other examples of this. Even this participant relativized her notions by recalling that there are problems in every part of the world and mentioning some of them in her own home country.

In contrast, some participants highlighted the cultural similarity between Europe, the Americas, and Japan. One of them perceived European identity as an outdated concept and preferred to speak of a 'Western identity' instead. He included the USA and Japan in this "Western cultural circle" (Interview II) because so much culture is imported to Europe from these countries. However, he noted that there are cultures with which he cannot identify and emphasized he was above all European and felt at home in European countries.

4.3   Geographical Borders

In addition, and related to history, unity, and diversity, the participants elaborated their conceptions of Europe in terms of geography and borders. Although participants often discussed Europe as the EU, their notions of Europe went beyond it: "Europe, after all, is bigger than the Union" (Interview V). Participants would have liked to include peers from Eastern, Southern, and Northern Europe in the ECC project "because that would really be Europe" (Interview V; also Interview 7; TW4). They hoped to meet participants from all over Europe, not only the EU member states, implying that their understanding of Europe was larger than the EU. Moreover, some of them thought that the project should have participants from other parts of the world, such as North and South America, Asia, and Africa (Interview II; IV).

One of the participants paid attention to the changes in the geographical perception of Europe between generations. This participant from Western

Europe assumed that for her grandparents "Europe does not go as far east as it does for me" (Interview 5). She was glad that in the current imaginaries, the eastern border of Europe was moving further east. She constructed an inclusive notion of Europe, saying that "we should not be afraid to let other people in" (ibid.).

The changing borders within and around Europe, discussed by the participants, can be seen as part of their conceptions of Europe. A piece of video art made in the Home lab represented how the borders in Europe have changed during centuries. For example, Germany was constituted from small states in the nineteenth century, and in the 1990s, Czechoslovakia was peacefully divided whereas Yugoslavia broke up through war, as a participant involved in the making of this artwork explained (Interview 11). Moreover, the morphing technique used in this video-art piece shows people's faces merging into each other. It represents a process of continuous, never-ending change, performing that "the Europeans are very similar", according to this participant (Interview 11).

Internal borders within the current states in Europe construct the participants' perceptions of the continent. For example, one participant pointed out that there are regional differences even within one country and one language (ML5). One interviewee observed a dynamic in which Europe first grows together due to the EU integration and then states (re-)emerge within Europe, such as Scotland, Catalonia, the Basque country, or Fleming and Walloon regions in Belgium (Interview 11). Moreover, if Turkey eventually joins the EU, "the Kurd question becomes a European question" (Interview 11). Such questions of regional sovereignty shape the image of Europe and its internal borders.

Several participants supported the idea of a 'borderless Europe'. For them, the ability to cross state borders without formalities makes everyday life easier for people like tourists, residents of the border areas, and exchange students (e.g. ML9). One interviewee had a vision of Europe in which the borders were erased altogether (Interview V). This idea again exemplifies a conception of Europe's shifting borders: they shifted in the past and they can shift in the future. While participants greatly appreciated the right to free movement across state borders, some of them regarded it as boundary-making, dividing EU citizens and non-EU citizens (Interview 5; 7). This issue was also raised by a participant speaking at the final conference, reminding listeners that free movement is not everybody's right. One participant specifically criticized the EU's "governmental institutions", such as FRONTEX, for granting "'our' freedom on the 'inside'" by drawing "a strong distinction against the 'outside' (meaning

FIGURE 5.4 Shifting geographies of Europe in the ECC art exhibition at the dissemination conference in Antwerp.
PHOTO: KATJA MÄKINEN

non-EU migrants and so on)" (TW4). In general, the participants were in favor of an inclusive Europe but some of them recognized that Europe is exclusive for many.

5   "Normal to Feel European": Transnational Mobility and Interaction

The participants' own relationship with Europe was commonly conceptualized through travelling, student exchange, youth exchange, international internships, and other international experiences. Participants firmly supported cross-border mobility without formalities, and mentioned the Euro currency as a factor that facilitates travelling. Interviewees saw it as important that projects, such as the ECC, enable travel for students who usually do not have enough money to do so (e.g. Interview 5; 6; 7; 10; 11).

Mobility was also significant for the participants' European identity and belonging, as one of them explained (Interview 9): "I really feel connected because of that [...] I really feel a citizen of Europe because of that". For instance, living and studying abroad and using foreign languages were perceived as fostering the feeling of Europeanness, as exemplified below (Interview 6):

> I don't know when it started but it started quite a time ago, and I started my studies [...] and because we are all so multicultural, and then I started to feel more European than German, and I really have the feeling now to be more European than German. And this language switching thing is not a problem anymore if we talk French or German or English to each other, and I even get some Italian words. It's quite a nice experience.

Similarly, another participant emphasized that her identity includes several aspects that are not mutually exclusive: "it's a personal identity thing [...] It was not either-or, it's not so black and white. I think it was very nice. And I love the whole language switching and being able to travel" (Interview 7). As these examples show, several participants discussed their European identity in relation to their national identity. It was typical to discuss both together, as this participant did: "I feel that I am French but I feel that I'm European too" (Interview 9). Some participants identified themselves rather as Europeans than their respective nationalities (Interview 6; 7; 11). In sum, as one of the participants expressed, for young people, it is increasingly "normal to feel European" (Interview 5).

According to the participants, mobility enables meeting people from different countries and learning about new cultures. Some participants already had experiences of mobility and transnational encounters through other EU projects, student exchange, or voluntary work, whereas for others the ECC project was a new experience of acting on this scale. Networking and interacting with new people and speaking foreign languages was one of the reasons that many participants wanted to join the project: "I joined this programme because I wanted to meet people, European people" (Interview 9).

The participants' notions of Europe were closely linked with their perception of other participants, whose different backgrounds were viewed as representing Europe (the audiences of the ECOC events had a similar approach to Europe, see Chapter 4). They saw Europe as consisting of encounters with other Europeans from different places (similarly to the younger EHL visitors, see Chapter 6). EU projects like the ECC were perceived as platforms for interaction and communication with people from different countries. According to the participants, "it's always interesting to confront our point of view with another, to just be with other people, to talk, to interact" (Interview 9). The language skills facilitating communication in the project were mentioned by several participants, as was an open-minded and interested attitude – the willingness to "have contact with the others" (Interview 1) despite language difficulties.

The participants felt that encounters with other participants brought them knowledge: "The fact that I have learned things just because we are talking, it's really good" (Interview 3). They repeatedly highlighted the role of other participants in learning: "I have experienced from others much about culture, cities, ways of life, eating, political systems of their regions or countries" (TW3). Such personal encounters could cause a positive clash, as one participant noted (Interview 11):

> Always when you meet people from other countries [...] you always learn something about yourself, about others, about cultural thinking, feeling, standards, morals. It's like a clash sometimes, but in a positive way.

The notion of clash implies that the encounters and the learning experiences they spark can expose participants to something new and different. Meeting new people and experiencing new places and situations also encouraged participants to appreciate cultural diversity, as explained by one of the interviewees: "we definitely do learn about each other and about being different. Cause we are all different" (Interview 1). Encountering this novelty, diversity, and difference effects participants' self-reflection, as highlighted by one interviewee (Interview 4):

> to find in myself a new source, to do new things, and to come back in my home bigger and enriched. [...] to see people from other countries permits me to re-evaluate myself and to know what I want and to confront to new cultures and new ways of thinking. To see with other eyes.

Personal interaction in the project could foster a sense of belonging. One participant explained how during the project, she had "been able to learn how to love other people, different people, different cultures" (Interview 3). Due to the encounters in the project, another participant felt "more able to connect with other places" (Interview 4). The participants conceptualized their encounters as contributions to developing openness, tolerance, understanding between people, co-existence, citizenship, and peace: "[w]e should not be prejudiced and not be afraid" (Interview 5).

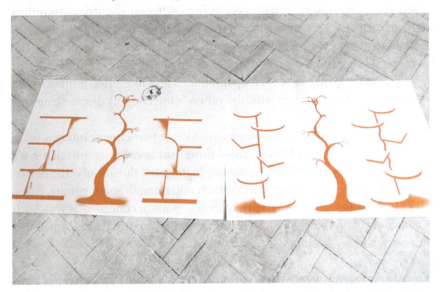

FIGURE 5.5   The empty trees in the illustration workshop are waiting for the participants' images and texts expressing their roots.
PHOTO: KATJA MÄKINEN

Some of the participants saw that the ECC affected their sense of belonging to Europe. The interaction in a group made up of members from different countries was conceived as a major factor here, as described by one participant: "Yes, of course it has developed. Because we created a European group and we acted and worked as it" (Interview VI). In a similar vein, another interviewee argued that projects like this are building entwined roots between different languages, cultures, and ways of thinking in Europe (Interview 9). However, other participants were more uncertain about this effect of the project: "I am not sure if I discovered there my identity as a European" (Interview V).

Nevertheless, the participants experienced that Europe becomes more concrete through the ECC and other similar projects. For one interviewee, the project proved that Europe is not just an abstract idea but can manifest itself in projects of considerable scope. "Thus, it has shown us that the partnerships are possible and feasible", she explained (Interview IV). The same participant argued that the "project can rehabilitate the vision that people have about Europe" and "give again belief in Europe" (ibid.). She contextualized the ECC in a situation after the election of the European Parliament, which had "showed that many people are against" (ibid.) Europe – that is, the EU. Similarly, another participant linked the project to EU integration pointing out that "besides the political and economic connections between states, it is the people who have to live and experience these connections in a small scale" (ML1). He thought that "the ECC seizes precisely this scenario" (ibid.) as it enables dialogue and cross-border networking on a human level. The participants explained that the European aspect of their own identities is attached precisely to this type of transnational practice.

However, as noted earlier, several participants regretted that all the project participants came from Western European countries, and one participant pointed out that the EU projects themselves, such as the ECC, can be interpreted as drawing a distinction between those who come from a "privileged country" (TW4) and those who do not. Admittedly, people from different member states do not have equal opportunities to participate in EU projects due to the burden of travel costs or other financial differences. Participation in EU projects – like any participation – requires resources that differ according to factors like economic or social background, class, education, and age. For example, the ECC was only aimed at students in higher education.

6   Citizenship as an Element of European Belonging

Launching the citizenship of the Union is a prime example of the EU's politics of belonging, and EU projects like the ECC can be seen as attempts to give practical contents to the concept of Union citizenship and thus also to the idea of Europe as citizens' community. Citizenship was a core term in the meso-level ECC discourses and closely intertwined with the notion of European identity. Similarly, the macro-level EU discourses endow citizenship with a major role in the EU's politics of belonging, aiming to bring citizens closer to the EU and each other (see Chapter 3). Next, we discuss how the participants understood the notion of citizenship in the EUropean context and in their own relation to Europe and the EU.

Although the theme of the ECC project was European citizenship, participants scarcely discussed citizenship itself. Nevertheless, some of them perceived Europe as a meaningful frame of citizenship. Mostly they were participants in the Roots lab, since their interviews included an explicit question about citizenship. However, most of the interviewees found it difficult to think about citizenship in the European context.

One participant explained that the idea of European citizenship is "difficult because Europe is so big and there're so many interests" (Interview 5). She felt that civic participation in general was more feasible in a smaller frame because it was easier to get to know the relevant information and actors related to the issues which one seeks to influence. Another participant agreed: "difficult to answer because [...] I have not a large vision of Europe. So, I don't know what it means to be citizen of Europe" (Interview 8). For her, citizenship was a way to live peacefully in a city and "to build projects about a better life, or maybe solidarity" (ibid., 8). Despite this local framing, she saw a correspondence between the local and the European scales when arguing that "maybe this kind of project we are living in this week is a way to do this more in a bigger vision" (Interview 8). She is the only interviewee who expressed that EU projects such as the ECC can have such a direct role in enhancing citizenship.

Participants very rarely recognized the political potential of citizenship. However, three interviewees (Interview 2; 5; 6) found it important that European citizens can elect members of the European Parliament. It needs to be noted, however, that the interviewer gave voting as an example of citizenship's political aspects when the interviewees asked her to clarify the question about citizenship. These participants argued that it is important to be involved in decision-making concerning the rules that we live by and voice one's opinions by voting.

Although the interviewees were asked whether they thought that participation in the ECC project will empower them to take public action, the effects of the project were mainly understood on an individual level, as demonstrated below (Interview 5):

> On a political level, I don't think it's gonna influence me, I think it's more gonna influence me on a personal level, it's again another help to for me to get more creative again [...] expressing myself [...] But being active politically, so far, I don't think this is gonna help me much.

Another participant agreed that participation in the project supported neither citizens' political involvement in the EU nor identity building (TW4):

> from my point of view the goal of construction a 'common European identity' or the idea of citizen participation is not achieved with programmes such as the ECC. Despite the fact that I am happy that EU granted me this treat, it does not make me feel as a citizen of a common European Union or as if I could with this get politically involved in it. I just got another confirmation that a lot of the privileges I enjoy are merely a product of

hegemonic inheritance. [...] Furthermore, there was never any critical reflection upon what it means to be European.

Even though the official ECC discourse emphasized the debate on Europe, this participant experienced that critical reflection about Europeanness was lacking in his laboratory. The participant observation in the Roots lab supports this impression that unlike the meso-level plans, the programme did not generate discussion about the idea of Europe or citizenship.

Some of the participants discussed citizenship in a way that reflects an understanding of Europe as a privileged place. They conceptualized their "privileges [as] a product of hegemonic inheritance" (TW4), emphasized that in Europe certain matters related to rights and equality are more advanced than in other places (Interview 1), and perceived citizenship as a right that their ancestors have fought for, and felt lucky "compared to [...] other countries" (Interview 4) to have this right, which is not necessarily available to people outside Europe. They noted that "European citizenship" does not apply even to all countries within Europe (Interview 7), thus distinguishing between Europe and EUrope and recalling the plurality of Europe. These comments reflected the fact that nationals of European states that are not EU members and third-country nationals in the member states are not entitled to EU citizenship.

Although some participants mentioned the power dynamics intrinsic in citizenship, they were more likely to discuss the effects of participating in the project on their personal lives, such as learning new skills and getting new information for their studies, forthcoming professions, plans for similar projects, student exchange, and making art. They also repeatedly highlighted that the opportunity to interact with other participants and learn about their backgrounds would have lasting effects on them. This was framed as interpersonal dynamics at the individual level in the private sphere rather than as joining forces for citizens' activity seeking to make claims, use power in the public sphere, or take part in decision-making.

Instead of political action in the public sphere, some participants understood citizenship as a status. For example, one participant with a multinational and multilingual family background was wondering why she could not simply have only the European citizenship, instead of needing to decide for one of multiple national citizenships (ML8). She also linked European citizenship to collective identity construction and felt European because of her background. In her specific case, the status of EU citizenship contrasted with the exclusive frameworks in which national membership is commonly defined, and offered an alternative way of experiencing full membership– with and despite her multiple affiliations and allegiances (see also Čeginskas 2016). Another participant explained how "holding EU citizenship was offering me benefits" (ML3) when living abroad. As discussed above, mobility rights were frequently emphasized as a concrete benefit to EU citizens, which indicates that the understanding of the Union citizenship as a status entitling free movement has consolidated in the public awareness.

As the examples demonstrate, Europe was primarily understood as the EU in the discussions related to citizenship. Some participants built an active relationship to this EUrope and saw themselves as agents in 'constructing Europe' (e.g. ML1). One of them explicitly framed European identity with the EU. She sought to develop and disseminate this identity and raise awareness of the EU as not dry, but thrilling. She was eager to be involved in enhancing the benefits provided by the EU in everyday life. She welcomed the "opinion differences of EU citizens" and saw Europe as a construction process involving joint problem-solving and increasing understanding and tolerance (ML9).

7 Conclusions: EU Projects as Politics of Belonging

Ethnographic research on implementing the EU's Culture programme, explored through an individual project, revealed various conceptions of Europe. Most importantly, it helped us to understand how the project participants themselves conceptualized Europe and their own relations to it. The role of Europe was central to their experiences, which reflects the importance of the notion of Europe in discursive identity building on the other levels. In the meso-level ECC discourses, Europe is a key concept through the project's core component, European citizenship, and the related aim of creating European identity. In the macro-level EU documents related to the Culture programme, the focus is naturally on Europe, and the most diverse issues are framed as European.

The participants depicted Europe as simultaneously united and diverse. There was thus a clear continuity from the discourse of the Culture programme, as well as other EU discourses, in which conceptualizations of Europe balance between unity and diversity, in the spirit of the official EU slogan "United in diversity". The participants drew on their own experiences to construct their understandings of and sense of belonging to Europe. Their constructions demonstrate that they saw the unity and diversity of Europe on a practical everyday level rather than as distant high-level EU institutions and abstract principles, or formal national and regional diversity (see also Chapter 6).

Several participants saw Europe as under construction, referring to the present and the future in this context, but also to the historical background of the construction process. In the participants' accounts, Europe often meant the EU, as is the case in the documents related to the Culture programme and in

other macro-level EU discourses. Similarly, in the meso-level texts on coordinating the ECC, the Europe usually meant the EU, because the terms Europe and
the EU were used interchangeably. Moreover, the core concept of the project,
European citizenship, referred to Union citizenship, which is an EU institution.

Despite the frequent overlapping of Europe and the EU in the participants'
discussions, their notion of Europe is broader and goes beyond the EU. They
framed their conceptions of Europe with the changing geographical perceptions of the continent and shifting borders within and around it. Mobility was
central to participants' conceptions of Europe and their own feeling of Europeanness. They supported the idea of a 'borderless Europe' and mobility across
the state borders without formalities. Using the Euro currency and foreign languages were also highlighted as building blocks of their feeling of Europeanness. Nevertheless, some participants regarded the right to free movement as
a means of establishing a boundary to keep out non-EU citizens and viewed
Europe as a privileged place as concerns freedom of mobility and some other
rights. Above all, participants expressed that European belonging develops
through personal relations and connections across state borders, enabled by
mobility. These views are connected to the discourses of the EU's Culture programme, in which mobility of cultural actors, products, and services is a key
objective. The goal of the Culture programme is to develop a European identity
"from the grass roots" precisely by fostering cross-state mobility and interaction (EC 2004, 4; see also EP&C 2006, 2, 4). In the meso-level discourses of the
ECC project, mobility was not explicitly discussed but obviously the project
itself enabled mobility and created cross-border interaction.

With few exceptions, the participants felt that the ECC project contributed
to the development of their European belonging. They conceptualized the
ECC as a space of mobility, making art, intercultural learning, networking, and
speaking various languages. They considered participating in the ECC project
as something 'European', and felt that doing so made Europe present to them.
The project as such can thus be viewed as creating a European "lived space"
(Lefebvre 1991, 362) that was enlivened through personal experiences. Hence,
EU projects have the potential to create European belonging as defined in the
objectives of the EU programmes through enabling interaction and connections between citizens across state borders – even if they do not include any
discussions or practices directly focusing on Europe. As such, the EU projects
engage citizens in the EU, and are thus inherent in the EU's politics of belonging. They are examples of "specific political projects" (Yuval-Davis 2006, 197)
seeking to construct EUrope and belonging to it simultaneously from above
and from below.

The ethnographic research revealed both continuities and disruptions
between the macro, meso, and micro levels in the ways in which citizenship

was understood in the European context. The documents regarding the Culture programme explain the role of cultural and linguistic cooperation in making "European citizenship a tangible reality by encouraging direct participation by European citizens in the integration" (EP&C 2006, 1). In the meso-level ECC discourses, this was explicit since European citizenship was taken as the project's core content. On this level, the ECC was envisioned as a platform to encourage public debate on citizenship and students' participation in it through art. The ECC project sought to contribute to the development of a European-level public sphere, trying to build Europe as a political community, as a community of citizens acting in a public sphere. The difference to the macro level is that even though the programme documents highlight the idea of citizenship of the Union, they do not pay attention to public debate and citizens' participation as political agency.

The aspiration to promote debate on the notion of citizenship was not present in the project practices observed in our ethnographic fieldwork in the Roots lab (but may have been present in other art laboratories). Concomitantly, citizenship was difficult for the participants to discuss, even though they were participating in a project with citizenship as its main topic. Only few of them saw themselves as political agents on the European scale, even though most if not all identified themselves as European citizens in some way. The majority did not refer to political action or public debate, which means that there is a considerable break between the meso- and the micro-level discourses within the project. The participants may have seen Europe as too broad a context for citizenship understood as civic action in the public sphere. The fact that participants discussed citizenship relatively little if at all underlines this break.

Common to the macro-, meso-, and micro-level discourses is the close link between citizenship and European identity. The decision of the Culture programme highlights European citizens' identity – consisting of common cultural values and roots as well as cultural and linguistic cooperation – and connects the key objective, creating a European cultural area, to "encouraging the emergence of European citizenship" (EP&C 2006, 1, 4). The meso-level texts follow and use this official programme rhetoric. Thus, the ECC can be interpreted as implementing the programme's key aims concerning identity and citizenship. In the micro-level discourses, identity and citizenship were also closely connected. For example, in response to the question about citizenship, interviewees often discussed their national and European identifications.

The notion of banal Europeanism, developed by Laura Cram (2009, 2012) can help us to interpret these findings. This notion is based on the well-known concept of banal nationalism by Billig (1995) that claims that nations are invisibly produced and reproduced in everyday lives through routine symbols and habits of language. Similarly, according to banal Europeanism, everyday routine practices and daily encounters with EU symbols may reinforce (unconscious) identification with Europe. Facing EU frequently and repeatedly through symbols, media discourses and other everyday situations may lead to the 'normalization' of the EU as a legitimate political authority. In the ECC interview data, the EU was primarily seen in terms of a functional actor often taken for granted. The project participants indeed closely linked the EU to their perceptions of Europe and their micro-level experiences related to Europe, such as the Euro currency and border-free mobility. When discussing Europe and their own relations to it, the participants combined their everyday experiences with the 'banal', well-known and frequently repeated representations and narratives, including values and 'universal' ideas such as peace and democracy, that are often related to Europe. In this respect, they echo the EU's grand narrative about the EU integration. The characteristics that the participants attached to Europe are also part of the official EU narratives, even though the participants discussed them through their own personal experiences.

It can be concluded that the EU's politics of belonging through identity building was present in the ECC at the macro, meso, and micro levels. Discourses at all levels, despite their differences, sought to create identity for both EUrope and its inhabitants primarily through cross-border interaction and interpersonal relations, enabled by the ECC project and other similar opportunities for mobility across state borders. These elements were seen more important than civic participation in bridging the gap both between the EU and citizens and between citizens themselves. The ethnographic research on this one project funded through Culture programme made visible the differences and similarities in the notions of Europe constructed at different levels of the project. As such, the analysis produced a more nuanced understanding of EU cultural policy and perceptions of Europe in the context of multilevel and participatory governance of the EU.

References

Antwerp Declaration. 2015. Antwerp Declaration for a Stronger Promotion of Student Culture. Received at the dissemination conference of the ECC project in Antwerp, 26 June 2015.

Arendt, H. 1998 [1958]. *The Human Condition*. Chicago: The University of Chicago Press.

Art Catalogue. 2015. Received at the dissemination conference of the ECC project in Antwerp, 25 June 2015.

Billig, M. 1995. *Banal Nationalism*. London, Thousand Oaks, New Delhi: Sage.

Čeginskas, V. L. A. 2016. "'I am Europe'. Experiences of Multiple Belonging." *Ethnologia Fennica*, 43: 72–88. Accessed 23 April 2020. https://journal.fi/ethnolfenn/article/view/65636/26505

Cram, L. 2009. "Identity and European Integration: Diversity as a Source of Integration." *Nations and Nationalism* 15 (1): 109–128.

Cram, L. 2012. "Does the EU Need a Navel? Implicit and Explicit Identification with the European Union." *Journal of Common Markets Studies* 50 (1): 71–86.

Detailed Description of the project European Citizen Campus (ECC). n.d. Received from the project coordinator by e-mail 15 May 2014.

EC (European Commission). 2004. Proposal for a Decision of the European Parliament and of the Council Establishing the Culture 2007 Programme (2007–2013). COM(2004) 469 final. Brussels: European Commission. Accessed 10 January 2020. http://www.europarl.europa.eu/registre/docs_autres_institutions/commission_europeenne/com/2004/0469/COM_COM(2004)0469_EN.pdf

EP&C (European Parliament and the Council). 2006. "Decision No 1855/2006/EC of the European Parliament and of the Council of 12 December 2006 Establishing the Culture Programme (2007 to 2013)." *Official Journal of the European Union* L 372: 1–11.

Fleck, J. 2015. "European Citizen Campus: Negotiating European Identity during an Intercultural Art Workshop." Master thesis in Learning and Communication in Multilingual and Multicultural Contexts, University of Luxembourg.

Lefebvre, H. 1991. *The Production of Space*. Oxford: Blackwell.

Mäkinen, K. 2019. "Interconceptualising Europe and Peace: Identity Building under the European Heritage Label." In *Dissonant Heritages and Memories in Contemporary Europe*, edited by T. Lähdesmäki, L. Passerini, S. Kaasik-Krogerus, and I. van Huis, 51–78. New York: Palgrave Macmillan.

Treaty of Rome. 1957. Traité instituant la Communauté Économique Européenne et documents annexes. 11957E/TXT. Accessed 20 April 2020. https://eur-lex.europa.eu/legal-content/FR/TXT/PDF/?uri=CELEX:11957E/TXT&from=EN

Walters, W., and J. H. Haahr. 2005. *Governing Europe. Discourse, Governmentality and European Integration*. London: Routledge.

Wiesner, C., A. Björk, H.-M. Kivistö, and K. Mäkinen. 2018. "Introduction: Shaping Citizenship as a Political Concept." In *Shaping Citizenship: A Political Concept in Theory, Debate and Practice*, edited by C. Wiesner, A. Björk, H.-M. Kivistö, and K. Mäkinen, 1–16. New York and Abingdon: Routledge.

Yuval-Davis, N. 2006. "Belonging and the Politics of Belonging." *Patterns of Prejudice* 40 (3): 197–214.

CHAPTER 6

Case 3: The European Heritage Label

1   The Construction of Europe in the European Heritage Label at the
     Macro and Meso Levels

The EU's most recent flagship heritage action, the European Heritage Label (EHL), contributes to the politics of belonging in EU cultural policy by seeking to form 'a community of Europeans' with an emphasis on common values and a shared past in Europe. As the EHL was developed with the aim to strengthen "European citizens' belonging to the Union", heritage sites have been awarded the Label on grounds of their "European significance" and contribution to Europe's history and development (see EC 2010, 2; EC 2011, 6; EP&C 2011, 3; Lähdesmäki 2014; Čeginskas 2018). The discourse of the EHL action emphasizes the European dimension of heritage, and instead of approaching heritage in terms of conservation, protection, and aesthetic or architectural quality, it treats it as a political instrument that serves identity-building purposes and expectations of economic benefit and sustainable development in the EU (Lähdesmäki et al. 2020). In this respect, the EHL approach corresponds to the recent EU cultural policy of approaching 'Europe' as a brand, promoting a sense of shared unity, commonality, and the benefits of EU membership in terms of 'products' to be mediated to the wider European public.

As one aim of the EHL action is to highlight Europe's cultural diversity, each labelled site has a different thematic context, and visitors interpret the history, heritage value, and meanings of the sites, including their European dimension, in different ways. The heritage sites vary in size, status, and structures depending on their functions as museums, exhibitions, archives, or historical sites, as well as their modes of cultural and educational engagement, practices, and activities. Therefore, the EHL sites manifest a broad temporal, geographical, and cultural variety that mediate events and process from different times, ranging from Roman archaeological remains and reconstructions at Carnuntum Archaeological Park, Austria, to an exhibition of EU integration and institutions in the European District of Strasbourg, France (see Annex 2 for an overview of the EHL sites). At first, it may therefore seem difficult to define any common denominator of 'European' heritage and Europe's past. However, our research shows that by recognizing only heritage sites (e.g. cultural monuments, cultural landscapes, memorials) and intangible heritage associated with a place that symbolizes European integration, common European values, and the history and culture of the EU, the EHL constructs a selective discourse of Europe and EU integration as an inevitable and positive trajectory, while retaining awareness of national and regional cultural differences. Furthermore, the EHL's transnational interpretation of cultural heritage challenges dominant national discourses of heritage and promotes a discourse on a common and shared cultural legacy to Europe's citizenry, in which World War II proves to be a turning point for the development of a European civic and political community (e.g. Lähdesmäki 2019). Thus, the purpose of the EHL is to safeguard and develop the process of European integration and to strengthen a unifying European narrative of belonging through the explicit claim to "improve the knowledge and dissemination of the culture and history of European peoples" (EP&C 2011), built upon the concept of a "shared", but not a homogenized, "European cultural heritage" (see also Niklasson 2017).

Embedded in the EU's multilevel governance, the EHL is based on an interaction between what we call the macro and meso levels of European discourse. The macro level is formed by the EU institutions and the civil servants of the European Commission who shape the EU's discourse on the EHL, and thereby on Europe, with their textual and visual materials, such as policy documents and websites. The main creators of the meso-level EHL discourse are professionals working day-to-day at the awarded EHL sites who formulate, interpret, and put into practice the 'European significance'. As our research shows, they

FIGURE 6.1   Alcide de Gasperi House Museum in Italy, an EHL site.
PHOTO: EUROHERIT

FIGURE 6.2   Camp Westerbork in the Netherlands, an EHL site.
             PHOTO: EUROHERIT

FIGURE 6.3   Franz Liszt Memorial Museum, part of the Franz Liszt Academy of Music in
             Hungary, an EHL site.
             PHOTO: EUROHERIT

FIGURE 6.4   The Carnuntum Archaeological Park in Austria, an EHL site.
              PHOTO: EUROHERIT

both follow the macro-level voice and contribute to it by creating contents for the EU discourse (Lähdesmäki et al. 2020). The designation process of the EHL sites exemplifies the interaction between the levels. Sites are pre-selected at the national level, designated at the EU level by an international expert panel, and finally awarded the Label by the European Commission (see Chapter 1).

Our analysis of the EHL data shows that the European Commission and the awarded heritage sites both try to promote 'European' values in terms of social and moral mindsets rooted in political ideals that connect cultural heritage with the promotion of unity, a sense of belonging, and democratic participation (see Lähdesmäki et al. 2020). In the process of constructing European narratives, the EHL discourse mixes local, national, and European scales (Lähdesmäki 2016; Kaasik-Krogerus 2019, 159). As the EHL action involves actors from 18 EU member states and diverse physical and cultural settings (e.g. urban and rural), we argue that the EHL discourse develops from and reveals different perceptions of how 'Europe' and 'the European' are imagined at various levels.

The EHL has a clear educative objective and according to its criteria, designated EHL sites should design pedagogical activities aimed specifically at young European citizens to support the process of European cultural and political integration. According to the EU documents, the designated sites are supposed to promote their European dimension and to 'bring to life' the European narrative (EC 2010, 2; EP&C 2011, 3; EC 2017). The heritage sites seek to follow these criteria by concretizing the European narrative from their specific perspective, in line with the thematic narrative of the heritage site. However, the views on the 'European' at the meso level do not always meet the views held by the actors at the macro level. This may lead either to candidate sites being rejected in the EHL selection process or to a request to strengthen the European dimension at awarded sites. For instance, the EHL monitoring report specifically asked the Great Guild Hall in Estonia to better place its narrative – perceived as mainly telling Estonian national history – in a wider European context by emphasizing the story of the Hanseatic League on its website and in its printed materials (EC 2016, 15).

In this chapter, we approach the EHL action as a means of pursuing politics of belonging. The explicit aim of positively influencing public perception of the EU and strengthening a sense of belonging to it and Europe, in particular among young European citizens, is at the core of the action (EP&C 2011). As part of this practice, an idea of a common European cultural heritage is formed and used to construct a particular European narrative (Borgmann-Prebil and Ross 2010; Lähdesmäki, Kaasik-Krogerus, and Mäkinen 2019; Čeginskas and Kaasik-Krogerus 2020). In this narrative Europe is constructed as a distinctive political, cultural, and economic entity that enables people to identify as Europeans and feel a sense of belonging to Europe (Sassatelli 2002, 436; Kohli 2000, 118). As regards politics of belonging, communities, in this case first and foremost 'Europe' and the EU, are continuously (re)imagined. 'European significance' as the key criteria of the EHL offers a good example of this process of (re)-imagining.

The promotional videos that introduce the EHL sites and their 'European significance' to the wider public exemplify how the entanglement of the macro and meso levels is enacted in practice in the EHL action. The videos are available on the website of the European Commission, which functions as its public forum to communicate cultural meanings related to Europe. Sixteen of these videos are fully or partly in English, the rest are in various national languages with English subtitles (see also Lähdesmäki, 2017). The videos focus on the respective site's 'European significance', whereas in them, practitioners at the sites commonly evoke an 'imagination' of three, partly overlapping communities: 'we' as contemporary Europeans, 'we' as a nation, and 'we' as a community of heritage professionals (Kaasik-Krogerus 2020).

However, the EU officials and European panel members at the macro level and the sites and heritage practitioners at the meso level are not the only actors involved in politics of belonging. We argue that the visitors to the EHL sites participate in 'doing' European cultural heritage and imagining Europe at the micro level. In this chapter, we therefore analyze imagining Europe at the micro level in the EHL action, i.e. the visitors and their engagement with the Label. We explore how visitors to the EHL sites engage with the specific EHL discourse on Europe in terms of a 'politics of belonging' on the one hand and, on the other, how visitors perceive 'Europe' in this process. The interviews with visitors allow us to explore various constructions of Europe and multiple understandings of belonging and non-belonging to Europe from below.

In what follows, we first introduce the research data and methods used. Then, the empirical analysis consists of three parts: Europe of people; Europe of nations; belonging to Europe. We finish with conclusions on the multiple constructions of Europe and (non)belonging to it in the EHL context.

2   Analyzing Europe from Below in the EHL Action: Research Data
        and Methods

Our research is based on fieldwork at the EHL sites, which included visits, observations, and interviews with both visitors and heritage practitioners working there. In this chapter, we focus on the interviews with the visitors, examining 271 visitor interviews from 11 EHL sites located in ten EU countries, which were conducted between August 2017 and February 2018 (see Chapter 1; Annex 1; Lähdesmäki et al. 2020). The interviews covered various topics, including the visitors' understanding of cultural heritage in general, European cultural heritage, 'Europe', European identity, and feeling European. The great number of interviews and the variety of interviewees make it possible to analyze how visitors from both EU and non-EU countries, and across different age groups, imagine, understand, and engage with Europe. Their responses help us to explore their personal views of Europe, of what constitutes the 'European' for them, and to interpret what specific experiences and attributes they relate with Europe. The qualitative interviews from the different sites enable us to analyze Europe from below, since they form discursive practices and subject positions in which people mobilize identities and a sense of belonging to explain, contest, or question the world around them (see also Wetherell and Potter 1992, 78; Siapera 2004, 131).

The visitors whose interviews are analyzed in this chapter include both EU citizens (n = 225) and non-EU citizens (n = 46). With the exception of one Russian, two Swiss, and two Ukrainian visitors, the non-EU visitors were not from member countries of the Council of Europe (see Annex 1). The EU visitors represented 19 nationalities, and we interviewed slightly more women visitors than men. Divided into three age groups, we had 98 younger visitors aged between 18 to 35 years, 112 visitors represented the middle-aged group (aged 36 to 65), and the group of older visitors (aged 66+) numbered 61 interviewees. The majority of interviewees had a higher (university) education, but others held diplomas from middle school, high school, college, and vocational school (see Annex 1). At some EHL sites, we interviewed many local visitors who lived near the site (e.g. Carnuntum Archaeological Park in Austria, Mundaneum in Belgium, or Robert Schuman House in France), while at others we met predominantly foreign visitors (e.g. Great Guild Hall, Estonia; Sagres Promontory, Portugal, and Franz Liszt Academy of Music and Memorial Museum, Hungary). The visitors' replies indicate that the vast majority of them were neither familiar with the EHL nor with the fact that the site they were visiting had been awarded it (see Čeginskas 2019). They had visited the sites for other reasons, such as leisure, vicinity, personal interest, and chance.

We conducted semi-structured qualitative interviews with the visitors. Depending on the length of answers, the interviews lasted from seven to almost 40 minutes. Since several researchers conducted the interviews at different sites, we agreed to keep the overall structure of the interview unchanged. However, depending on the interview situations, the actual order of the topics and themes varied from interview to interview, and sometimes required additional questions. In our analysis, we went through all the visitor interviews and focused on topics and themes related to interpreting European cultural heritage and European identity at the sites and in the exhibitions, and then analyzed the visitors' understandings of Europe, their (non-)belonging to Europe, and their feeling of being European. We used close reading and a qualitative content analysis of language use and discursive meaning making in our data. Consequently, our interpretations stem from our subjective readings and contextualizations of the data, which we addressed in joint discussions and intensive exchanges of views within our team of researchers.

The interviews engaged with people's perceptions of both the site and the notion of European heritage, which we understand as a dialogic process of meaning making between the visitors and heritage sites. We enquired how the interviewees engaged with the EHL and in this context perceived Europe and the EU (see also Lähdesmäki et al. 2020). The similarities and differences depicted in the process of close reading formed a basis for organizing the answers into specific categories (about the method, see also Kvale 1996, 192) for further analysis. The background questions about age, education, and nationality were mainly intended for constructing the social profile of the interviewees. In our analysis, the visitor interviews (V) appear with a specific code that indicate the respective heritage sites (S1–11), where the interviews were recorded, followed by a number that expresses the chronological order in which the interviews were conducted. For instance, VS3/11 refers to the eleventh visitor interviewed at Camp Westerbork. A more detailed overview of the EHL sites and their codes can be found in Annex 3; information on the social, educational, and ethnic backgrounds of the visitors to the sites is in Annex 1.

In the interviews, we also asked the visitors about their associations related to the EHL logo and two of its slogans 'Europe starts here' and 'Europe starts with you' (see also Lähdesmäki et al. 2020). The former is the official slogan of the EHL, which is used for presenting the EHL action at all sites, with the exception of Camp Westerbork, which uses the slogan "Europe remembers Camp Westerbork". The slogan 'Europe starts with you' is found in the brochures and other promotional material informing interested heritage sites about the application aims and procedures. Both of these slogans are formulated by the Commission and used by the national coordinators of the action and the EHL practitioners at the awarded sites. The question about the slogans, thus, enabled us to explore the reception of the intertwined macro and meso-level EHL discourse at the micro level. During our interviews, most of the interviewees compared the slogans and usually preferred one to the other. Their interpretations of the slogans opened up a very interesting understanding about

FIGURE 6.5   The EHL logo, photographed at Camp Westerbork, the Netherlands.
PHOTO: EUROHERIT

Europe based on location and/or individual disposition and participation. The simple and catchy formulations of the slogans provided a good basis for interpreting both the visitors' answers to their imaginaries of Europe and to questions directly connected with the EHL. During the process of data analysis, we realized the potential of the EHL slogans as a basis for discussing the EU's politics of belonging and decided to structure our chapter according to the 'Europe of people' and 'Europe of nations' positioned in the visitors' answers. It is important to emphasize that by analytically dividing the data, we do not intend to categorize visitors. As our data shows, interviewees gave controversial or multiple answers to the interview questions. The following sub-sections are mostly based on people's responses to each of the EHL slogans, whereas the third sub-section focuses on answers given about Europe throughout the interviews.

FIGURE 6.6   Collage of information brochures, flyers, and promotional material from various EHL sites and in multiple languages.
PHOTO: EUROHERIT

Various scholars have pointed out how the term 'Europe' is continuously 'owned' and used by the EU, its institutions and representatives, and they have explored how Europe is constructed in EU policies as a synonym for the Union (e.g. De Cesari 2017; Lähdesmäki et al. 2020; Turunen n.d.). The EHL is a good example of this common overlapping usage and understanding of the two entities. The questions we asked the visitors were affected by this conception. Since we asked about both the EU and the idea of European cultural heritage in the interviews, interviewees, partly unintentionally, intertwined Europe and the EU while elaborating on the EHL and Europe. Some interviewees claimed to be "European-minded" and "supportive of Europe" and explained that their "pro-European attitude" was linked to their studies of "European Law" or belonging to a generation "who believed in Europe" (e.g. VS3/3 and VS3/4). What these visitors meant is that they support the EU's politics and integration project. To tackle this phenomenon in our analysis, we use the term 'EUrope' for the cases where no clear distinction between the EU and Europe is made. As we explained in the introduction, this term combines 'Europe' the geographical continent and the political institutions and member states of the EU (see also Lähdesmäki et al. 2020).

3   Europe of People: Europe Starts with You

The analysis of the interview data showed that most visitors, both from the EU and outside, interpreted the EHL slogan 'Europe starts with you' as a mixture of possibility and responsibility. Feeling 'ownership' of Europe strengthened both people's personal agency and the idea that everybody is capable of contributing to Europe, to make it work. "If you want change, start with the man in the mirror," as one Dutch man in his fifties put it, referring to the EU (VS3/7). Some emphasized the individual approach and personal touch of the slogan (e.g. VS8/19; VS8/20), saying that it conveyed a sense of affiliation or solidarity and a participatory approach, which expressed an appeal of becoming active. This made the interviewees often feel personally addressed (e.g. VS2/12; VS2/13), something which we interpreted as engaging with the EHL's politics of belonging. As one of the interviewees claimed, the emphasis on 'you' made it clear that Europe is about people (VS2/17). Another interviewee, a retired German professor of law visiting Hambach Castle, suggested an understanding of Europe in terms of uniting people and creating a sense of community based on shared activities. Referring to the EHL slogan, he explained (VS7/15):

> I mean, why would I want to juxtapose myself with others, instead of bringing them closer to me? Well, that's indeed a problem, I want everyone to be involved... It's rather "We are Europe", and we drive through Neustadt an der Weinstraße – of course, coincidences don't exist – and there, in the church, we experienced European youth playing music together. It was spectacular! There you could say "Europe starts with us" or "within us" – or something like that.

This emphasis on people as actively participating in and being the essence of Europe renders the idea of EUrope a community that is both alive and in flux. A similar understanding of Europe and being European was reflected in the rejection and critical evaluation of the concept of identity that some visitors expressed, regardless of their gender, age, nationality, or visited heritage site. For them, the concept of European identity was too restrictive and carried excluding and static connotations with belonging. In their view, identity implied a rigorous understanding of belonging, based on distinguishing between those who are included and excluded, both physically and symbolically. For some visitors such an understanding came dangerously close to discourses about (racial) superiority and (national) exclusiveness. These visitors expressed the fear that a misuse of identity for political and nationalistic reasons could cause more harm than good. For instance, at Camp Westerbork, a Dutch visitor with a university degree in his early fifties explained (VS3/21):

> I don't like the idea. We love discussing in the Netherlands about our identity. I think it's a dangerous idea of trying to formulate an identity on the level of a nation or the level of a continent.

A Belgian visitor in her late forties at Mundaneum explained that the use of the concept of identity in connection with Europe raised uncomfortable feelings in her; in contrast, she perceived 'culture' as an enclosing concept that enabled a broader sense of commonality between people (VS9/22):

> Because the name, the word, 'identity' sounds to me like something that is inclosing people, that is just, you know, yeah, closing doors. It is 'MY identity' and if we need a 'common identity' – it means that we have to accept people in, or they are out. And that is something that is quite sad. While culture is not like that. Culture is like a common ground.

Besides identity, the concept of Europe(an) as a fixed and closed entity was criticized by some visitors, since it "is not good to create divisions", as a young Polish woman put it (VS8/19). These interviewees defied clear boundaries of what and where Europe is or why Europe has to 'start from here' (e.g. VS3/29; VS3/30; VS2/2). For instance, a man in his early fifties of Belgian origin, who had lived and worked for many years on other continents, elaborated at the Mundaneum: "Where does Europe end? Humanity is arbitrary anyway. So, where does Asia begin, where does Europe begin? Well, there is an ocean next to it, but I mean, it's a continent" (VS9/27).

Against this criticism of defining clear territorial boundaries of Europe, many of the interviewees consistently pointed out that the experience of mobility was one of the key reasons why they felt European and had a sense of belonging to Europe. The important role of mobility and free movement for European integration has been noted elsewhere (e.g. Favell 2008; Recchi and Favell 2009; Favell and Recci 2011). In our data, mobility was connected to free movement and travel across borders within Europe. It was also about being able to talk and communicate with fellow Europeans, share common interests and concerns, and, in a quite literal and practical sense, directly get in touch with them. Many interviewees spoke of their own mobility experiences, which had led to their meeting, exchanging views, or forming personal relationships and friendships with other Europeans. These experiences led some interviewees to argue for a common awareness as Europeans and construct belonging to EUrope in emotive ways, despite their simultaneous observation of existing linguistic, cultural, historical, and geographical differences. Such intertwined experiences of mobility and encounter seemed to reduce the 'felt' distance between Europeans of different national, regional, or cultural backgrounds.

Scholarly discussions highlight the fact that people need enough money and valid passports or identity cards in order to benefit from 'borderless Europe' (see also Rumford 2008, 41–42; Lähdesmäki et al. 2020). The interviewed visitors did not mention this, but conveyed the impression that mobility was a normal condition and taken-for-granted practice in contemporary EUrope. Visitors referred – explicitly or not – to institutional developments in the EU in recent decades, such as the Schengen Agreement, which opened borders and enabled free movement of people, capital, goods, and services within this space. Other important aspects mentioned in this context were the harmonization of regulations and services in connection with the single currency (the Euro) or mobile data roaming. Thus, the interviewees referred to the construction of a common European space that encouraged unlimited personal mobility within it, and referred to political processes that helped to connect member states and spread ideas and phenomena all over EUrope. For instance, a German woman in her late forties visiting Robert Schuman House in France explained (vs10/14):

> I mean, I have the impression that I benefit from the way in which Europe is today, that's how I experience it. For example, I can freely move across borders, or these small everyday advantages, like the common currency, which is really very useful here in the borderland. [...] So, I find it very useful in everyday life, especially if you live here. I find it very nice that it is in general possible to move from one country to another without problems.

Like many other visitors, this interviewee equated Europe with (the Schengen area of) the EU, in which the borders between the member states have become invisible. Some other visitors constructed Europe as a shared space based on their educational and professional experiences (gained e.g. through Erasmus, other university or school exchange programmes, or working abroad or in international environments) as well as their personal opportunities for leisure travel. A young French student described her perception of Europe as follows (vs4/4):

> It is to be able to speak with English people, Germans... lots of countries of Europe. And to have common things in the sense that we all belong to the European Union. We can freely travel from one country to another without necessarily crossing any real border. That's it. It is freedom of exchange, of expression between all the member countries. And to know that we are, so to speak, 'allied'. We are all together reunited around the EU.

EUrope as a common space constituted by mobility becomes associated with a feeling of connecting with people, friends, and family members across Europe. A man in his early fifties visiting Hambach Castle highlighted the relevance of cultural and real experienced mobility by reflecting on his personal situation (vs7/19):

> Yeah, first, we have this partnership, he is Flemish, I am German. I have Finnish roots; my mother is Finnish. So, it was always about different cultures and identities at my home, however, rather European-American.

A sense of belonging to Europe was strengthened by travelling not only within, but also outside the EU, especially to other continents. Ideas about the 'other' did not emerge from juxtaposing one European state against another but rather from identifying Europe's 'other' and locating it to Africa, Asia, America, Australia – places that were further away than a neighboring European state, and separated by geographical distance and boundaries. In this context, 'being European' was seen as having "always been different from the way of being African, the way of being Asian, the way of being American" (vs1/9). The visitors often perceived the difference between Europe and other non-European places as 'real'. As a Dutch woman in her late forties argued, it was easier to feel "at home" in different places across Europe than in Asia, Africa, or America, increasing the perception of a unity among Europeans (vs3/27). Other

interviewees explained that travelling and staying outside Europe felt different because of the unknown currencies, cultural practices, or language (e.g.
vs6/19; vs7/12; vs9/7; vs9/23; vs9/28). For some visitors, this difference in the
perception between European and non-European countries served as proof of
the existence of a common European culture (vs9/23). As one Belgian man in
his late forties at the Mundaneum put it (vs9/7):

> Once we go beyond, as I said, Europe, and we get to, be it in Asia... or the
> United States, America. North America, South America: You travel enor-
> mously, you see at once that they have another identity, another culture.

Similarly to the visitors from EU countries, those from non-EU countries
referred to mobility as a main aspect of what defined today's EUrope. As a
young PhD student from the US, visiting the Great Guild Hall in Estonia, confirmed, "[b]ut if there's one kind of [common] thread through all of them, it
would be the four principles [freedoms of movement] that are kind of stated in
the EU's charter, and the concept of solidarity is very important" (vs6/18). Some
visitors from outside the EU used mobility to boost their case for constructing a personal connection with Europe. They often interpreted the mobility
of their ancestors from various parts of Europe to the USA, Canada, Australia,
New Zealand, or South America as something that enabled them to imagine
Europe as a specific community that they could engage with because of their
heritage and 'roots'. For instance, a US visitor to the Great Guild Hall in Estonia
explained that his "great-grandparents came from Germany and Wales, and I
grew up in a city that was predominantly German, very German. So, I've always
had a sense of connection back with Europe" (vs6/2). However, in some cases,
this imagined link with Europe based on roots and shared culture went beyond
the idea of forming a community only with EU citizens. As a Chilean visitor to
the Carnuntum Archaeological Park, a man in his fifties, argued (vs2/2):

> if the culture that passed on to your parents is of European roots, then
> that's European heritage. So, it doesn't have to be only Europe, within the
> continental European mass, but it could be maybe from somebody from
> Australia that might have identity with us. [...] Because I was raised with
> very strong Spanish values, and always reminded in Chile, being a coun-
> try, which is itself multiracial, I was always reminded that this is your
> background, it's... mostly, mostly Spanish, yeah.

As these quotes show, mobility was largely understood as positive: the vast
majority of the visitors related it to the wider context of modernity and their

own (rather privileged) position in this world. Mobility implies the potential to create new connections, which does not necessarily need to be restricted to Europe but may help to construct an imagined community with different people in various places. However, not all visitors shared such an 'unproblematic' view of mobility. For instance, some visitors interviewed at Camp Westerbork saw people's forced mobility during World War II as a warning example for today. Similarly, at the Great Guild Hall in Tallinn, where the permanent exhibition displays the harsh conditions, violent conquests, and foreign rule throughout Estonian history, some visitors widened the concept of mobility. They discussed critical issues connected with mobility, including deportations and fleeing wars in the past, but connected these to life in the world today. While visitors addressed the current solidarity crisis among EU member states about receiving refugees from various (mainly non-European) countries, they often approached mobility as a political and humanitarian challenge. Some saw it as a security problem for contemporary Europe – not necessarily taking into account the refugees' perspective on the trauma of forced migration.

4   Europe of Nations: Europe Starts Here

The interviewed visitors frequently interpreted the EHL slogan 'Europe starts here' in both spatial and temporal terms. Their understanding that Europe was linked with certain personalities and started with a specific event or at a particular geographical point corresponds to how the EHL action and the awarded sites present Europe and European cultural heritage. These interpretations had one thing in common: understanding Europe as an entity consisting of bounded geographical areas with cultural characteristics considered as 'European'. At sites like Alcide de Gasperi House Museum or Robert Schuman House, visitors mentioned the role that its 'Founding Fathers' had played in the establishing the EU. Similarly, the visitors to Carnuntum – a site that is dedicated to the Roman past – created a connection between the Roman Empire and contemporary Europe (e.g. VS2/1). Some visitors explained their European belonging by referring to the towns or regions where they lived; others perceived themselves as European as their "country is European", as a Slovak visitor to Carnuntum simply put it (VS2/1). The visitors interviewed in Tallinn, Estonia, and Sagres, Portugal, referred to the specific geographical location of both sites at the 'spatial edge' or political border of the EU (e.g. VS6/2; VS11/8). Similarly, visitors to sites that were situated in national border areas often emphasized the meaning of borders and the experience of transgressing them, as for instance at Hambach Castle (Germany), Mundaneum (Belgium), Carnuntum

(Austria), Lieu d'Europe (France), Alcide de Gasperi House Museum (Italy), and Robert Schuman House (France).

Hence, these visitors contextualized Europe by entangling local, regional, national, and European scales, which allowed them to claim belonging to Europe alongside sensing belonging to their home country, nation, region, and town. In this respect, the visitors' sense of belonging closely resembled the 'marble cake' model, in which culturally diverse states constitute 'Europe', and their community within the EU determines and conditions citizens' belonging to EUrope (Risse 2004, 251; see also Breakwell 2004). However, the role of the individual citizen is rather limited in such a 'Europe of nations', since their agency is largely tied to, and thus subordinate to, the agency of the state. This means that Europe is imagined as a normative community (the EU) with specific 'rules and regulations' that bind together different states and thus the people who live there. However, the normative character neither abolishes existing controversies between European countries or cultural communities, nor renders 'Europe' uniform. As the interview data from the EHL sites shows, visitors from both within and outside the EU alike imagine such a 'Europe of nations' as a culturally diverse community united by shared values.

The visitors commonly understood Europeanness in terms of a strong sense of spatiality, which enabled them to feel a sense of connection to and draw a distinction between different places at the same time. The majority of the visitors greatly valued the cultural and national differences inside the EU and regarded them as worth preserving. Several visitors claimed: "When I think about Europe, I think about all different kind of cultures everywhere. That it's actually good" (vs6/13, Dutch man under 25); or argued: "I mean there are different cultures, too, in parts of Europe and in knowing that it's still Europe, so it's important to keep this parity" (vs11/28, young French woman). Some visitors emphasized that Europe created a common cultural space consisting of differences based on the diversity of culture and heritage in the various European countries (e.g. vs9/16, Belgian woman under 25; vs8/18, Polish woman in her early thirties). Hence, different languages, peoples, cultures, states, and landscapes are viewed as decisive and defining aspects of Europe, as outlined for the ECC project in Chapter 5. In the words of one visitor, Europe is both "multicultural" and "rich" (vs10/9, French man in his fifties), and unites diverse elements: "As if Europe is one, but it consists of different elements, regions that have their own characteristics" (vs8/18, young French woman). Visitors from both EU and non-EU countries described Europe in similar ways as being different, diverse, manifold, progressive, possessing common goals, and a place where no animosity existed between neighbors (e.g. vs11/32; vs11/33), thereby often overlapping with the EU narrative. As a visitor from Canada claimed:

"I mean it's a real mix of cultures, Europe, from the Scandinavian countries through the Baltic, through the Iberian Peninsula, all different. Italy's different, France – European culture is a blend of all of that to me." (VS11/13).

In some cases, the discussion of Europe's cultural richness developed into admiring its perceived cultural uniqueness. Eurocentric views emphasized the superiority of Europe, too. Visitors from both inside and outside the EU held these views. Visitors from the USA, Canada, and Australia, in particular, tended to construct an "Old World" discourse that underlined the Europe's cultural richness, long history, and great cultural heritage compared to their home countries. After her visit to the EHL site in Hungary, an American woman in her mid-eighties described Europe as the "predecessor to the new world. We all come from here, although some come from Asia, but the majority come from the whole Europe, to America, to the new world" (VS5/13). Another American man of the same age, interviewed at the Great Guild Hall in Estonia, explained: "We in America look at anything 300 years old is really, really old. Really old. In fact, I happen to live in one of the oldest towns in America. We were founded in 1638. For you that stuff is all over the place here, it's twice that old" (VS6/9). The visitors' discourse contributed to reinforcing the narrative of Europe's cultural diversity and historical cultural richness at the expense of the cultural richness of other cultures and communities, such as the native first nations in the USA and Canada or the Aborigines in Australia.

The temporal aspect of 'Europe starts here' was strongly related to values stemming from the past that many visitors regarded as being supposed to unify the culturally diverse European countries. As a young French couple interviewed together at Lieu d'Europe in Strasbourg, France, pointed out, although each European country has a different culture, history, and identity, "we still share the same values" (VS4/4; VS4/5). The EHL documents refer to "freedom, democracy, respect for human rights, cultural and linguistic diversity, tolerance and solidarity" as the core values of the EU (EP&C 2011, 1), and unsurprisingly, the visitors, like the participants in the ECOC project (see Chapter 4), point out the same intangible meanings and universal values. The visitors referred to values such as "tolerance, freedom, independence, history, learning from history" (VS2/9, Austrian woman in her early fifties), "understanding for others" (VS2/13, Austrian man in his early forties), the "rule of law" (VS2/11, Austrian man in his late thirties) and "democracy" (VS8/13, man from the UK in his twenties). Interviewees also frequently mentioned freedom, equality, peace/maintaining peace, human rights, and openness, while some connected well-being and welfare with the construction of a social Europe (VS4/2; VS4/3). For instance, one Austrian woman visiting the Carnuntum Archaeological Park explained (VS2/9):

> I think Europeans, no matter where they are from, from the West or from the East, we all have... well, history has basically moved across the whole continent through all centuries and millennia. And in my opinion what makes us today European, is that – that we fought for our freedoms, for tolerance, equality of women, and religious freedom.

Several interviewees also referred to the EU as a peace-project, creating thus a close link between Europe and the EU, like a young male visitor at the Alcide de Gasperi House Museum (e.g. vs1/13). The same young Italian visitor also cautioned that we should not take these values for granted due to Europe's past conflicts, including World War II, the time of the Iron Curtain dividing Europe into 'East' and 'West', and before the creation of the EU. In his opinion, "the aim of Europe" is based on "equal principles: that of freedom, of guaranteeing culture, of guaranteeing healthcare, and therefore the theme of citizens' rights" (vs1/13), which need to be safeguarded. Many visitors at different sites repeated the EHL rhetoric of learning from the past and stressed that it was important to ensure that 'these times will never come back'. This reference to the past arose again when some visitors discussed the future of Europe in terms of maintaining what 'we have achieved'. This type of rhetoric is a good example of identifying with EUropean narratives and connects to the issue of dual loyalty between the national and European: whether a person identifies more strongly or frequently with local, regional, national, or international (including European) communities (see also Hermann and Brewer 2004, 12).

In the interview data, some visitors elaborated on the controversies between cultural diversity and the notion of a common Europe. Europeanness was sometimes interpreted as threatening to homogenize the particularity and originality of national cultures in Europe. Yet other visitors underlined how different nations, languages, cultures, and people complicated the formation of a common Europe. For instance, a middle-aged German visitor to Hambach Castle argued (vs7/8):

> Yeah, I think it can't work with all these different cultures, different languages to have one Europe, like being one country... It's good that there is a European community for sure, 'cause we never had that long time of peace, I think. So, it's good to, that it's there, but it's not... you cannot understand it as being one country.

Various interviewees claimed that they felt national, in terms of being "more Poles than Europeans" (vs8/14, Polish woman) or did not feel European "as strongly as I feel Dutch." (vs3/1, Dutch woman) whereas some 'chose their sides' and identified only with the nation state (e.g. vs3/5, Dutch man in early thirties) or only with Europe (e.g. vs2/18, Czech woman in her late sixties). This indicates that people have multiple and highly varied priorities as regards national and European belonging (see also Citrin and Sides 2004, 164). However, while right-wing parties appropriate the 'Europe of nations' as a positive identity for their own agenda, to distinguish it from the EU and EUrope as a negative identity (see also Niklasson and Hølleland 2018; Lähdesmäki 2019b), in our data these two were considered as complementary rather than contradictory.

5   Belonging to Europe: From Purposeful Vision to Banal Normality

During the interviews, we asked visitors about their social backgrounds, including their nationality, level of education, country of residence, and age. Distinguishing between non-residents/tourists and EU citizens/residents of EU member states, our data shows that the vast majority of the interviewed visitors sensed belonging to Europe. While the interviews did not include any questions on the EU, the visitors often brought up their – mostly positive – associations with Union. Only a small minority felt negative or a lack of belonging to EUrope. As the visitors engaged in various ways of imagining Europe and constructing belonging and non-belonging, nationality and country of residence did not appear to strongly influence their answers. Similarly, we did not see a marked difference in answers based on the interviewees' gender. As regards their educational background, our data confirmed that people with higher education (a college degree or higher), had only positive associations with Europe and the EU. However, there is a strong bias in our sample towards higher-educated interviewees (see Annex 1); most of them held at least a college degree or were students. Among those with lower levels of education, both sentiments (e.g. approval/disapproval of Europe; belonging/non-belonging to Europe) were almost equally represented. In short, nationality, residence, gender, and education may have affected some narrations and views on Europe, the 'European', and belonging, but were neither the most decisive nor the most conclusive factors in constructing interviewees' views. However, age proved significant for constructing specific narratives and notions of belonging (see Chapter 7). We divided our data into three age groups: (1) older visitors (aged 66+), (2) middle-aged visitors (36–65), and (3) young visitors (aged 18–35). With a few exceptions, the visitors' responses on belonging were somewhat similar within these age groups. We now focus on the predominant views about Europe, the 'European', and notions of belonging to Europe that we found in these three age groups.

The visitors belonging to the older generation most frequently referred to peace as the most important motive for sensing and working towards European belonging. As many of them still remembered the destruction and the process of rebuilding society and infrastructure in the decades immediately following World War II, they often claimed to have a personal interest in belonging to Europe for maintaining peace and developing closer collaboration between Europeans.

Older visitors believed it was possible to achieve imaginary unity with other Europeans based on shared historical experiences, which included the 'utilitarian' function of the EU in creating peace and prosperity, as this older German visitor to Hambach Castle explained (vs7/4):

> When I was born and a child during the war, I witnessed the bomb-ings, and if I count back as a historian how many peace gaps were there between each war, then I have to say that Germany, we, never did better, based on this development.

This group of visitors often stressed that people across different European states shared a common vision of creating peace and sustainable develop-ment. The visitors explained that they personally believed in and were con-vinced of the particularly political and economic necessity of the European project, which remained a legitimate way of providing more opportunities and creating a peaceful stability despite the cultural differences and the problems between European nation states. For instance, an older Italian man argued that "at the political level, it's important to try to reason because divisions are never good for anyone and this is what we learn from history" (vs1/10). Like-wise, a French visitor to the Franz Liszt Academy of Music spoke of Europe as a "communed continent, a communauté" making it possible "to build something together, in order to remove the conflict and also in order to be more powerful against the other economic systems". He continued that when he was young "we were really into it, and now, personally, I'm surprised by the discussion and so on, and including my children" who seemed to be more critical towards belonging to EUrope (vs5/5).

While the experience of mobility was less of a personally decisive factor in their sense of belonging to Europe, the older generation recognized and highlighted mobility as a decisive factor in creating opportunities for younger people to share ideas and practices and to develop a sense of commonality.

Two elderly French women (vs10/20 and vs10/21), who were jointly interviewed and mutually completed their thoughts at the Robert Schuman House, expressed a clear connection between sensing belonging to EUrope and the experience of mobility:

> – It's a mixture of all the people, all these students who go and study in Spain, go on exchanges, the Erasmus programme, and all that.
> – *There is a lot of exchange now.*
> – There is a lot of exchange...
> – *When you see the young people...*
> – ...at university level and all that. It's very good.

In contrast, the group of middle-aged visitors were often more critical of the idea of creating a shared European belonging. They shared with the visitors in the older generation an approach to Europe that was closely intertwined with the developments of the EU. Frequently, they referred to their sense of Europeanness in terms of the added value of being part of the EU, in terms of a functional sense of belonging: the EU is beneficial for the individual but also for the state in which the individual lives. In other words, the visitors recognized the utility of the EU as it offers a structure that helps unite and form a community to face economic, political, environmental, and other challenges collectively in today's globalized world but beyond this, they often lacked a personal approach towards Europe. As a middle-aged French woman at the Robert Schuman House pointed out (vs10/3):

> We are nevertheless anchored in our language, our heritage as well, everything that represents culture, so well... what's more European for me is the currency. It's this freedom now... in any case I feel as I do, having known the franc. [...] Even if you go over the German or English border, or if you go to other countries, the Euro is accepted and exchanged anyway, but indeed it's a great freedom, additionally to the freedom of movement.

The group of middle-aged visitors did not witness the reconstruction of states after World War II, but their generation was familiar with the European integration process (e.g. the introduction of a common currency) and their countries becoming part of the European Community and/or the EU. They grew up in a time when the EU focused its efforts on expanding its ideas and policies in the member states and created the motto 'united in diversity' to bridge cultural and national gaps. While visitors in this age group shared memories of the transformation from national currencies to the Euro, which for some involved ambivalent experiences, unlike the older generation, they did not share personal recollections or memories of the immediate post-war period. The middle-aged visitors referred to the peace narrative in their discourses, but they were not necessarily able to connect or construct a personally meaningful memory of it as it was too distant from their own lives.

Although some referred to shorter school exchanges, the majority of this age group had not personally benefited from longer stays abroad, unlike many of the younger visitors. However, this does not mean that they were not mobile. Many middle-aged visitors had travelled and their answers expressed a great appreciation of cultural differences in Europe, which they had encountered on their travels and which they considered to constitute the essence of Europe. Based on their experiences, cultural diversity, in particular the lack of a common European language, was nevertheless viewed as an obstacle to creating a sense of belonging to Europe, as a German woman in her late forties explained (vs10/14):

> Well, I think the European identity is essentially nourished by this diversity. I mean that we have different regions with different traditions, languages, foods, clothing, whatever, and that it combines this diversity. [...] Well, I think it [European identity] can only develop for real if everyone had a second, I mean for the most of us a second, additional official language, and nowadays that's only English.

As a result, many visitors in this age group were skeptical about the possibility of constructing European belonging as, in the words of a Dutch man, "the interests in southern Italy are very different from the interests of northern Norway, just to give an example. The distances are too big" (vs3/12).

On the contrary, young people who grew up as EU citizens benefited of the experience of open borders and mobility. Such experiences were often part of their ordinary life and everyday practices and therefore taken for granted (see also Chapter 5). The young interviewees were often familiar with passport controls, border checks or currency exchanges in different European states only as stories told by their parents and grandparents, and in exhibitions. One young German visitor to Lieu d'Europe spoke of Europe as "sort of instinctively part of my identity, more on a day-to-day basis" (vs4/17) upon which she did not need to reflect. She explained (vs4/17):

> I grew up with the Euro, I mean. I think I was like eight, when we got the Euro starter kit and we were all standing around the kitchen like "oooh". Yeah, but having the Euro, being able to travel, being part of the Schengen

zone, never needing a visa, being able to do Erasmus, these are things that come very natural to me, and therefore I would always intuitively say that I'm European without having to reflect hard or having to adapt to new circumstances. I just grew up in this environment, so it's part of who I am and how I perceive my environment.

Visitors belonging to this younger age group often referred to bottom-up experiences of being European through participating in longer exchanges and mobility (e.g. the Erasmus Programme), which influenced their perception of Europe and their emphasis on sharing commonalities in Europe despite observing and experiencing cultural differences. Similarly, they did not think about belonging in the same national categories as middle-aged interviewees, tied with language, territory, or nationality. As one young Belgian interviewee explained, "Let's say that we stay human, no matter what happens. As for the rest, it varies" (VS9/11).

Young visitors often referred to common values when discussing Europe, the 'European', and belonging to Europe. As a young Italian student (VS1/11) at the Alcide de Gasperi House Museum explained, Europe constituted "[d]iversity of culture and the respect of culture, liberty, democracy. Differences from a cultural point of view and in particular the respect of other cultures, other people, other nations". However, for the visitors in the youngest age group, values were not the most dominant aspect of their notions of and relations to Europe. References to values were frequently linked to concrete political provisions and actions – like the Schengen area or the Eurozone – that contributed to constructing a taken-for-granted Europeanness among many of the younger visitors. However, for some, Europeanness was not an individual choice but something they had inherited by birth, as a young French student put it: "Yes [I feel European], after all, we were born in Europe" (VS10/10). Among these interviewees, the conflation between Europe and the EU became obvious. When asked whether and why they felt European, a young Austrian couple (he was a carpenter, she a student), simply answered: "Because I was born here (VS2/15); Yes" (VS2/14). To a certain degree, such answers show how Europeanness may be commonly perceived through contemporariness – as a sense of belonging shaped by interaction with people in the present and in relation to dominant discourses (see Chapters 4 and 5).

The conception of a 'day-to-day European reality' or the experience of Europe as a 'normal entity', as revealed in the answers of the youngest age group, is the key aspect of a 'Europe of people'. This conception is formed by the social, economic, and political benefits of EU integration for the individual. Drawing on Billig's (1995) concept of 'banal nationalism', Cram (2009, 110, 114;

2012, 83) suggests that everyday practices and daily encounters with Europe's symbols produce banal, serendipitous, and contextual processes that facilitate unconscious identification with EUrope (see also Deutsch 1966, 117; Billig 1995, 42; Sassetelli 2009). The perception of a 'European reality' relates to the development and implementation of EU-wide binding policies and norms in the framework of European integration (see Risse et al. 2001; Trenz 2015). This makes it possible to understand the EU visitors' belonging to Europe in terms of manifold processes and engagements with Europe in the everyday, and may increase their sense of belonging to Europe. Mobility is one significant factor in imagining EUrope as a space and community of possibilities, whereas controversial issues are frequently left out of the scope of this everyday belonging. European visitors also confirmed that with geographical distance, the idea of being European was more accepted, as the term 'European' was better recognized from outside than within specific European states. Unlike 'Europe', which commended itself as a 'brand', neither 'Austria' nor 'Austrian', sparked immediate associations outside Europe, as a male Austrian visitor in his twenties noted at Carnuntum (VS2/20).

6   Conclusions: United in Plural Europes

According to some scholars (Mummendey and Waldzus 2004, 69), a sense of belonging to Europe may increase commonality and tolerance between Europeans at different levels. The fact that people from outside Europe perceive Europeans as somehow similar and representing one entity, despite their cultural and historical differences, facilitates the construction of a shared sense of belonging to Europe. As our study highlights, there are several 'Europes' depending on who you ask, and it is therefore important to consider in which contexts these 'Europes' occur and are constructed. At the same time, the concept of Europe is often perceived as vague. In our data, the visitors both from EU and non-EU countries wondered whether the concept referred to a geographical (the continent) or a political and economic entity (the EU), whether Europe had to be understood in cultural terms (referring to the experience and knowledge of historical, cultural, and linguistic diversity), or whether Europe was defined by their personal experiences. When engaging with the politics of belonging of the EHL, Europe, the EU, European identity (least by the fact of EU citizenry), and European cultural heritage all seemed to become intermingled and intertwined.

Visitors referred to cultural diversity as a defining feature of Europe in almost all interviews. The EU motto 'united in diversity' hence described the notion of belonging and attitudes of many visitors to the EHL sites in our study (see also Lähdesmäki et al. 2020). Thus, the macro- and micro-level discourses on Europe seemed to include similarities. As our analysis showed, the interviewees' notions of Europe resonated with how the EU defines itself. The EU value discourse found its way into almost all our interviewees' answers about European values, albeit in an indefinite way. While lack of concreteness in a discourse is often perceived as a shortcoming, it can also help to strengthen the reception and adoption of a discourse by a broader public. Although the values discourse remains vague and contains a variety of interpretations and understandings, at the same time it can give people the impression of sharing 'something' in common. Commonality is often constructed through narratives of personally meaningful experiences. The interview data shows that being able to understand and imagine Europe in multiple ways enables different people to engage with EU's politics of belonging, and the reverse is also true: the EHL as politics of belonging associates with different understandings of 'EUrope'. Through its emphasis on a European dimension, the EHL enables a transnational interpretation of cultural peculiarities, similarities, and commonalities. Furthermore, immaterial aspects of the heritage awarded with the EHL make it easier for different groups and individuals to identify with this heritage.

References

Billig, M. 1995. *Banal Nationalism*. London, Thousand Oaks and New Delhi: Sage.

Borgmann-Prebil, Y., and M. Ross. 2010. "Promoting European Solidarity: Between Rhetoric and Reality?" In *Promoting Solidarity in the European Union*, edited by Y. Borgman-Prebil and M. Ross, 1–22. Oxford: Oxford University Press.

Breakwell, G. M. 2004. "Identity Change in the Context of the Growing Influence of European Union Institutions." In *Transnational Identities. Becoming European in the EU*, edited by R.K. Hermann, T. Risse, and M.B. Brewer, 25–39. Lanham, Boulder: Rowman & Littlefield Publishers.

Čeginskas, V. L. A. 2018. "The Added European Value of Cultural Heritage. The European Heritage Label." *Santander Art and Culture Law Review* 21 (4): 29–50.

Čeginskas, V. L. A. 2019. "The Challenges in Creating Visibility of European Cultural Heritage: A Case Study of the European Heritage Label." *Ethnologia Fennica* 46: 109–134.

Čeginskas, V. L. A., and S. Kaasik-Krogerus. 2020. "Politics of Solidarity in the Context of European Heritage. The Cases of the European Solidarity Centre and Hambach Castle." *International Journal of Heritage Studies* 26 (10): 998–1012. doi: 10.1080/13527258.2019.1663235

Citrin, J., and J. Sides 2004. "More than Nationals: How Identity Choice Matters in the New Europe." In *Transnational Identities. Becoming European in the EU*, edited by R.K, Hermann, T. Risse, and M. B. Brewer, 161–185. Lanham, Boulder: Rowman & Littlefield Publishers.

Cram, L. 2009. "Identity and European Integration: Diversity as a Source of Integration." *Nations and Nationalism* 15 (1): 109–128. doi: 10.1111/j.1469-8129.2009.00367.x

Cram, L. 2012. "Does the EU Need a Navel? Implicit and Explicit Identification with the European Union." *Journal of Common Markets Studies* 50 (1): 71–86.

De Cesari, C. 2017. "Museums of Europe: Tangles of Memory, Borders, and Race." *Museum Anthropology* 40: 18–35.

Deutsch, K. 1966 [1953]. *Nationalism and Social Communication*. Massachusetts: MIT Press.

EC (European Commission). 2010. Proposal for a Decision of the European Parliament and of the Council Establishing a European Union Action for the European Heritage Label. COM (2010)76 final, 2010/0044 (COD). Brussels: European Commission.

EC (European Commission). 2011. European Heritage Label. Guide for Candidate Sites. European Commission 2011, Brussels.

EC (European Commission). 2016. European Heritage Label. Panel Report on Monitoring. 19 December 2016. Brussels: European Commission.

EC (European Commission). 2017. European Heritage Label. 2017 Panel Report. 5 December 2017. Brussels: European Commission.

EP&C (European Parliament and the Council). 2011. "Decision No 1194/2011/EU of the European Parliament and of the Council of 16 November 2011 establishing a European Union action for the European Heritage Label." *Official Journal of the European Union* L 303: 1–9.

Favell, A. 2008. *Eurostars and Eurocities. Free Movement and Mobility in an Integrating Europe*. Malden: Blackwell Publishing.

Favell, A., and E. Recchi. 2009. "Social Mobility and Spatial Mobility." In *Sociology of the European Union*, edited by V. Guiraudon and A. Favell, 50–75. Basingstoke: Palgrave Macmillan.

Hermann, R., and M. B. Brewer 2004. "Identities and Institutions: Becoming European in the EU." In *Transnational Identities. Becoming European in the EU*, edited by R. K. Hermann, T. Risse, and M. B. Brewer, 1–22. New York: Rowman & Littlefield.

Kaasik-Krogerus, S. 2019. "Politics of Mobility and Stability in Authorizing European Heritage: Estonia's Great Guild Hall." In *Dissonant Heritages and Memories in Contemporary Europe*, edited by T. Lähdesmäki, L. Passerini, S. Kaasik-Krogerus, and I. van Huis, 157–181. New York: Palgrave Macmillan.

Kaasik-Krogerus, S. 2020. "Identity Politics of the Promotional Videos of the European Heritage Label." *Contemporary Politics* 26 (1): 1–16. doi: 10.1080/13569775.2019.1611207

Kohli, M. 2000. "The Battlegrounds of European identity." *European Societies* 2 (2): 113–137.

Kvale, S. 1996. *InterViews: An Introduction to Qualitative Research Interviewing.* Thousand Oaks: Sage.

Lähdesmäki, T. 2014. "The EU's Explicit and Implicit Heritage Politics." *European Societies* 16 (3): 401–421. doi: 10.1080/14616696.2014.894547

Lähdesmäki, T. 2016. "Politics of Tangibility, Intangibility, and Place in the Making of European Cultural Heritage in EU Heritage Policy." *International Journal of Heritage Studies* 22 (10): 766–780.

Lähdesmäki, T. 2019a. "Founding Myths of EU Europe and the Workings of Power in the EU Heritage and History Initiatives." *European Journal of Cultural Studies* 22 (5–6): 781–798.

Lähdesmäki, T. 2019b. "European Culture, History, and Heritage as Political Tools in the Rhetoric of the Finns Party." *In European Memory in Populism*, edited by C. de Cesari and A. Kaya, 191–209. London: Routledge.

Lähdesmäki, T., Kaasik-Krogerus, S., and K. Mäkinen. 2019. "Genealogy of the Concept of Heritage in the European Commission's Policy Discourse." *Contributions to the History of Concepts* 14 (1): 115–139.

Lähdesmäki, T., V. L. A. Čeginskas, S. Kaasik-Krogerus, K. Mäkinen, and J. Turunen. 2020. *Creating and Governing Cultural Heritage in the European Union: The European Heritage Label.* London: Routledge.

Mummendey, A., and Waldzus, S. 2004. "National Differences and European Plurality: Discrimination or Tolerance between European Countries." In *Transnational Identities. Becoming European in the EU*, edited by R.K. Hermann, T. Risse, and M. B. Brewer, 59–72. New York: Rowman & Littlefield.

Niklasson, E. 2017. "The Janus-Face of European Heritage: Revisiting the Rhetoric of Europe-Making in EU Cultural Politics." *Journal of Social Archaeology* 17 (2): 138–162. doi: 10.1177/1469605317712122

Niklasson, E., and H. Hølleland. 2018. "The Scandinavian Far-Right and the New Politicization of Heritage." *Journal of Social Archaeology* 18 (2): 121–148. doi: 10.1177/1469605318757340

Recchi, E., and A. Favell, eds. 2011. *Pioneers of European Integration. Citizenship and Mobility in the EU*. Cheltenham: Edward Elgar Publishing Inc.

Risse, T. 2004. "European Institutions and Identity Change: What Have We Learned?" In *Transnational Identities. Becoming European in the EU*, edited by R. K. Hermann, T. Risse, and M. B. Brewer, 247–271. New York: Rowman & Littlefield.

Rumford, C. 2008. *Cosmopolitan Spaces: Europe, Globalization, Theory.* London: Routledge.

Sassatelli, M. 2002. "Imagined Europe. The Shaping of a European Cultural Identity through EU Cultural Policy." *European Journal of Social Theory* 5 (4): 435–451.

Sassatelli, M. 2009. *Becoming European. Cultural Identity and Cultural Policies.* Basingstoke: Palgrave Macmillan.

Siapera, E. 2004. "EU Correspondents in Brussels: Between Europe and the Nation-State." In *Transnational Identities. Becoming European in the EU*, edited by R. K. Hermann, T. Risse, and M. B. Brewer, 129–157. New York: Rowman & Littlefield.

Trenz, H.-J. 2015. "The Saga of Europeanisation. On the Narrative Construction of a European Society." In *European Integration, Processes of Change and the National Experience*, edited by S. Börner, and M. Eigmüller, 207–227. Palgrave Studies in European Political Sociology. London: Palgrave Macmillan. doi: 10.1057/9781137411259_10

Turunen, J. n.d. "Borderscapes of Europe – Cultural Production of (Colonial) Border Imaginaries through European Heritage." (Unpublished manuscript)

Wetherell, M., and J. Potter. 1992. *Mapping the language of Racism: Discourse and the Legitimation of Exploitation.* Hemel Hempstead: Harvester-Wheatsheaf.

CHAPTER 7

Cross Analysis of the Case Studies

1 Bringing the Case Studies Together

Our methodological innovation, ethnography of Europeanization, offers a multi-dimensional and intersectional approach to how people construct Europe and their notion of belonging to it at different social and cultural locations. We explore this in data sets from three EU cultural initiatives – the European Capital of Culture (ECOC), the European Citizen Campus (ECC), and the European Heritage Label (EHL). In our three case studies, various social locations and demographic aspects, such as age, gender, education, nationality, country of residence, and level of active engagement in cultural participation, had a major impact on our research participants' answers dealing with Europe and the 'European'. These socio-demographic factors affected both people's agency and their imaginations of Europe, and intersected with other social and cultural phenomena that participants addressed, such as mobility, cultural diversity, and ideas of participation. People's social location plays a role in deepening and/or creating opportunities for engaging in such phenomena and contributing to processes of belonging.

In this chapter, we bring together the core findings from our three case studies and cross-analyze them in relation to spatial and temporal contexts, including the specific contexts in which the EU cultural initiatives occurred. While we address the overlap in our data, we have no intention to conduct a comparative study. Our qualitative analysis takes into account only the answers of EU citizens and of citizens of Russia, Ukraine, and Switzerland, which includes all respondents and participants in the ECOC and ECC data sets and 230 interviewed visitors to EHL sites.

In order to interpret and understand our data and its meanings more extensively, we have quantified certain answers from our interviews and survey. These findings are valid and representative only for the respective case study in which the responses were collected. Bearing in mind the small numbers of informants, particularly in the ECC and EHL cases, we do not claim that our results are as representative as larger surveys like Eurobarometer. However, grouping the answers enabled us to discuss belonging to Europe from different perspectives and in various contexts, and to consider the factors affecting the answers that referred to the respondents' relationship to Europe and views on the 'European'. Grouping answers also helped us to identify important topics in the debates about Europe and belonging to it. While our findings suggest a connection between European identity and support for European integration, we noted that this was not the case for all interviewees and respondents, some of whom either considered themselves European but were critical of the EU's policy or who rejected the idea of a European identity but were nevertheless supportive of the Union's policy and goals. This suggests that a variety of factors, including the extent of transnational experiences, are important determinants that influence people's self-identification as European and their support for European integration (see Kuhn 2011, 2019, 1215). In our discussion, we relate our participants' social locations and backgrounds to how they constructed Europe and the 'European'. The analysis allows us to link their views and backgrounds to various cultural and social phenomena occurring in Europe in the 2010s.

2   The Impact of Social Locations and the Research Setting on Notions of Europe

2.1   *Gender*
In all our three case studies (Chapters 4–6), more women than men participated in the questionnaire surveys or qualitative interviews. Although we are aware of more than binary gender conceptions, we did not perceive any potential conflict based on the traditional gender division during our data collection and we will therefore continue to refer to men and women only. In the ECOC data, eight respondents did not (for several possible reasons) reveal their gender. Based on our data, we noticed that female participants and interviewees tended to hold neutral to positive views on the 'European' and Europe more often than men did, particularly participants in the ECOC and EHL case studies (see tables 7.1 and 7.2). The ECC case is slightly different as all interviewees had volunteered to participate in a European project with thematic workshops dealing with European issues, and we therefore assume that the participants had positive associations with Europe and the EU. While male interviewees and respondents also had a high approval of Europe and the EU, in particular on economic and political issues, they more often voiced criticism towards the EU and its current state of affairs and politics in their answers.

Drawing on our EHL interview data, more women than men expressed the view that something like a European identity might exist and it seemed to be easier for women to describe what this was (see Table 7.1). They often connected it to notions and ideas that highlighted family and roots on the one hand, and the importance of peace and strengthening rights and equality, on the other. In contrast, among these interviewees, men were more often critical of the whole concept of European identity, or approached it from a constructivist perspective, as a project, or as something still under construction that may emerge in the future. Very few interviewees of each gender (i.e. seven or less) either had negative associations with European identity or did not think that a European identity exists, so we cannot say anything valid based on these numbers. However, as the EHL data shows, gender had an impact on the ability to construct notions of what represents Europe and the 'European', which in turn may contribute to less negative associations with the concept of European identity.

TABLE 7.1   Notions of European identity and feeling European in relation to gender among EHL visitors from EU countries, Russia, Switzerland, and Ukraine (123 women and 107 men)

	Women	Men
Strongly feels European	62%	66%
Feels both European and membership of a specific nation, region, or city	22%	21%
Does not feel European	13%	10%
Positive associations with the concept of European identity	19%	19%
Neutral associations with the concept of European identity	64%	50%
Negative associations with the concept of European identity	6%	9%
Other associations with European identity (e.g. views that it is a project, still needs elaboration, or may emerge only in the future)	11%	22%
Is able to describe what European identity is	65%	51%
Does not think that European identity exists	7%	17%

In the following, we refer to our detailed analysis of the ECOC case as an example that supports the findings on the interrelation between gender and views of Europe from our EHL case. The questionnaire survey used in the ECOC study allowed us to cross-reference gender with respondents' views on Europeanness. Our analysis of the ECOC case indicated that women identified with Europeanness more often than men (see Table 7.2). When calculating how much the respondents considered Europeanness as an important element for their identity, women had a higher score in all case ECOCs (mean score of a scale of 1–3 [not at all / to some extent / a lot]: for respondents in Pécs, women

2.47 and men 2.24; Tallinn, women 2.43 and men 2.32; Turku, women 2.28 and men 2.27). The difference between genders was biggest in Pécs and smallest – almost equal – in Turku. The data analysis also suggested that women had more positive perceptions of the concept of Europeanness. The mean score of a scale of 1–5 (very negative / negative / neutral / positive / very positive) for women was higher in all case ECOCs (Pécs women 3.90 and men 3.75; Tallinn women 4.11 and men 3.93; Turku women 4.07 and men 3.93). We noted that in this score, the difference between genders was biggest in Tallinn and smallest in Turku.

TABLE 7.2   Views on Europeanness among the respondents from Pécs, Tallinn, and Turku based on gender (968 women and 451 men)

	Women	Men
Identifies a lot with Europeanness	44%	38%
Positive or very positive impressions on Europeanness	76%	70%
Sees that ECOC events represent a lot or very much Europeanness	63%	55%
Sees that ECOC events should represent a lot or very much Europeanness	74%	67%

The respondents' views on how the ECOC events represented Europeanness, or how they should represent it, followed similar gender bias. We calculated how much the respondents perceived that the ECOC events represented Europeanness using the mean score on a scale of 1–5 (not at all / a little / to some extent / a lot / very much), and found that women scored higher than men (Pécs women 3.82 and men 3.68; Tallinn women 4.01 and men 3.64; Turku women 3.68 and men 3.58). Here, the difference was biggest again in Tallinn and smallest in Turku. Moreover, women saw more often than men that the events should represent Europeanness (in Pécs women 4.15 and men 3.96; Tallinn women 4.22 and men 4.01; Turku women 3.78 and men 3.69). Again, the biggest difference was in Tallinn and the smallest in Turku.

These geographical differences in our findings on gender and Europeanness are difficult to explain but may connect to the influence of broader social and cultural phenomena, such as the experience, attributed significance, and implementation of gender equality. We found that in Pécs and Tallinn, both the ECOC programmes and the ECOC audiences often emphasized and dealt with the aim and interest of 'becoming' and being taken more seriously as

European. Although EU integration has increasingly extended to various societal sectors since the Eastern enlargement of the Union, the old division of Europe into 'East' and 'West' continues to influence notions of Europe. The Central and Eastern European countries that joined the EU in 2004 and 2007 have not been always perceived to be as European as their Western counterparts (Lee and Bideleux 2009). Many of these countries have, therefore, sought to 'become' more European. Cities have used the ECOC action as a tool to become better-known as European on a wider European and global scale. However, becoming European has proved challenging for many smaller Central and Eastern European cities, as it has been equated with modern infrastructure and the polished appearance of city space. The ECOCs in Eastern and Central European countries have also aimed to broaden the whole notion of the 'European' by narrating their socialist history, heritage, and experience as part of it. Both in Pécs and in Tallinn, the ECOC programme included this historical layer and heritage in their 'European dimension' but this layer was not emphasized in the audiences' responses on the 'European'.

The findings from the ECOC data suggest a connection between Europeanization and the political and socio-cultural traditions in the respective countries. Compared to Estonia and Hungary, Finland has a longer tradition of gender equality dating from the introduction of women's right to vote and stand for election in 1906. With other Nordic countries, Finland is commonly perceived to score high on gender equality politics (Lähdesmäki and Saresma 2014). Unlike the former Eastern bloc countries – Estonia and Hungary – Finland was more strongly influenced by EU politics, even before becoming member state. The European Community and then Union has emphasized equality between men and women as a fundamental value and sought to advance gender equality from its beginnings (Jacquot 2015; EC 2019; see also Lähdesmäki et al. 2020). While broad public discussion of women's rights and gender equality began in Western countries in the late 1960s, this did not occur in the Soviet Union and its satellite states, even though the communist imagery and rhetoric characterized women as 'equal to men', emphasized the importance of women in the society, and offered greater opportunities and expectations for them to participate in the workforce. This different development may have shaped each society's dominant perceptions on gender. In turn, it influences people's relations and associations with Europe.

Thus, gender and the experience of gender politics may be more relevant for forming people's views on Europe and their relationship with the EU in some societal contexts than in others. The extent and ways in which certain social phenomena are addressed in societies can reflect their citizens' views on Europe as a whole. Social environments and the experience of everyday life and practices are relevant to how people construct their relations with Europe, their expectations of the EU, and their views on the desirability of 'European-ness'. In countries where gender rights are more of an issue, Europeanization may become intertwined with attempts to change the perceived status quo and to strengthen women's social and political positions. This may result in a higher approval of Europeanization among women, as indicated in our ECOC data. In contrast, in countries where there is a broad public perception of gen-der equality, like in Finland, gender may have less impact, and the difference between women's and men's views on Europe may be influenced by other fac-tors than gender.

2.2 *Age*

Another factor that affected the interviewees' and respondents' views on Europe and 'the European' was their age. In the ECOC data, respondents to the questions on Europeanness born in the 1970s and 1960s were more reserved towards it than younger or older respondents (see Figure 7.1). The youngest respondents, born in the 1990s or later, and the oldest ones, born in the 1950s or earlier, had the most positive attitude towards the 'European'.

We noted similar findings in the EHL data, although this was collected seven years later – the ECOC data was collected in 2010 and 2011 and the EHL data in 2017 and 2018. However, the ECC data was less conclusive on age, as the inter-viewees were all younger (students) and had consciously decided to participate

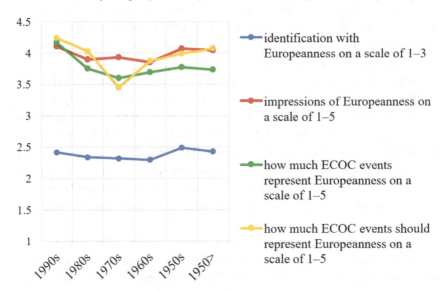

FIGURE 7.1 Views on Europeanness among the ECOC respondents (N = 1,425) from Pécs, Tallinn, and Turku based on age

in a programme on Europe and the EU. Thus, their higher identification with and sense of belonging to Europe did not come as a surprise (see Chapter 5). Nevertheless, the ECC data shows that younger people who have grown up as EU citizens consider Europe and the EU as relevant topics but have a different way of accessing them, as outlined in our EHL case study (see Chapter 6).

Based on our analysis of the interviews from the EHL sites (see Chapter 6) we divided visitors into three age groups: young (aged 18–35), middle-aged (aged 36–65), and older (66+). In general, high numbers of people in all age groups felt European (in response to the question 'Do you feel European?', see Table 7.3). Among young interviewees, 60% strongly felt European, while 24% considered themselves both European and national citizens – and sometimes also felt belonging to a certain region or city. In the group of middle-aged interviewees, 64% strongly felt European and 22% both European and a national citizen, while in the oldest age group, 74% felt strongly European, 16% both European and national citizens, and only four interviewees did not feel European. The younger the age group, the more positive the associations with European identity (young: 24%, middle-aged: 20%, older: 8%), while older interviewees seemed to have more negative associations with the idea of a European identity. Older interviewees also more frequently highlighted European identity as a project. To a certain extent this resonates with the findings that the two younger age groups were both better able to describe what a European identity represented and more ready to accept that a shared European identity existed.

This relationship between age and feeling European was slightly surprising to us. Similarly to the ECOC data, younger and older visitors to the EHL sites generally spoke in far more positive terms about European identity and the EU in the interviews. Middle-aged visitors generally voiced more frequent and often harsher criticism of the EU and the notion of a unified Europe. However, middle-aged interviewees were more likely than young people to give positive responses to the direct question on feeling European. This is one example of participants' contradicting and contested notions in our case studies. One simplified explanation might be that young people are still in the process of finding their way, while middle-aged people are more critical and looking for immediate solutions to current problems, and members of the older generation are more relaxed and less tense about future projects. Another explanation is that there were unequal numbers of interviewees in each age group in the EHL case.

Our cross analysis showed that the EHL visitors in the youngest age group most frequently had positive associations with European identity (24%, see Table 7.3), while interviewees aged 66 and over seemed to have more negative associations with the idea of a European identity. Interviewees in the

TABLE 7.3   Notions on European identity and feeling European in relation to age among
EHL visitors from EU countries, Russia, Switzerland, and Ukraine (N in age
groups from the youngest to oldest: 87, 93, and 46)

Age group	18–35	36–65	66+
Strongly feels European	60%	64%	74%
Feels both European and membership of a specific nation, region, or city	24%	22%	16%
Does not feel European	12%	12%	10%
Positive associations with the concept of European identity	24%	20%	8%
Neutral associations with the concept of European identity	60%	57%	56%
Negative associations with the concept of European identity	7%	5%	12%
Other associations with European identity (e.g. views that it is a project, still needs elaboration, or may emerge only in the future)	9%	18%	24%
Is able to describe what European identity is	61%	62%	44%
Does not think that European identity exists	9%	13%	14%

middle-aged visitor group had fewer positive associations with the term and concept of European identity than the young interviewees, despite more strongly feeling European. However, this rejection often circled around the term 'identity', which was regarded as too excluding, rather than the idea of commonalities between Europeans from different backgrounds. We also noticed that the older the visitor, the more often the opinion was voiced that Europe, the 'European', and European identity were not a finished process but still under construction. This view did not affect older interviewees at EHL sites in a negative way, and they more frequently felt European than members of the younger groups. In contrast, younger people seemed to strongly connect the idea of being European to being both national and European citizens. Young and middle-aged Europeans were significantly better at describing what European identity meant to them and they more readily voiced the opinion that something like a shared European identity existed (see Table 7.3). These findings suggest a change in the way in which the EU has become accepted and incorporated in people's social location in recent decades. The younger the age group, the more the EU seems to have become a normal and influential factor in people's everyday and banal practices of belonging in Europe.

Our results indicate that the older generation of Europeans should not be generally considered, or automatically dismissed, as conservative and reluctant to belong to Europe and build its unity. As discussed in Chapter 6, this generation has had a reason to work towards European belonging as part of rebuilding and developing European societies and consolidating peace, trust, and welfare in them after World War II – particularly in Western European democracies. For young people in Europe today, the EU, transnational experiences, and everyday exchanges in Europe are part of normality, which assumedly becomes reflected in their positive views on Europe.

When analyzing the views to Europe in different age groups between countries, our data did not indicate clear differences between the 'East' and 'West' of Europe. This can be illustrated by the results from the ECOC case study. When calculating how much the respondents considered Europeanness as an important element for their identity, based on the mean of a scale from 1–3 (not at all / to some extent / a lot), the oldest age group, born in 1949 or earlier, scored highest (2.57) in Tallinn, but the figures were not much lower for Turku (2.40) and Pécs (2.38). The youngest respondents, born in the 1990s, also scored highest in Tallinn (2.49) and similarly in Turku and Pécs (both 2.37). The perception of the concept of Europeanness was not clearly different in 'East' and 'West' – at least in the youngest age group. The mean perception of a scale of 1–5 (very negative / negative / neutral / positive / very positive) for the youngest respondents was 4.31 in Tallinn, 4.14 in Turku, and 3.92 in Pécs. Among the oldest respondents, the scores were 4.11 in Turku, 3.93 in Pécs, and 3.90 in Tallinn. However, the number of respondents in this age group was relatively low, so it is not possible to draw meaningful conclusions for this question based on age.

2.3 Education

Another important socio-demographic factor affecting our research participants' views on Europe, the EU, and belonging is their educational background. In general, interviewees who participated in the ECC project and an overwhelming majority of visitors to the EHL sites had a higher education. The interviewees from the ECC workshops were all university students, while almost three quarters of the interviewed EHL visitors either held a bachelor's, master's, or doctoral degree (or equivalent diploma) or were university students. In the ECOC data, almost half of the respondents had a university degree (see Annex 1).

As Risse (2004, 256) writes, based on earlier studies, education and income have a positive impact on levels of attachment to Europe (see also Citrin and Sides 2004). According to Risse, attachment to Europe is linked with support for the EU and willingness to cede authority and sovereignty to EU institutions in various policy domains. We acknowledge that our discussions of belonging to Europe are largely based on data gathered from people with a higher education and shed less light on the notions of belonging to Europe among people with a lower level of education. Despite this educational bias, we are nevertheless able to discuss a wide range of notions and imaginations regarding Europe and the European among European citizens.

The detailed questionnaire study in the ECOC data enabled more detailed cross-tabulation of the impact of education on the respondents' views. Our analysis indicated that education was a relevant factor in the respondents' identification with Europe and their notions of Europeanness. The respondents with lower levels of education appeared to have also lower interest in Europeanness, and less often connected Europeanness with the ECOC events. The data enabled us to conclude that the higher the educational background of the respondents, the higher their identification with Europe and the more positive their impression of Europe (see Table 7.4). Moreover, identification with Europeanness seemed to reflect ease to interpret the European dimension in the ECOC events (see Lähdesmäki 2013, 2014a).

TABLE 7.4   Views on Europeanness among the respondents from Pécs, Tallinn and Turku based on educational level (A = comprehensive or elementary school, vocational course, or in-job training, N = 155; B = high school, polytechnic, or other higher vocational degree, N = 622; C = higher education [bachelor's, master's, or doctoral degree], N = 630)

	A	B	C
Identifies a lot with Europeanness	39%	40%	44%
Positive or very positive impressions on Europeanness	69%	71%	78%
Sees that ECOC events represent a lot or very much Europeanness	54%	64%	60%
Sees that ECOC events should represent a lot or very much Europeanness	64%	74%	72%

Levels of education also affected how respondents answered the open questions on the representation of Europeanness in the ECOC events. This was explored using thematic codes, based on the themes listed in the Table 4.1. We calculated how many of these codes were included in each open response on Europeanness in the events. Many of the respondents found difficult to describe Europeanness and did not, thus, answer the open questions regarding it. We considered, however, these 'empty answers' as meaningful data and included them in our calculations with a number zero. The more educated the respondents were, the more often they answered the open questions and the

TABLE 7.5   Means of the number of different ways of perceiving Europeanness in the ECOC events given by respondents in different educational groups in Pécs, Tallinn and Turku, including empty answers (A = comprehensive or elementary school, N = 45; B = vocational course or degree or in-job training, N = 110; C = high school, N = 462; D = polytechnic or other higher vocational education, N = 163; E = bachelor's degree, N = 215; F = master's degree, N = 340; G = doctoral degree, N = 36)

	A	B	C	D	E	F	G
Number of different ways to perceive Europeanness in the ECOC events	0.40	0.47	0.59	0.60	0.64	0.70	0.81

more broad and varied descriptions they gave of how they perceived Europeanness in the events (Table 7.5).

Similarly, the EHL data revealed that notions of feeling European or being able to describe ideas about what Europe and the 'European' represents was linked with the interviewees' educational background (see Table 7.6). People who did not have a higher education struggled more frequently with describing notions of Europe, while interviewees with an academic background had greater linguistic and cognitive competence (and courage) to describe abstract concepts, and hence to explain what Europe and European identity might mean. Interviewees with a university education seemed to feel strongly European more often but, at the same time, they more frequently referred to both positive and negative associations with 'European identity'. Interviewees with a higher education more often described Europe as being open-minded, borderless, culturally and linguistically diverse, tolerant, and guaranteeing human rights and freedoms. However, many of them found the term 'identity' problematic and negatively connoted with exclusion, as implied in our findings in relation to age groups. From their studies, they were familiar with the rejection of the concept as too exclusionary and limiting. However, this did not affect their general sense of belonging to Europe, feeling European, and belief that Europeans from different cultural and ethnic backgrounds had things in common. This rejection of the term identity did not reveal the interviewees' relationship to the EU; in fact, most of them identified with the Union's political and economic goals.

Our analysis of the EHL data suggests that visitors with a higher education tend to feel a higher level of belonging to Europe, but their appreciation of the EU is based on multiple and diverse factors, including personal experiences, such as mobility, international work environments, bicultural partnerships, or mixed family backgrounds. Many of the interviewees who held academic degrees had had more opportunities for mobility and had spent some time abroad more frequently than the interviewees who had not gone to university. Furthermore, interviewees who had a higher educational background judged their transnational mobility experiences more positively (67%) and also were more likely to work in international or multilingual environments than those who had a basic education or vocational training (50%). Such diverse experiences can be assumed to impact on these interviewees' feeling of being European and their ability to describe what they viewed as European.

TABLE 7.6   Notions on European identity and feeling European in relation to education level among EHL visitors from EU countries, Russia, Switzerland, and Ukraine (A = basic education, high school, or vocational training, N = 47; B = higher education, bachelor's, master's, or doctoral degree, N = 177)

	A	B
Strongly feels European	59%	65%
Feels both European and membership of a specific nation, region, or city	17%	23%
Does not feel European	24%	8%
Positive associations with the concept of European identity	16%	20%
Neutral associations with the concept of European identity	64%	57%
Negative associations with the concept of European identity	4%	8%
Other associations with European identity (e.g. views that it is a project, still needs elaboration, or may emerge only in the future)	16%	15%
Is able to describe what European identity is	49%	61%
Does not think that European identity exists	19%	10%

2.4   National Background

In all three case studies, most of the interviewees were EU citizens. In the ECOC case study, the majority of the respondents originated from three host countries in Central, Eastern, and Northern Europe; Hungary, Estonia, and Finland. The ECC project involved university students from six Western European countries; Belgium, France, Germany, Italy, Luxembourg, and Portugal. West European interviewees dominated the EHL data set, which was partly due to the higher mobility of visitors from some West European countries. For instance, at almost all EHL sites we interviewed Dutch, French, or German tourists. In total, we interviewed EHL visitors representing 34 nationalities (see Annex 1). The selection of the EHL sites for our fieldwork was based on the specific, predetermined criteria of our research project (see Lähdesmäki et al.

2020): the year of awarding the Label, the site's theme, our linguistic competences, and the need to balance the sites on a North-South / East-West axis. As a result, six of the selected eleven EHL sites were situated in Western (and core) EU member states. Hence, the majority of our EHL interviewees were from Western European countries, most notably from Germany (16% of total visitor numbers), France (15%), the Netherlands (15%), Belgium (14%), Italy (10%), and Austria (7%) (see Table 7.7).

TABLE 7.7   Frequency and percentage of nationalities among all EHL visitors from EU countries, Russia, Switzerland, and Ukraine (N = 230)

Nationality	Total number of visitors	Total percentage of visitors	Nationality	Total number of visitors	Total percentage of visitors
Austria	16	7%	Russia	1	<1%
Belgium	33	14%	Slovakia	1	<1%
Czech Rep.	1	<1%	Spain	1	<1%
Denmark	3	1%	Sweden	2	1%
Finland	3	1%	Switzerland	2	1%
France	35	15%	UK	15	7%
Germany	37	16%	Ukraine	2	1%
Greece	2	1%	Austrian-Polish	1	<1%
Ireland	2	1%	Dutch-American	1	<1%
Italy	22	10%	French-German	1	<1%
Luxembourg	1	<1%	Russian-French	1	<1%
Netherlands	35	15%	Swedish-Dutch	1	<1%
Poland	9	4%	Hungarian-British-German	1	<1%
Portugal	1	<1%			

In all our data, Europe is often identified with 'Western' Europe and reflects a certain bias to reproduce ideas and notions of citizens from core Western EU member states. These narratives may significantly differ from those of citizens from Central and East European states. The wealth of backgrounds in the EHL data allowed us to observe considerable differences in the discourses about Europe and the 'European' from different parts of Europe. While for some Western European interviewees, East European countries served as examples of the 'European Other', the vast majority of all interviewees and respondents in the case studies – EU citizens and tourists from non-EU countries alike – associated the 'other' with non-European contexts. For them, the USA, Australia, Africa, Asia, and South America represented different political and social models and opposing examples of what constituted Europe and the 'European'.

The EHL visitors pinned specific social meanings on Europe, very similar to the official EU value discourse, and often interpreted the EU in terms of a social welfare model. Moreover, they often understood Europe as a social construction and closely associated it with the EU and its legal and political provisions. As a result, traditional and historical constructions of ingroups and outgroups, based on national and ethnic differences and enmities between European countries, were replaced by new categories of inclusion and exclusion. The new outgroups were usually situated or viewed as originating from outside Europe or the EU. Nevertheless, the visitors expressed historically and culturally embedded differences in how they understood the significance of national sovereignty and the citizens' relationship to the EU, which influenced their ways of constructing (or not constructing) belonging to Europe. In this, our data reflects similar findings from earlier studies of political discourses and interpretations of European integration in European countries (see Marcusssen et al. 1999; Risse et al. 1999; Breakwell 2004).

Quantifying the qualitative responses in our EHL data enabled us to compare attitudes towards Europe and feeling European based on a four-point scales (feel strongly European / feel also European in addition to national or other scalar allegiance / do not feel European / cannot say or not answered) in relation to the seven biggest visitor groups: Germany, France, the Netherlands, Belgium, Italy, Austria, and the UK (see Table 7.8). Italian interviewees (88%) and Austrians (81%) felt most strongly European, followed by Germans (75%) and French interviewees (73%). At the lower end of this group were Belgian (50%), British (50%), and Dutch (47%) visitors. Dutch visitors had the largest numbers who did not feel European (31%), followed by British visitors (17%) and Belgian and Austrian visitors (13% each). In contrast, relatively few French and German interviewees (8% and 3%, respectively) did not feel European and not a single Italian interviewee expressed not feeling European at all.

When looking at the answers about feeling European among visitors from Ukraine, Switzerland and Russia, we noticed that they predominantly strongly felt European (60%) or also felt European (40%) in addition to feeling allegiance to their home countries. However, their total number was too small (see Table 7.7) to draw any valid conclusion or generalize our findings. While Poles constituted a comparatively small proportion of the interviewed visitors to the EHL sites, they were the biggest group among Central and East European nationals. Of the Polish interviewees, 17% expressed strongly feeling European versus 83% feeling both Polish and European. While the first figure was lower than for nationals of West European countries, the second figure was much higher than among West European nationals. Furthermore, not a single Polish interviewee avoided addressing the issue of feeling European or claimed not to feel European, showing that this issue had some relevance to all of them.

TABLE 7.8 The seven biggest nationality groups in relation to their notion of feeling European among interviewed EHL visitors from EU countries, Russia, Switzerland, and Ukraine (those who were asked/answered)

Nationality	Strongly feels European	Feels also European	Does not feel European	Unable to say
Austria	81%	6%	13%	0%
Belgium	50%	29%	13%	8%
France	73%	15%	8%	4%
Germany	75%	22%	3%	0%
Italy	88%	13%	0%	0%
Netherlands	47%	16%	31%	6%
UK	50%	33%	17%	0%

The quantification of the qualitative data from the EHL case study supported our reading of the interview data: that for most Europeans we interviewed, feeling European was an important issue. At the same time, the interviews revealed that feeling European is very complex. In some cases, Europe and belonging to Europe were interpreted as desirable but not necessarily linked with EU membership, whereas other visitors, particularly those who positioned themselves as feeling both European and citizens of an EU member state, often referred to the membership of their home country in the EU. Considering the small number of interviewees, we cannot draw strong conclusions but our data enables us to reflect on and interpret the responses in their wider (national, cultural, historical, societal) context.

Despite their rather skeptical attitude towards Europe, as exemplified in their comparatively low scores of feeling European (47%) and high scores of not feeling European (31%), Dutch interviewees displayed a curious example of in-betweenness. Depending on the EHL site at which they were interviewed, Dutch visitors differently integrated Europe and notions about the 'European' in their construction of belonging. At Camp Westerbork, we interviewed many local Dutch visitors and often noticed that they expressed Eurosceptic narratives. However, Dutch visitors interviewed outside the Netherlands felt more connected to Europe and more often emphasized feeling European. As we observed that other interviewees with a higher degree of mobility often viewed Europe and belonging to Europe more favorably than people who were interviewed in their home countries, we decided to scrutinize mobility more closely as a relevant factor in interviewees' and respondents' perceptions of Europe. The case studies (Chapters 4–6) highlighted how personal experiences of mobility impacted on participants' answers and views; we return to this issue towards the end of this chapter.

The fact that Italian visitors strongly affirmed feeling European seemed surprising at first glance, given the rise of the populist party Lega Nord and the Cinque Stelle movement in Italy at the time of the EHL fieldwork. However, our results reflected the EHL site where most Italians were interviewed, which was a museum to one of the founding figures of the European Community and Union, Alcide de Gasperi. The majority of the visitors at this site were Italian students at university and in their final year at high school who participated in a project about Europe. The other Italian visitors were interviewed at EHL sites abroad, and we assume that the same effect of mobility, as observed among mobile Dutch visitors, applied to them as well.

Most Belgian visitors were interviewed at the EHL site in Belgium, which may have contributed to the aforementioned scores on strongly feeling European (50%) and not feeling European (13%). These answers may reflect a double-edged attitude to the European project in the Belgian public. Support for EU integration is not equally strong in all language communities across Belgium but reflects the divergent demands of different political forces, parties, and poles (see Sinardet 2013). Migration was addressed in many interviews we conducted in Belgium. However, increasing public opposition in Belgium to the EU's social and economic agenda, in particular regarding further EU enlargement, coupled with concerns about social inequalities for Belgian nationals arising from inner-European mobility and migration to Europe from other countries, seem to reduce the willingness to support European integration and European solidarity (see Baute et al. 2019; Brack and Crespy 2019).

According to the qualitative analysis of our EHL data, UK visitors were more often skeptical about belonging to Europe and spoke more critically about ideas of solidarity and unity within the EU than visitors from other European states, which confirms the findings of earlier studies (e.g. Knopf 2002; Wyn Jones et al. 2013; Jeffery et al. 2014; Ormston 2015). Our interviewees from England tended to emphasize an antagonism between their sense of nationality (Englishness) and Europeanness, which was addressed in many interviews. The contrast between these two poles of belonging constructed their discourse of Europe and the European, and often amounted to feeling more distant from Europe. Scottish visitors also often distinguished themselves from the English. These interviewees often constructed a closer sense of connection and belonging to both Europe and the EU. In principle, our findings confirm the different and divided positions towards the EU revealed in UK voting behavior during the referendum on leaving the EU (June 2016) and the parliamentary elections (December 2019).

Europe and the EU resonated in a different way for the interviewed German visitors to EHL sites (both in Germany and abroad). They constructed a link between feeling German and being European, in which Europe and a concern for preserving European unity seemed to be strongly embedded in their understanding of belonging. The discourse of these interviewees strongly reflected the post-war, West German political discourse on overcoming the country's nationalist and militarist history (see Risse 2004, 252) – in contrast to the discourse of many UK interviewees. This discourse favored European belonging over German identity. While most of the German interviewees were West Germans, the few East German interviewees seemed to share this discourse – but as it turned out, they either resided in West German federal states or had a critical attitude to the former German Democratic Republic.

The answers of the ECOC respondents in Pécs, Hungary and interviews with the Polish EHL visitors to the European Solidarity Centre in Gdańsk, Poland partly reflect the openly nationalistic turn in Polish and Hungarian politics in the past decade. The current attempts to rewrite Hungary's 'golden past' conflicts with the experiences of the early 1990s, when Hungary strove to join 'Europe' and to 'become European'. Similarly, the national populistic policy of the Law and Justice (PiS) party has recently led the government in Poland to openly and strongly collide with EU politics and values, resulting in a European Court of Justice ruling against Polish judicial reform. The Polish interviewees at the European Solidarity Centre partly referred to the critical legal and political situation in their country and, depending on their personal positions, this influenced their views on Europe and the 'European'.

It is noteworthy that the few people who said they had dual citizenship or an ethnically mixed family background always felt strongly European, suggesting that multiple ethnic, national, and cultural allegiances and everyday transnational practices can facilitate a stronger allegiance to Europe (see Čeginskas 2016). Our findings confirm the importance of social experiences for making Europe to an important object of identification, as also proposed by the transactionalist theory, which suggests that patterns of transnational interaction and communication can lead to a growing sense of community among citizens, and hence increase support for further political integration (see Deutsch 1957, 1966, 1969, 34–35). However, our quantified findings about feeling or not feeling European do not aim to represent the actual sentiments and attitudes of European citizens in their respective countries. Moreover, our interviewees sometimes revealed rather unexpected answers that needed contextualization. For instance, the only person from Luxembourg who was interviewed at an EHL site did not feel European. The interviewee addressed the fear of small countries becoming politically crushed between big powers but it became obvious during the interview that the visitor was having an 'off day', which affected the interview at large. If the same person had been interviewed at another time, the answer about feeling European could have been different. This interview crystallized the fact that all research dealing with informants' opinions, views, experiences, and feelings are always situational and context-dependent, and may change.

Far from wishing to essentialize our findings about notions of Europe and feeling European in relation to the nationality of the visitors, these examples reveal how nation-specific contexts and personal disposition based on culturally and historically embedded notions become relevant for understanding the responses in our data. Europeanization is not an isolated process: when addressing and examining Europeanization, it is important to pay attention to processes of regional, international, or supranational integration and to processes of globalization, as relations and interaction between states. A transnational approach must use different levels of analysis, namely, the local, the national, the European, and the global level, and, equally, the interplay between these levels must also be analyzed, as connecting points for transnational transactions can be found at each level (see Kuhn 2011; Faist 2014; Delhey et al. 2014). Similarly, the analysis of the ECOC data in relation to gender showed interesting regional differences, which appeared to intersect with various social aspects, such as gender and age. For historical reasons, the notion of Europe is understood differently in today's states, which have developed as sovereign entities over centuries than in those, which were part of larger multi-ethnic empires in the years leading up to World War I. In addition, experiences with World War II and with the Socialist regime until 1989/1991 forged different mnemonic communities in West European and Central and East European countries. These historical experiences contributed to affect both their divergent understandings of the past and of their contemporary positions in the EU (see Mälksoo 2009, 2014). Hence, a notion of belonging to the EU – also in terms of a federal model of cohesion – can be interpreted against the fact that half of the twentieth-century these countries have been either occupied by the Soviet Union or situated in the Soviet bloc. This period of forced belonging affects their current notion of holding a liminal position within EUrope and is a factor in the increased nationalism in states like Poland and Hungary today. While West Germany had to undergo a complete reorganization and face its nationalistic past after World War II, other Western states, and later the states, which regained independence when the Soviet Union collapsed, continued to draw on their national past, and this resonates in their citizens' views and attitudes.

Similarly, the public debates on the current state of the EU highlight the many crises the Union is facing. People draw different conclusions from this: while some foresee disintegration of the EU, others assume that the Union's future lies with even closer integration. However, the entanglement of national and European discourses in our participants' answers makes it difficult for us to distinguish what they mean by Europe, as different interpretations of the concept are interrelated and mutually influence people's perceptions. Therefore, the relation between the EU and its citizens needs to be examined in context – which may yield contradictory findings.

2.5   Location and Thematic Focus

The geographical locations and the thematic narrative of the researched EHL sites both matter for our pool of interviewees and their answers on Europe. Some EHL sites hold a different attraction to local or national visitors than to foreign tourists. For instance, the Great Guild Hall in Tallinn is more frequented by foreign visitors than by local Estonians who avoid the touristic old town where it is located. During our fieldwork, we did not manage to interview a single Estonian visitor to the Great Guild Hall. Other sites – such as Hambach Castle, Robert Schuman House, Alcide de Gasperi House Museum, or Carnuntum Archaeological Park – appeared to be of greater interest to local or national visitors than to foreigners. Furthermore, the specific themes of some EHL sites (e.g. Franz Liszt Academy of Music) did not necessarily attract a mainstream but rather a select audience.

The respondents interpreted our interview and survey questions in terms of the thematic narratives set by the respective exhibition at the heritage site, cultural event, or project, which consequently affected their views and answers. For instance, at EHL sites situated in border areas or near national borders – such as Hambach Castle, Lieu d'Europe, Robert Schuman House, Carnuntum Archaeological Park, or Alcide de Gasperi House Museum – visitors more often referred to borders and explained the impact of open borders on their lives. At Camp Westerbork, a former transit camp to Auschwitz and other extermination camps, visitors discussed mobility in critical terms, while at the Sagres Promontory they discussed nature and the environment, which they experienced there, and in Gdańsk most visitors referred to Eastern

Europe. The thematic influence on interview answers was most noticeable at the home museums of EU founding figures (Robert Schuman and Alcide de Gasperi) and Lieu d'Europe in Strasbourg, an exhibition space on the EU institutions and the historical development of the EU. The experience of these sites often prompted visitors to relate their answers to notions of crisis in Europe or the relevance of personal involvement for transforming and advancing the European project but they also often expressed strongly feeling European, as the previous section showed. In this respect, the thematic narrative and the extent to which a site or event was visibly associated with Europe impacted on how visitors approached and understood our questions, and on the way they answered.

Although the thematic narration of a site or cultural event provided an initial trigger for answering our questions, it did not necessarily constrain the interviewees' narratives. This could be observed at some EHL sites, such as the Mundaneum in Belgium, where the exhibition on secret codes did not provide most visitors with any explicit relation to Europe or European cultural heritage. Interviewees moved freely in and out of the spatiotemporal and emotional frame suggested by the site's narrative on secret codes. Equally, for some visitors, our questions stimulated long narratives, while others provided no more than a short reply. Chapters 4–6 discussed how the EU's politics of belonging intertwines with individual and collective efforts and aspects that situate humans in time and space. Our case study participants revealed different processes of creating (non-)belonging and our analysis of the data showed that these processes are shifting, multiple, continuously constructed, and context-bound, enriched by personal narratives, positions, and experiences.

2.6   Personal Engagement in Cultural Activities

In our EHL fieldwork, we asked our interviewees about their notions of the importance of cultural heritage in general and European cultural heritage in particular (see Lähdesmäki et al. 2020). The responses enabled us to see a strong connection between personal views on the cultural heritage and imagination of Europe as a cultural space based on specific discourses. However, we did not ask the EHL interviewees in detail about their engagement with culture *per se*. In contrast, the questionnaire survey in the ECOC case study allowed us to specifically analyze respondents' willingness to engage in cultural activities and their level of immersion, which revealed that this factor played a role in their views on the 'European'. One question in this survey was: 'How often do you participate in difference cultural events (such as festivals, concerts, exhibitions, theatre plays)?' The analysis showed that culturally active respondents more often identified with Europeanness and had more positive impressions of it than the less active ones. They also tended to connect the ECOC events with Europe more often than the culturally less active respondents, and considered it important to create Europeanness through these events (see Table 7.9). Activeness in cultural participation also affected how respondents answered the open questions on the representation of Europeanness in the ECOC events. This was explored in the same way as in the case of education (see Table 7.5). The more culturally active the respondents were, the more often they answered the open questions and the more broad and varied descriptions they gave of how they perceived Europeanness in the events.

TABLE 7.9 Views on Europeanness among respondents from Pécs, Tallinn and Turku in relation to their activeness in cultural participation (A = hardly ever N = 18; B = once a year or less, N = 53; C = a couple of times a year, N = 321; D = every other month, N = 244; E = 1–3 times a month, N = 555; F = once a week or more, N = 209), including the mean number of ways in which they perceived Europeanness in the ECOC events

	A	B	C	D	E	F
Identifies a lot with Europeanness	29%	40%	38%	36%	44%	54%
Positive or very positive impressions of Europeanness	31%	60%	72%	73%	75%	83%
Sees that ECOC events represent Europeanness a lot or very much	37%	67%	56%	62%	61%	67%
Sees that ECOC events should represent Europeanness a lot or very much	50%	77%	67%	70%	72%	79%
Number of different ways of perceiving Europeanness in the ECOC events	0.00	0.34	0.43	0.64	0.69	0.77

The questionnaire data has been previously analyzed by creating a Cultural Competence Index based on the respondents' level of education, immersion in cultural events in general, immersion in the ECOC events, immersion in the organization of the ECOC events, and source of livelihood in the arts and cultural sector (Lähdesmäki 2014b). This index aimed at enabling the analysis of the open responses guided by Bourdieu's (1984, 1987) notion of cultural capital. The study indicated that the respondents with a high score in Cultural Competence Index related various contemporary phenomena and issues to the representation of Europeanness. In addition, they were more likely to interpret Europeanness in terms of international connections, which they recognized between the host city, its cultural scene, and Europe, and in relation to the cultural features they considered as common to Europe. In general, describing Europeanness as a shared cultural identity based on common cultural grounds was relatively rare in the data. Only some respondents with a very high score in the above-mentioned Index related the display of historical issues to Europeanness.

Based on the analysis of the ECOC case study in particular, we suggest that willingness to (actively) engage with cultural activities is another element of negotiating belonging that affects attitudes towards Europe. People who are willing to visit and immerse themselves in certain cultural events or sites marked as European might be more willing to construct belonging to Europe. For instance, we assumed that participants in the ECC project were interested in issues and themes related to Europe and the EU, which was behind the project. The interviewees' answers were therefore more likely to confirm or possibly strengthen the interviewee's existing set of attitudes and ideas. We were not able to analyze the connection between personal engagement in cultural activities and stronger sense of belonging to Europe in the EHL data, since the majority of the interviewed visitors were not aware that the Label had been awarded to the EHL site they were visiting (see Lähdesmäki et al. 2020; Čeginskas 2019). Based on this data, we suggest that personal engagement in European-themed cultural events and activities is more likely to be interconnected with various reasons and motivations.

2.7   *Mobility*

In the three case studies, our interviews and survey did not include specific questions on mobility, movement, and migration but mobility crystallized as an important theme and social phenomenon to which people referred in manifold ways during the qualitative interviews and in survey responses. We understand mobility experiences referring to experiences with cross-border mobility, which influence people's individual transnational practices in terms of "individual ties, interactions, and mobility across borders" (Kuhn 2015, 31) that enable them to develop specific transnational skills or affect their choices in life (see Favell 2008; Kuhn 2011).

Mobility experiences equally affected visitors' views on belonging to Europe, as we particularly noted in our EHL data set. While not all interviewees referred to personal experiences of transnational mobility, or mentioned explicitly their lack of them in the interviews, 29% of the EHL visitors (68 out of a total of 230) across all age groups integrated their personal experiences with various forms of mobility in their answers (see Table 7.10). These experiences included long-term migration experiences, periods studying or working abroad, extensive and frequent travels, or possessing summer cottages abroad, all of which enabled the interviewees to learn more and talk about other people and practices. We noticed that if an interviewee had personal experiences of mobility, she or he was more likely to refer to mobility and to relate it to issues such as European heritage, identity, and belonging. This suggests that people consider their personal mobility experiences as having a profound impact on themselves, their views and positionings in the world, and as giving them another perspective to that of those who did not move. Our findings suggest that transnational mobility experiences are a marker of difference akin to other social and cultural factors, such as age, gender, or education (see Favell 2008; Faist 2014, 212).

The group of interviewees aged 66 and over addressed personal mobility experiences most (72% of this age group); they referred to extensive travels or long-term stays abroad for professional reasons, but also to memories of displacement during or right after World War II. The middle-aged interviewees made the least reference to their personal mobility experiences (or lack of them) in their answers (43%), while more than half of the interviewees under the age of 35 years referred to such experiences. There was an equally high number (92%) of interviewees in the young and middle-aged age groups who linked their answers to personal mobility experiences (see Table 7.10). Middle-aged persons often highlighted extensive travels or longer professional stays abroad. In contrast, younger people more frequently referred to exchanges (most notably Erasmus) or internships abroad, which testifies to the rise and attractivity of such programmes over the recent decades (Cairns 2017). They often explained their motivation for participating in exchanges with an increased interest in encountering people from different countries and learning more about their lifestyles in terms of 'seeing and getting to know the world'.

TABLE 7.10   Personal mobility experiences (explicit mentions of a stay abroad; Erasmus or equivalent; migration experience; extensive travel, N = 68) versus non-mobility experiences (explicit mentions of being non-mobile, N = 4) among EHL visitors from EU countries and from Russia, Switzerland, and Ukraine in relation to age groups

Age group	Mentions being mobile	Mentions being non-mobile
18–35	92%	8%
36–65	92%	8%
66+	100%	0%
Total	94%	6%

We noticed that mobility duration often affected the extent to which the interviewees felt European. People who mentioned longer stays abroad or who travelled extensively and frequently in Europe and other parts of the world more often expressed that they strongly felt European, and often found the national framework limiting for constituting belonging. In this respect, mobility strengthened self-reflection about who the 'others' are and transformed views on the issue of belonging by emphasizing its personal aspects. However, our data set included too few interviewees (just four visitors) who explicitly mentioned having no or not enough mobility experiences to draw any reliable conclusion based on how limited mobility may affect people's sense of being and feeling European.

We also noticed that a great number of the EHL interviewees with transnational mobility experiences judged mobility as a (even very) positive experience (see Table 7.11). Within this, we perceived age-related differences: young adults were the most likely to view mobility positively. While the oldest age group often had positive associations with mobility, they differentiated more carefully between voluntary (positive) and forced (negative) movement. Happy memories of meeting one's future partner abroad or residing and working in different countries were contrasted in the same interviews with experiences of displacement and deportation during and shortly after World War II. Some interviewees also spoke critically about mobility in the current political climate in Europe and linked it with the humanitarian crisis of receiving refugees in Europe. Others, particularly middle-aged visitors, also referred to negative effects of inner-European migration and revealed concerns for safeguarding social standards and rights. In contrast, the younger generation often

TABLE 7.11   Mobility associations in relation to age group among EHL visitors from EU countries, Russia, Switzerland and Ukraine in four groups (positive N = 90, neutral N = 43, negative N = 2, both positive and negative associations N = 8)

Age group	Positive associations with mobility	Neutral associations with mobility	Negative associations with mobility	Both positive and negative associations
18–35	70%	23%	2%	4%
36–65	57%	38%	2%	3%
66+	60%	27%	0%	13%
Total	62%	31%	1%	6%

viewed mobility and movement less critically and focused in their narratives on (recent) personal benefits and concrete experiences of privileged mobility.

Moreover, our analysis revealed that those interviewees who expressed positive associations with mobility also often strongly felt European (72%, see Table 7.12), which confirms mobility as an important factor and social phenomenon in both European integration and feeling belonging to Europe (see e.g. Favell 2008; Recchi and Favell 2009). Interpersonal relationships, travel, and exchanges across European countries contribute to deepening awareness of cultural diversity in Europe, which interviewees commonly viewed as an important and descriptive feature of what represents Europe. At the same time, individual mobility enables cross-border encounters and transnational interaction that often have the psychological effect of mitigating national boundaries or political, cultural, and social differences within Europe (see also Kuhn 2011), and thereby help individuals feel that they share commonalities with citizens of other European countries.

TABLE 7.12   Mobility associations in relation to feeling European (strong feelings N = 122; feeling several belongings N = 41; no feelings N = 22; unable to say N = 5) among EHL visitors from EU countries, Russia, Switzerland and Ukraine

Feeling European	Strongly feels European	Feels also European	Does not feel European	Unable to say
Positive associations with mobility	72%	21%	4%	4%
Neutral associations with mobility	50%	28%	19%	3%
Negative associations with mobility	0%	50%	50%	0%
Both positive and negative associations with mobility	71%	29%	0%	0%
Total	65%	24%	8%	3%

The ability to establish positive associations with (manifold forms of) mobility played a role across all age groups among those interviewees who strongly felt European, but it was a particularly important aspect among young interviewees as the interviews revealed (see Table 7.13). Younger interviewees often considered mobility as a right – and display of their personal freedom – that they took for granted, and which determined their space of movement and belonging. In this context, the European integration becomes a relevant factor for guaranteeing the continuation and extension of this right.

TABLE 7.13   Positive associations with mobility according to age (N in age groups from the youngest to oldest: 22, 21, 15, and 58) and strongly feeling European among EHL visitors from EU countries, Russia, Switzerland, and Ukraine

Age group	18–35	36–65	66+	Total
Strongly felt European and had positive associations with mobility	85%	64%	68%	72%

Our analysis suggests that the quality of mobility experiences affected the extent to which interviewees felt European. Similarly, the more positive associations with mobility the interviewees had, the better they were able to describe what European identity represented (see Table 7.14). While the people with the most mobility experiences in our data set, the interviewees aged 66 and over, expressed feeling European (74%) the most (see also Table 7.3), they were often less able to describe what a European identity is. However, the older group contained the smallest number of interviewees with a higher education, which might have affected their ability to express their notions and thoughts on Europe and the European. European integration has increased over the past decades and through banal practices (Billig 1995) the ability to describe Europe has increased. The younger interviewees were born into a different framework and more readily adopted new practices than the middle-aged and

TABLE 7.14   Mobility associations and ability to describe European identity (able N = 106; unable N = 55; thinks it does not exist N = 21) in EHL visitors from EU countries, Russia, Switzerland, and Ukraine

	Is able to describe European identity	Unable to describe European identity but believes it exists	Thinks that European identity does not exist
Positive associations with mobility	69%	17%	14%
Neutral associations with mobility	47%	40%	13%
Negative associations with mobility	50%	50%	0%
Both positive and negative associations with mobility	57%	43%	0%
Total	61%	26%	13%

older generations. The interviewees in the older two age groups had seen the implementation of new European symbols, such as the common currency and European citizenship, alongside existing national symbols and practices, as discussed in Chapter 6.

Mobility is an important social factor in the EU's politics of belonging and connects to practices of EU citizenship, processes of integration, and social equality concerns, making the context of mobility experiences important for the individual, too. Increasing mobility is a central aim of the EU cultural policy (see Chapter 2). Our findings reveal that mobility is an important phenomenon in constructing belonging and intersects with the interviewees' social locations. Diverse experiences of mobility, such as extensive travel, study exchanges, and migration for work or for love can make European citizens feel more European. Mobility often leads to meaningful relationships between people from different backgrounds. This enables learning about cultural and social practices that provide insight into Europe's cultural diversity, without it becoming viewed as a source of friction and new conflict. Among young people in particular, positive experiences of mobility increase their sense of belonging to Europe and to the EU as a political, economic, and socio-cultural entity. The analysis of our case studies confirms that mobility has become increasingly significant in recent decades. It stands for globalization and collective networking in both positive and negative ways – maintaining and increasing personal freedoms but deepening social inequalities between people. Transnational mobility experiences seem to construct a cleavage between mobile and less mobile EU citizens, creating new forms of social inclusion and exclusion based on citizens' unequal and stratified involvement in transnational interactions (Kuhn 2019, 1222; see also Faist 2014). Thus, it has an impact on the visitors' answers, and conditions their relationship to and understanding of Europe and the 'European'.

References

Baute, S., K. Abts, and B. Meuleman 2019. "Public Support for European Solidarity: Between Euroscepticism and EU Agenda Preferences?" *Journal of Common Market Studies* 57 (3): 533–550. DOI: 10.1111/jcms.12833

Billig, M. 1995. *Banal Nationalism.* London, Thousand Oaks and New Delhi: Sage.

Bourdieu, P. 1984. *Distinction. A Social Critique of the Judgement of Taste.* Routledge, London.

Bourdieu, P. 1987. "The Forms of Capital." In *Handbook of Theory and Research of the Sociology of Education*, edited by J. G. Richardson, 241–258. New York: Greenwood Press.

Brack N., and A. Crespy 2019. "Belgium in Search of a Stance on Today's EU Integration Dilemmas." In *The Future of Europe*, edited by M. Kaeding, J. Pollak, and P. Schmidt, 5–8. Cham: Palgrave Macmillan. doi: 10.1007/978-3-319-93046-6_2

Breakwell, G. M. 2004. "Identity Change in the Context of the Growing Influence of European Union Institutions." In *Transnational Identities. Becoming European in the EU*, edited by R. K. Hermann, T. Risse, and M. B. Brewer, 25–39. Oxford: Rowman & Battlefield.

Cairns, D. 2017. "The Erasmus Undergraduate Exchange Programme: A Highly Qualified Success Story?" *Children's Geographies* 15 (6): 728–740. doi: 10.1080/14733285.2017.1328485

Citrin, J., and J. Sides 2004. "More than Nationals: How Identity Choice Matters in the New Europe." In *Transnational Identities. Becoming European in the EU*, edited by R. K. Hermann, T. Risse, and M. B. Brewer, 161–185. Lanham, Boulder: Rowman & Littlefield Publishers.

Čeginskas, V. L. A. 2016. "'I am Europe'. Experiences of Multiple Belonging." *Ethnologia Fennica* 43: 72–88. Accessed 23 April 2020. https://journal.fi/ethnolfenn/article/view/65636/26505

Čeginskas, V. L. A. 2019. "The Challenges in Creating Visibility of European Cultural Heritage: A Case Study of the European Heritage Label." *Ethnologia Fennica* 46: 109–134.

Delhey, J., E. Deutschman, T. Graf, and K. Richter. 2014. "Measuring the Europeanization of Everyday Life: Three New Indices and an Empirical Application." *European Societies* 16 (3): 355–377. doi: 10.1080/14616696.2014.904916

Deutsch, K. W. 1957. *Political Community and the North Atlantic Area: International Organization in the Light of Historical Experience*. Princeton: Princeton University Press.

Deutsch, K. W. 1966. *International Political Communities*. New York: Anchor Books edition Garden City.

Deutsch, K. W. 1969. *Nationalism and Its Alternatives*. New York: Alfred Knopf Inc.

EC (European Commission). 2019. *2019 Report on equality between women and men in the EU*. Brussels: European Commission. doi: 10.2838/395144

Faist, T. 2014. "On the Transnational Social Question: How Social Inequalities are Reproduced in Europe." *Journal of European Social Policy* 24 (3): 207–222. doi: 10.1177/0958928714525814

Favell, A. 2008. *Eurostars and Eurocities. Free Movement and Mobility in an Integrating Europe*. Malden: Blackwell Publishing.

Jacquot, S. 2015. *Transformation in EU Gender Equality. From Emergence to Dismantling*. Gender and Politics Series. Houdsmills, and Basingstoke: Palgrave Macmillan.

Jeffery, C., R. Wyn Jones, A. Henderson, R. Scully, and G. Lodge 2014. *Taking England Seriously: The New English Politics*. ESRC Scottish Centre on Constitutional Change. Accessed 7 January 2020. https://www.research.ed.ac.uk/portal/files/20030688/Taking_England_Seriously_The_New_English_Politics.pdf

Knopf, H.-J. 2002. "Britain and European Integration between 1950 and 1993: Towards a European Identity?" PhD diss. Department of Social and Political Sciences. Florence: European University Institute.

Kuhn, T. 2011. "Individual Transnationalism, Globalisation and Euroscepticism: An empirical test of Deutsch's transactionalist theory." *European Journal of Political Research* 50 (6): 811–837. doi: 10.1111/j.1475-6765.2011.01987.x

Kuhn, T. 2015. *Experiencing European Integration: Transnational Lives and European Identity*. Oxford: Oxford University Press.

Kuhn, T. 2019. "Grand Theories of European Integration Revisited: Does Identity Politics Shape the Course of European Integration?" *Journal of European Public Policy* 26 (8): 1213–1230. doi: 10.1080/13501763.2019.1622588

Lähdesmäki, T. 2013. "Identity Politics of the European Capital of Culture Initiative and the Audience Reception of Cultural Events Compared." *The Nordic Journal of Cultural Policy* 16 (2): 340–365.

Lähdesmäki, T. 2014a. "The Influence of Cultural Competence on the Interpretations of Territorial Identities in the European Capitals of Culture." *Baltic Journal of European Studies* 4 (1): 69–96.

Lähdesmäki, T. 2014b. "European Capital of Culture Designation as an Initiator of Urban Transformation in the Post-socialist Countries." *European Planning Studies* 22 (3): 481–497.

Lähdesmäki, T., V. L. A. Čeginskas, S. Kaasik-Krogerus, K. Mäkinen, and J. Turunen. 2020. *Creating and Governing Cultural Heritage in the European Union: The European Heritage Label*. London: Routledge.

Lähdesmäki, T., and T. Saresma. 2014. "Reframing Gender Equality in Finnish Online Discussion on Immigration: Populist Articulations of Religious Minorities and Marginalized Sexualities." *NORA—Nordic Journal of Feminist and Gender Research* 22 (4): 299–313.

Lee, C., and R. Bideleux 2009. "'Europe': What Kind of Idea?" *The European Legacy* 14 (2): 163–176.

Mälksoo, M. 2009. "The Memory Politics of Becoming European: The East European Subaltern and the Collective Memory of Europe." *European Journal of International Relations* 15(4), 653–680. doi: 10.1177/1354066109345049

Mälksoo, M. 2014. "Criminalizing Communism: Transnational Mnemopolitics in Europe." International Political Sociology 8 (1): 82–99. doi: 10.1111/ips.12041

Marcussen, M., T. Risse, D. Engelmann-Martin, H.-J. Knopf and K. Roscher 1999. "Constructing Europe: The Evolution of French, British and German Nation-State Identities." *Journal of European Public Policy* 6 (4): 614–633.

Ormston, R. 2015. *Disunited Kingdom: Attitudes to the EU across the UK*. Accessed 7 January 2020. http://whatukthinks.org/eu/wp-content/uploads/2015/12/Analysis-paper-3-Disunited-kingdom.pdf

Recchi, E., and A. Favell, eds. 2009. *Pioneers of European Integration. Citizenship and Mobility in the EU*. Cheltenham: Edgar Elgar Publishing Inc.

Risse, T. 2004. "European Institutions and Identity Change: What Have We Learned?" In *Transnational Identities. Becoming European in the EU*, edited by R. K. Hermann, T. Risse, and M. B. Brewer, 247–271. Oxford: Rowman & Battlefield.

Risse, T., D. Engelmann-Martin, H.-J. Knopf, and K. Roscher 1999. "To Euro or Not to Euro. The EMU and Identity Politics in the European Union." *European Journal of International Relations* 5 (2): 147–187.

Sinardet, D. 2013. "How Linguistically Divided Media Represent Linguistically Divisive Issues. Belgian TV-Debates on Brussels-Halle-Vilvoorde." *Regional & Federal Studies* 23 (3): 311–330. doi: 10.1080/13597566.2013.773895

Wyn Jones, R., G. Lodge, C. Jeffery, G. Gottfried, R. Scully, A. Henderson, and D. Wincott. 2013. "England and Its Two Unions: The Anatomy of a Nation and Its Discontents." Accessed 9 January 2020. http://www.ippr.org/publications/england-and-its-two-unions-the-anatomy-of-a-nation-and-its-discontents

CHAPTER 8

Conclusions: Europe's Lived Space

1 Constructing Europe from Below

In this book we explored how the participants in EU cultural initiatives construct notions of Europe and the 'European', what concrete meanings they give to them, and how they build their own relations to Europe. Hence, the focus was the construction of Europe and belonging to it from below. The analysis of our three cases, the European Capital of Culture (ECOC), the European Citizen Campus (ECC), and the European Heritage Label (EHL), clearly showed that there are many competing narratives of Europe and, concomitantly, people's narratives of belonging comprise wide-ranging, mutually interdependent, and accumulative constructions, including discrepant ones. As exemplified by our case studies, Europe means different things to different people, which suggest that it has different overlapping territorial, political, cultural, and ideological connotations. The multitude of notions of Europe among the interviewees and respondents reflects the variety of linguistic and cultural practices and historical pasts in Europe. These notions assist in creating and confirming a vague and contradicting perception of Europe as 'united in diversity'. The most frequent elements that participants used to discuss their conceptions of Europe in all our three cases included values, borders and cross-border experiences, mobility, and diversity. These elements were used in various combinations and resulted in several types of constructions of Europe, the 'European', and belonging to Europe.

The discussion of values in our data echoes the value discourse found in the EU policy documents. In this value discourse, the EU is closely linked to the development of the market economy and parliamentarian democracy over the course of the past 200 years as well as to general efforts at keeping peace between European countries. Furthermore, this discourse places the EU in the intellectual tradition of the Enlightenment and French Revolution, emphasizing human rights, freedoms, democracy, and solidarity. The values that our respondents and interviewees referred to include tolerance, the rule of law, various freedoms (e.g. opinion, press, religion, movement), human rights, openness, equality, and solidarity. However, the same values can be used for both drawing and crossing boundaries within Europe and between Europe and 'non-Europe'. Some of our respondents and interviewees highlighted these values as a way of overcoming the internal European divisions caused by past wars, conflicts, and invasions. They understood these values as symbolizing

© TUULI LÄHDESMÄKI ET AL., 2021 | DOI: 10.1163/9789004449800_008

belonging to Europe in the age of globalization, interconnection, and Brexit, and as a means of facing common concerns and challenges, such as climate crisis. Some framed these values as tightly 'European' and a few interpreted them even as a basis for perceiving Europe as a progressive and morally highly developed, and thus a more exclusive entity. Others emphasized values as an inspiration for more inclusive attitudes towards 'others' in terms of non-Europeans and non-EU citizens. However, in general, Europe was still frequently identified with 'Western' Europe and its specific value discourse, while East European countries continued to represent the 'European other' for many West European interviewees. In other contexts, the Americas, Africa, Oceania, or Asia were repeatedly referred to as the main group of what constituted 'the real others'. Usually, the discourse included references to the European social welfare system or model of parliamentarian democracy, which were viewed as marking Europe as distinctive from other countries and continents.

Other commonly used tropes in our data deal with borders, bordering, and movement across borders. In the case of the EHL data, many of our fieldwork heritage sites are situated close to national borders, which might have prompted many interviewees to allude to borders and how unrestricted mobility helps overcome national and cultural boundaries and thereby defines their perception of today's Europe (see also Lähdesmäki et al. 2020). Mobility was frequently referred to in our ECOC and ECC data as well, so it can be seen as central to how participants in the EU cultural initiatives constructed Europe and their relations to it. The emphasis on mobility was also closely linked to another central element, cultural diversity, which was commonly raised in discussions on Europe and the 'European'. Europe was often characterized as culturally diverse, and this diversity was seen as manifested through cultural exchanges in Europe and personally experienced while travelling in Europe.

Although our focus is on participants and visitors with a privileged background to three central EU cultural initiatives, we believe that our book offers new findings about the construction of a cultural discourse of Europe. In sum, our findings suggest that the participants in EU cultural initiatives emphasized a cultural dimension in their relationship to Europe and constructed 'Europe' as a historically grown or contemporary-focused cultural space with a social responsibility towards its community of people, rather than in terms of a clearly bounded territorial entity (see also Risse 2004, 256).

2   Two Narratives of Europe

In our empirical data, experiences of mobility and cultural diversity are significant for characterizing today's Europe and perceiving it as an 'object of identification' (see also Delhey et al. 2014, 357). According to our analysis, the interrelation of these two phenomena, mobility and cultural diversity, helps to produce belonging to Europe imagined as a cultural and social entity. A culturally diverse Europe corresponds to most of our interviewees' and respondents' conception of Europe and reflects the socio-spatial embeddedness of people and their practices. However, the notions of cultural diversity in our data resulted in two different ways of understanding Europe, and the personal experience of mobility is a decisive factor here. To put it bluntly: on the one hand, cultural diversity was viewed as preventing the emergence of European identity; on the other hand, diversity was considered a core element of European identity shaped by transnational experiences that also involved personal mobility and various forms of cross-border interactions. Therefore, based on our data, we have formulated two narratives capturing the main elements that our interviewees and respondents used when constructing their conceptions of Europe and their relations to it, focusing particularly on cultural diversity and mobility.

These narratives inform a spatial and cultural discourse of Europe between "spaces of places and flows" (see Sassatelli 2010; Castells 1999, 2000). Sassatelli draws on Castells' (1999, 2000) theory of the network society for explaining how a complex interplay and interrelation between a 'space of places' (e.g. the EU) and a 'space of cultural flows' (e.g. new communication processes, technological change, information) shapes contemporary social organization, and affects the transformation of social relationships and people's situatedness in the context of European politics of belonging. According to Castells, social organization and political representations, just like many personal experiences, take place within spatially defined places "whose form, function, and meaning are self-contained within the boundaries of territorial contiguity" (Castells 1999, 296). However, influential societal networks and systems as well as personal networks are organized around the space of cultural flows that enable a "simultaneity of social practices without geographical contiguity" (Castells 2000, 14) through producing hubs of interaction and connection between different flows, which can lead to processes of decentralizing responsibilities and resources in the space of places. As Sassatelli (2010) points out in the context of the European Landscape Convention, the cultural policies of the EU, and the notions of belonging they bring about through the creation of a specific cultural discourse, seem to function as a 'space of flows', while the (nation) state remains the 'space of places'. We see the same phenomenon grounded on the emphasis on cultural diversity and mobility in our data. While the two narratives constitute distinct discourses, people may draw on both to construct their personal narratives of belonging. In our previous chapters (Chapters 4–7) we provided evidence how these narratives interact with each other in constructing notions of Europe and the 'European' based on travel and manifold transnational and interpersonal interactions, which helped to produce an experience of cultural difference that shaped people's notion of cultural diversity and equally affected the meanings they gave to Europe.

In the first narrative, Europe is understood in terms of different nation states and cultures, and the cultural differences between Europeans are seen as a decisive factor that prevents the development of a 'true' community of Europeans despite political and legal harmonization across EU member states. In this narrative, the interviewees and respondents refer to examples of experiencing difference in their everyday lives, such as the multitude of European languages, but they also repeat the EU's grand narrative about a shared history and appreciate the values embedded in it, such as peace, freedoms, and democracy. Belonging to Europe is predominantly understood in terms of creating normative and functional relations with Europe, for instance based on sharing common political and economic interests or practical benefits in the EU framework. Hence, Europe is conceived as a culturally diverse but essentially political and economic entity. At the same time, this conception emphasizes that power relations between European countries are unequal based on perceived economic and political differences. The cultural aspect remains abstract, and a personal dimension of constructing belonging to Europe or to an imagined community across 'fixed' national boundaries seems to be missing here. Frequently, this narrative includes the fear that a European belonging may lead to the homogenization of Europe's cultural differences. While this narrative depicts Europe as being under construction, it simultaneously conveys the opinion that the goal of European identity will never be attained because of witnessed cultural diversity. The respondents and interviewees frequently used emotionally loaded terms such as identity, roots, and home, which shows the relevance of the affective dimension in the discussion of belonging to Europe. But the reference to identity, roots, or an emphasis on a common history also serves to construct narratives of exclusion.

In the second narrative, the notion of a culturally diverse Europe supports the acceptance of communality among Europeans across national borders despite persisting cultural differences. While the 'European' still incorporates the notion of a common history of wars and invasions that used to separate Europeans in the past, the personal experience of mobility, e.g. travel and various forms of cross-border interactions, indicates a shift in the understanding of the past and its significance for people today. Cultural differences are not considered as creating decisive antagonism between Europeans, but they are regarded as defining Europe in a positive way. This cultural diversity represented the 'charm' and 'essence' of Europe for both European citizens and non-European citizens alike. The association of Europe and Europeans with existent cultural and linguistic plurality is further reinforced by people's individual mobility, in terms of travels or student and professional exchanges.

In the second narrative, personal, individual, and first-hand encounters and social relationships with other Europeans – through work, studies, travel, family links, or friendships – have an important influence on how our interviewees and respondents perceive and describe belonging to Europe. In this narrative, Europe is often associated with everyday practices of 'doing Europe': taking part in dialogue, exchange, and encounters across plural boundaries. The narrative stresses the possibility of developing and sharing cross-cultural commonality based on experiences and encounters in everyday situations. First-hand transnational encounters enable the construction of a sense of 'lived' European reality, based on the legal and political harmonization of frameworks in the EU and associated states in Europe. In this respect, the relation to Europe goes beyond the functional aspect of the EU, reflecting a personal approach to belonging and connecting with feelings towards fellow Europeans that are used to construct a notion of a transnational 'shared space' in Europe. This space is not territory-specific but brings together Europe's various 'others', including citizens of other EU member states, citizens of non-EU member states in Europe, and, in some cosmopolitan or humanist views, even 'non-European others', such as third-country citizens residing in a EU country and refugees. In this narrative, the EU is understood as a social entity and personal signifier that both guarantees the necessary social and civic rights and facilitates cultural and personal experiences of Europe as a "lived space" (Lefebvre 1991, 362).

Both narratives share the idea that the national antagonism between European states, which used to fuel European wars in the past, has been overcome. Participants in the EU cultural initiatives no longer thematize cultural differences as a potential source of future military conflicts between European states. In both narratives, the perceptions connect to legal and political harmonization of frameworks in the EU and its associated states. Another commonality to both narratives is that values, such as equality, social justice, human rights, peace and rule of law, are a central means of depicting Europe. Participants in the EU cultural initiatives thus use both legal and political integration as well as values to construct Europe in terms of a shared cultural space in both narratives. However, in the second narrative, the emphasis on mobility and interpersonal interaction enables the participants to conceive Europe as a more tangible social space that is concretely experienced in their lives and has a greater personal relevance for them. This emphasis challenges people's nation-based territorial socio-spatial attachments and instead can help to create a transnational notion of a cultural community of Europeans. Such an idea of transnational cultural community does not exclude simultaneous place-specific or local, regional, and national attachments. However, the notion of Europe as a transnational cultural community is characterized by multifarious interpretations of Europe in various European countries and economic, social and political inequality may deepen the gap between them.

A significant difference between the two narratives lies in the perception of who is included in, or excluded from, and, hence, entitled to belong to this cultural space. While values are used in both narratives, the second narrative emphasizes that they can help to unite different groups, including non-European citizens who have moved to Europe for various reasons. This narrative is more common among young people who seem more likely to have early experiences of and with mobility (such as exchanges), among people with transnational family links, and among older participants (particularly in Western European countries) who often described themselves as the generation that supported the visionary beginnings of the EU after the experiences of World War II. In contrast, many middle-aged interviewees and respondents follow the first narrative and predominantly connect the construction of Europe with an identity discourse analogue to national identity discourses. Cultural differences, the lack of a common language, as well as a history of violent conflicts, wars, and antagonism are viewed as real and continuing obstacles to creating a 'united Europe', and thus affect people's construction of belonging to Europe and views on the EU.

The two narrative strands reveal that views on European belonging and integration are polarized along the lines of mobility. While some Europeans share such experiences, others do not. Mobility experiences provide a different access to Europe and the EU and promote a more concrete and affective way of constructing belonging than narratives of common values or legal and political harmonization, which may remain remote and abstract. Particularly for the younger generation, narratives that stress personal experiences of intercultural dialogue, peaceful exchanges, and experiences of mobility across national borders seem to have become new powerful, empowering, and more concrete narratives. Thus, mobility is a key aspect in EU cultural policies that function as a means for reflecting the interdependencies of belonging between places and flows on the one hand and at the same time enable to re-conceptualize diversity and change as compatible with unity on the other (see Sassatelli 2010, 80). The latter is achieved by defining diversity and change as part of a 'lived experience' of Europe that additionally has the effect of softening and relativizing these multiple cultural differences in Europe. The emphasis on mobility and dialogue does not replace the frequently repeated 'grand narratives' on peace and values as a foundation of EUrope but helps to broaden them and give them a new tone. Through this emphasis, then, mobility becomes an important component in the EU's value discourse. At the same time, mobility poses a new challenge to understanding Europe in the context of current (im-)mobilities of migrants, refugees, and asylum seekers in Europe, and intertwines with issues of social justice, participation, EU citizenship, and belonging. The two narratives therefore speak of the challenges in building Europe as a cultural and social entity, which our interviewed and surveyed European citizens were concerned about and in which they themselves played an active part.

3   Europe in the Making: Multilevel Dynamics of Europeanization

Our analysis shows that the participants of the EU cultural initiatives actively participated in the meaning-making of Europe as a socio-cultural space in all its dimensions that goes beyond a passive reception of the EU rhetoric into their construction of a socio-cultural discourse of Europe. However, their various narratives on Europe that help to construct their imaginary and subjective notion of community and belonging to Europe do not drastically differ from the ways, in which dominant EU narratives are produced.

In all our cases, Europe and the EU overlapped very frequently. The close connection between Europe and the EU has a formative influence on how people living in Europe construct belonging to Europe from below – including their images of Europe and how they want it to develop in future. The interviewees and respondents often referred to the EU when they discussed European identity or their own feelings of 'Europeanness'. For example, the participants in the EU cultural initiatives commonly discussed Europe by referring to institutional arrangements established by EU integration, such as the Euro currency, EU citizenship, freedom of mobility, and common policies in the fields of international relations, the economy, and trade. In addition, the EU was entwined more indirectly with other types of discussions on Europe and belonging to it in our data. In turn, sometimes they used the term Europe even when clearly discussing matters related to EU integration and institutions. The notions of Europe constructed from below are closely connected with the EU but also go beyond it. Thus, in our data Europe and the EU formed an ambivalent entity of EUrope (see Chapter 1).

Our ethnography of Europeanization enabled us to explore the interrelations between the micro, meso, and macro levels and their impact on constructions of Europe from below. Our findings show that regarding the politics of belonging in EU cultural policy, these levels intermingle and connect in various ways. Our analysis indicated that the interviewees and respondents often repeated EU rhetoric and used EU symbols when discussing Europe and belonging to Europe, which suggests that they have adopted the EU discourse of 'shared values' and a 'common future'. However, many of them rejected the concept of identity, thereby detaching themselves from the macro-level EU discourses that explicitly used the concept in their politics of belonging. As we discussed in Chapter 6, rejection of the concept did not necessarily entail negative attitudes to Europe in general. Many of our interviewees and respondents depicted Europe as a 'community in the making', and while they often acknowledged the EU's top-down endeavors to construct Europe, they also highlighted citizens' personal contributions and active participation in its construction. Thus, they perceived belonging to Europe as based on activity, agency, and participation in a community (of people) of which they felt part.

Perceptions of Europe created from below are reflected in the EU's official policy ideas and in turn, these EU discourses are adopted in people's everyday practices and lives. As our findings demonstrate, Europe is understood at the micro level in terms of individual situatedness and belonging, as well as expectations and ideas that refute understanding Europe as a mere top-down political project. The EU discourse does not only reach the micro level through top-down diffusion. This discourse also emerges from the bottom up. It is important to remember that EU civil servants and experts who help to design policy documents are themselves European citizens and therefore their policy discourse replicates the narratives they experience in their everyday lives (Risse 2004).

As discussed above, the participants in the EU cultural initiatives repeatedly referred to legal and political harmonization within the EU in their accounts on Europe and their own relations to it. At the same time, despite many interviewees and respondents characterizing the EU as an economic and institutional entity, the analysis of the data revealed more nuances to this view and showed that many people take a cultural approach to the Union. In our data, the imagination of Europe as a cultural space is closely interrelated with perceptions of a social reality in Europe that is strongly shaped by actual EU policies and provisions. Since the 1990s the EU has become more tangible in people's everyday lives, starting with the single market, the introduction of EU citizenship, the implementation of a single currency (the Euro), and the promotion of free movement of EU citizens in the framework of the Schengen Agreement. The public debates about Eastern enlargement and about institutional reform and an EU Constitution have contributed to increase the public visibility of the Union since the early 2000s. At the same time, the EU has consolidated its role as a political actor for and 'voice' of Europe's states, going beyond the perception of the Union as an economic market. Attempts to construct the EU as a significant global player include both the development of the EU institutions and the efforts to promote identification with the EU narrative and value discourses (see also Risse 2004, 267).

EU cultural policy seeks to further increase the EU's visibility in citizens' lives and to create a greater sense of belonging to Europe through its programmes and initiatives, as we have discussed in this book. For example, the EHL is envisioned to cover 100 heritage sites within and outside EU member states by 2030 (EC 2017a). By doing this, the original aim of the Label as a cultural action of the EU is extended to help construct a notion of a shared, transnational 'European cultural space' across the bounded space of the EU. At the same time, EU cultural policy contributes to blurring the boundaries between the EU and its member states as well as between EU and non-EU countries. The multi-layered discourse of the European dimension in the ECOC and the insistence on European significance in the EHL avoid addressing the national layer, which is often perceived in the EU policy discourse as a challenge to the construction of the European (Lähdesmäki and Mäkinen 2019; Lähdesmäki et al. 2020). As a result of the increasing visibility of the EU in the media and everyday life, through its cultural initiatives and numerous other channels, citizens engage in a process of constructing 'banal Europeanism', which is enabled by similar triggers and processes as seen in banal nationalism (Billig 1995; see also Cram 2012 and previous chapters in this book), as our data also indicates.

Previous studies have highlighted the high psychological reality of the EU observed among Europe's political, economic, and social elites, whose dealings and business in Europe make them constantly aware of and refer to EU rules and regulations (see Hermann et al. 2004). Castano (2004) argues that processes of political and economic integration can make the EU become real and supports the conception of Europe as community arising from shared cultural values, a perceived common destiny, increased salience, and boundedness. In this respect, the EU and its policies shape European citizens' social reality. Equally, we can see people taking specific EU provisions and regulations, such as mobility or social equality policies, for granted, which increases the perceived normality of the EU in people's everyday practices and lives. In the context of mobility, the EU plays a significant role in facilitating movement and encounters between European citizens, which in turn makes the EU become a real psychological existence and a personal signifier for some people (see also Cram 2012).

As our analysis of cultural Europeanization in this book manifests, notions from above and below mutually influence each other in people's imagination of Europe as a cultural space. Thus, we see EU politics of belonging playing a role in people's constructions of belonging, attachments, and interests, which suggests that Europeanization is a complex process, in which the micro and

macro levels of discourses and narratives about Europe conflate and mutually reinforce themselves. Our findings show that Europeanization cannot be
viewed as an isolated phenomenon that only takes place through processes
from above bringing multiple outcomes on European citizens. It needs to be
put in relation to how transnational cultural flows and processes change our
relationship to space and time, and how various forms of movement allow for
social decentralization by establishing a hub of interconnections between various spaces at different levels, and how they become reflected in politics of
belonging (see Castells 2000; Urry 2003; Sassatelli 2010). Our findings in our
previous chapters speak against a distinct separation between top-down and
bottom-up processes in how belonging and community in Europe are constructed at the micro level. Rather, we find evidence that links exist between
the construction of spatial and cultural dimensions in the narratives at the
micro, meso, and macro levels that imply multiple interrelations between
them. Thus, Europeanization includes both top-down and bottom-up processes and a circulation of ideas between various positions and levels, in which
citizens actively engage with the idea of Europe through their own agency and
thereby co-construct conceptions of what Europe is that also can impact the
cultural discourse at the EU level.

In the context of EU cultural initiatives, we therefore suggest that 'Europe'
and the 'European' are constructed in an interrelated process that refers to
networked diversity and connectivity between different notions of Europe.
Moreover, such a networked connectivity allows European citizens to associate Europe and the 'European' with everyday experiences and 'banal' representations, as well as with discourses about Europe and its people and manifold
history. The conflation of the EU and Europe in various social, political, and
economic spheres has led scholars to argue that "[o]ne could not be a 'real'
European without being an EU member", as Risse (2004, 255) has noted. As a
result, "the EU increasingly is Europe" (Risse 2004, 263) and, hence the wider
public within and outside Europe perceives European states and the EU as
pursuing similar objectives. Our findings suggest that the European integration process may have left a mark at various social and political levels, defining
both state- and nationhood in Europe. At the same time, the EU constitutes a
meaningful resource and social entity for the individual (see also Risse 2004,
255).

4   Mobility: An Answer and a Challenge to Politics of Belonging

As the core principle of the integration process, mobility is an important factor
in the EU's politics of belonging and connects to several areas of its cultural

policy, practices of citizenship, and social equality concerns. In all our three cases, mobility is at the core of how people understand contemporary Europe. Our data reveals an interrelation between the experience of culturally diverse Europe and mobility. Our interviewees and respondents commonly used this interrelation to elaborate their sense of belonging to Europe. Many of them emphasized direct connections with EUrope, that is, belonging to a borderless European space with harmonized systems where they can travel freely. Our findings thus support the assumption that the extent of individual transnational interaction is key to 'feeling European' (see also Kuhn 2011).

Mobility has changed people's personal identification and relationship with Europe and the ways they think about fellow Europeans. It has transformed the notion of who (and what) 'we' are and who the 'others' are. Individual experiences of mobility – whether studying, working, or living in other European countries, and binational partnerships and ethnically mixed families – support the construction of cross-cutting and overlapping multiple allegiances that may also strengthen individuals' sense of belonging to Europe (see also Risse 2004, 251; Čeginskas 2015) while preserving distinctive local, cultural, and national allegiances. Mobility can contribute to new and lasting memories and create new connections that may foster processes of belonging and place-making, in which 'Europe' becomes meaningful and positively loaded. Some of our interviewees and respondents associated the practical effects of the EU politics of integration (such as the borderless Schengen area) with their own, personally meaningful memories and experiences. Although they had different and manifold understandings of what they associate with Europe and the 'European', our participants seem to suggest an interrelation between a 'lived' European integration and the increasing acceptance of the EU as a relevant social entity in the lives of Europeans. Particularly in the context of mobility and travel, this can produce a 'European experience' for some. The materialization of personal benefits connected with the EU may strengthen a sentiment of belonging to Europe and the EU, in particular if threats to acquired social and economic standards and security become concrete and real (see Cram 2012, 80), for instance in the contexts of the Brexit negotiations or the current political alienation between Europe and the US.

In general, according to surveys, most European citizens have positive personal experiences and associations with mobility across European borders. For instance, in a recent survey, European citizens highly valued their freedom of movement, and it is listed as a very positive result of EU integration along with 'peace among the EU member states' (Eurobarometer 2015). EU citizens' free and unrestricted mobility is usually associated with the experience of different places and cultures in Europe that enable people to learn about and to become acquainted with different practices, places, and people. Moreover, encounters between citizens of different European states often result in acknowledging the far-reaching harmonization of systems (including roaming regulations, ease of travel in the Schengen area, the common currency, standardization of various citizens' rights, etc.) and cultural interrelation between European states and people, as our data reveals.

The idea of restricting EU citizens' movement in various spheres of their public and private lives has commonly become regarded as an unpopular socio-political move, only acceptable under very specific circumstances, such as limiting the outbreak of the COVID-19 pandemic. As a result of Brexit, national-populist movements and parties in France, Sweden, and Italy no longer seek to dissociate their countries from the amenities and securities of a European single market, the Euro currency zone, and Schengen area, while they remain highly critical of the EU membership and the EU itself. This again emphasizes the extent to which individual mobility experiences and the right to free movement have a significant social impact and direct consequences for politics of belonging.

The right to free movement was one of the controversial political issues in the Brexit negotiations between the European Commission and the UK government. The apparent difficulties with 'decoupling' the UK from the EU reveal the extensive institutional, social, economic, and political interconnections between the EU and its member states. However, the highly emotional political debates and speeches in both the UK and continental media and parliaments reveal that the ties between the EU and its member states are often interpreted in terms of a specific 'cultural' connection. In this respect, the events and experiences connected with Brexit since the referendum in June 2016 prove relevant for Europe's reinvention and crucial for how the EU constructs and positions itself in the future, as well as for how belonging to Europe is perceived and constructed among European citizens.

The relevance of the right to free movement can be also seen in terms of posing new problems and hazards, as the spread of the COVID-19 pandemic across the world shows. At the time of writing (March 2020), many EU countries have taken far-reaching governmental measures to restrict movements of people across and within their borders. The new restrictions on movement, together with the call for people to practice 'physical distancing' during the health crisis, have made EU citizens notice how essential free movement has become for them, and how closely it connects to the exercise of their essential rights and civil liberties. The restriction on movement makes people directly vulnerable as regards supply chains and the economy at large, but also as individuals as regards issues, such as rise in addictions, domestic violence and abuse, or racism, and limited personal range of movement. It also connects to limitations on (national and EU) citizens' democratic rights, as seen in Hungary, where Viktor Orban has used the pandemic to increase political control over the country for his own political agenda. Similar situations can be observed in other European countries, which exemplifies the general political importance of free movement for individuals and collectives as a determining feature of our contemporary societies.

Mobility is generally associated with positive stereotypes in the context of elite mobility and privileged border-crossing, however, movement in terms of migration often still carries a stigma. The recent Brexit discussions in the UK media revealed openly xenophobic and racist views about citizens of Central and East European countries, such as Romania, Bulgaria, or Poland, and provided new insights into the stigma of mobility. Whether mobility is perceived as a positive or negative factor also affects the relationships between the EU, its citizens, and its member states. Hence, mobility has important implications for European societies and for people's constructions of belonging to Europe. On the one hand, it increases individual freedom, offers citizens new perspectives, and can favor the formation of transnational identification, rather than emphasizing membership and participation in a single political community such as the nation state (see Witte 2019, 93). These factors are particularly important for mobile people whose lifestyle challenges traditional modes of constructing belonging as well as for the socio-cultural construction of Europe (e.g. Favell 2008; Čeginskas 2016; see also Koikkalainen 2019). On the other hand, mobility in the European context is also associated with distinct social, economic, and political disadvantages. In some countries, it connects to the brain drain of young, highly educated people and loss of necessary manual laborers, while in other countries it links to increased competition for social rights between national and foreign residents and invokes fears about maintaining certain standards.

The experience of mobility reveals a new political cleavage between mobile and non-mobile EU citizens, which affects people's attitudes to European integration, their extent of association with the EU, and their willingness to transfer sentiments usually associated with the national to the 'European' (see also Bauböck 2019a; Fine 2019, 130; Kuhn 2015; Risse 2004). Several studies suggest that unequal access to resources and opportunities of transnational practices can deepen the imbalance between those people who can participate and who cannot participate in cross-border interactions (see Kuhn 2011, 815; Fligstein 2008; Faist 2014; Delhey et al. 2014). This view is supported particularly by our EHL data, which indicates that interviewees with mobility experiences were more likely to feel European and support the EU than those with limited or no mobility experiences. According to empirical research, transnational interactions have become increasingly frequent over the past decades but there is a great difference in the numbers of European citizens who engage in transnational interactions and in the extent to which they engage in them, which can result in their unequal socialization as Europeans (e.g. Favell 2008; Recchi and Favell 2009; Kuhn 2015). Also our data showed an interrelation: those people who were able and willing to engage in transnational interaction and practices were also more likely to embrace European integration as a new source of personal opportunities (see also Kuhn 2011, 2019; Faist 2014, 212). While individual experiences of transnational mobility may shape positive attitudes towards European integration, our analysis suggests that other personal dispositions or social locations, such as family background, gender, and education, also impact on people's notions of EUrope. Moreover, not every European citizen who has lived or worked abroad feels transnational and European but, on the contrary, these people can hold strong nationalistic views (the former British MEP Nigel Farage is an excellent case in point).

The right to free movement is at the core of democracy (Witte 2019, 98). It therefore closely connects with the practices and the rights of EU citizenship. In fact, the first right mentioned in the article establishing the citizenship of the European Union is the "right to move and reside freely within the territory of the Member states" (EC 2016, article 20). However, as Bauböck (2019a, 127) argues, "[a]s long as European citizenship is nearly exclusively about free movement, immobile Europeans will not perceive it as a value and as an important aspect of their identity." In the citizenship article, the only rights not about mobility are the rights to petition the European Parliament, to apply to the European Ombudsman, and to use any (official) EU language in the communication with the EU institutions and advisory bodies. In a recent edited volume (Bauböck 2019c), many prominent scholars discuss the current cleavage between mobile and immobile European citizens and address the civil, social, and political dimension of EU citizenship in the light of mobility. Their contributions add to the ongoing debates about extending voting rights in national elections to resident EU citizens from other member states. While citizenship and its practice are fundamental democratic principles, the present provision at the national and EU levels is contradictory: promoting free movement of EU citizens on the one hand and, on the other, restricting their political participation in the EU member states where they choose to reside without being citizens there. In the context of mobility, EU citizenship can change existing constructions of national identity and belonging to Europe, but being a 'mobile European' does not imply the same rights and duties as being a citizen of the EU member state in which one resides (Breakwell 2004; see also Witte 2019; Paskalev 2019).

EU citizenship and freedom of movement as one of its core aspects reveal the limits on participation and the danger of exclusion and social inequality. As Witte (2019, 95) argues:

> The construction of EU citizenship, in particularly [sic!] within the context of the rights to free movement and nondiscrimination, has the potential to lead to more inclusive ways of thinking about what freedom, justice, equality and participation should mean in the EU. It also has, however, the potential to lead to more practices of exclusion. The fact that EU citizenship and free movement are not embedded in a sufficiently sophisticated, responsive and democratic institutional structure makes it very difficult for the EU to mediate the social conflict that practices of inclusion and exclusion produce, and to legitimise the choices made.

Mobility as a social phenomenon is bound to produce divisions by assisting in creating images of first-class and second-class EU citizens and third-class migrants in the European context. Hence, it has the potential to undermine democracy. As regards third-country nationals, despite its transnational design with the aim to ensure a "new – less ethnic – way of thinking about the role on the individual in the EU" (Witte 2019, 98), EU citizenship has a strong national impetus, since it is not possible to obtain EU citizenship without first being a national citizen of one of the EU member states (see Neuvonen 2019). Several contributors to Bauböck's edited volume therefore advocate for a stronger social dimension of EU citizenship by increasing the visibility of a social Europe in order to reconcile mobile and non-mobile Europeans (see Bauböck 2019d, Part III).

5   Belonging and the Social Dimension of Europe

The cultural understanding of Europe and the EU, produced by the participants of the EU cultural initiatives in our data, includes a social dimension (see also Bruter 2004) that goes beyond the mere economic and institutional integration of Europe. The imagination of Europe as a cultural space connects to the perception of Europe as a relevant and unique space that provides social welfare. The connection of cultural and social dimensions was particularly manifest in our data through the emphasis on social rights and values, such as freedoms, equality, and justice. Freedom of mobility and peace among the EU member states were commonly highlighted as positive aspects of EU integration (see also Eurobarometer 2015). Both aspects are interconnected as the ability to move freely across national borders symbolizes peaceful relations and enables participation in a community.

The discussion on the social dimension of Europe in the EU policy discourses is part of a broader debate around Europe's future. In its White Paper on the Future of Europe (EC 2017b), the European Commission sets out a number of options for collective actions to respond to the transformations of contemporary European societies and their worlds of work. The actions are targeted at issues such as the precarity of work and housing, restructuring of work conditions, falling wages, social insecurity in the face of rising rental and purchase prices, social inequality, and poverty. The EU Charter of Fundamental Rights (Charter), which was proclaimed in 2000 but became legally binding with the Treaty of Lisbon in 2009, incorporates fundamental legal rights into EU law to ensure common standards of social justice and equality for EU citizens and residents consistent with the European Convention on Human Rights (CoE 1953). However, the Charter is not a replacement for the national systems for protecting and interpreting rights, as the recent open conflict between the Polish government and the EU on legal reform in Poland has shown.

Similarly, the European Pillar of Social Rights (Pillar) outlines a notion of Europe as a social entity that both involves EU member states and has consequences for countries in Europe that are associated with the EU. The Pillar refers to EU citizens' rights regarding the labor market, working conditions, gender equality, and social protection and inclusion, especially the rights of disabled citizens, the elderly, and children (EC 2017c). The Pillar also calls for social rights to be reinforced in order to create a "promising future for all" that should help to "build a more inclusive and sustainable growth model" that will contribute to fostering social cohesion (EC 2017c, Articles 7 and 9).

The four freedoms of movement are underpinned as a core value and right for "the peoples of Europe" in both the Charter and the Pillar (EC 2012, preamble; see also EC 2017c). As stated in the preamble of the Charter (EC 2012, 395):

> The Union contributes to the preservation and to the development of these common values while respecting the diversity of the cultures and traditions of the peoples of Europe as well as the national identities of the Member States and the organisation of their public authorities at national, regional and local levels; it seeks to promote balanced and sustainable development and ensures free movement of persons, services, goods and capital, and the freedom of establishment.

The emphasis on EU social policies fosters the perception of Europe as a social entity. The objective to increase the significance of the EU for European citizens is intertwined with cultural policy measures to increase and strengthen belonging between EU citizens and the EU. Indeed, the social dimension is embedded in various ways in EU cultural policy. The decisions of the core EU cultural programmes and initiatives call for promoting social cohesion, inclusive societies, engagement of different people, and social equality. The social dimension has recently been given a more central role in EU cultural policy discourses. In 'A New European Agenda for Culture', the European Commission has identified the social dimension as the first of its three strategic objectives for "harnessing the power of culture and cultural diversity for social cohesion and well-being" (EC 2018, 2). Interconnection between European cultural and social dimensions, thus, "brings people together", "empower[s] people", "increase[s] self-confidence", enables "community regeneration", "improves health" and "psychological well-being", and promotes "opportunities for all to take part and to create", as the Agenda envisages (EC 2018, 2–3).

Mobility (and free movement as a fundamental principle) is a factor that intertwines economic and social dimensions in the European context. The political question as to who should be able to access social rights, and who should be discouraged from doing so, reveals the dilemma inherent in the EU's politics of belonging. This question is at the core of the conflict between EU countries about immigration and asylum policies, security interests, and social (in)equality concerns and relates to the topical discussions about open and closed borders of the EU. The political dilemma about endorsed versus unwanted mobility also reveals a tension between transnational belonging to Europe as proposed by the EU and national belonging as lived in practice by many European residents (see Bauböck 2019b). This tension will not be solved in the near future, as the ongoing conflicts between EU member states on the issue of receiving refugees and migrants from poorer countries suggests. In the context of 'migration crisis' discourses, we are faced with growing practices and processes of policing mobility and securing borders within the UK-EU-Schengen area that reshape (im)mobilities across the EU, and affect both non-EU migrants and asylum seekers, as well as Europe's 'undesirable' mobile citizens, such as the Roma.

A transnational "vision of social justice" (Thym 2019, 103) based on equal and fair treatment could help to bridge the gap between immobile residents in Europe and mobile EU citizens as regards their attitudes to belonging to Europe and the EU (see also Neuvonen 2019, 114). If Europe is increasingly associated with a European social model surpassing national models of social welfare by representing harmonized social regulations on employment, health, social protection, welfare, social rights, and so forth, then European integration becomes a significant aspect of the lives of mobile and immobile residents of Europe. Indeed, our data showed that participants in the EU cultural initiatives construct belonging to Europe through value-based discourses that include references to a 'social Europe'. Thus, their imagination of Europe as a cultural space is interconnected with the imagination of Europe as a social entity, which in turn has consequences for the EU's politics of belonging.

Mobility and migration create new challenges for social rights and new categories of citizenship that transcend the traditional context of nation states (see Bauböck 2005, 2007, 2019c; Wiesner et al. 2018, 11). Mobility as a social phenomenon that defines belonging links not only to EU citizenship but also to participation – and participation enables inclusion, while limited participation increases exclusion. Belonging in the light of mobility also raises the problem of how inclusive such a 'social Europe' is and who participates in it and is entitled to claim social rights. We found some evidence that constructing boundaries is no longer seen to be as relevant among 'fellow Europeans' as against citizens from outside 'cultural Europe'; as a result, specific cultural and religious groups of people, such as Muslims, are singled out.

To construct belonging to Europe around the right to free movement equally justifies providing non-discriminatory access to social benefits to everybody in every European country (Ferrera 2019, 196). However, the social reality shows that "the mobile citizens are losing a significant aspect of their freedom due to their movement", as Paskalev (2019, 119) points out. This concerns practices of social rights and inclusion, which applies not only to mobile EU citizens but equally to permanent, long-term EU citizens residing in another EU country and migrants and refugees from outside EU countries (see Rodríguez 2019, 71; Swoboda 2019, 56). Some EU citizens may perceive the act of extending social rights to citizens from another EU country or to non-EU immigrants as reducing the value of nationals' rights and opportunities. This may result in alienation from the EU and fuel inner-societal conflicts. Therefore, confining the imagination of Europe to mobility and EU citizenship potentially replicates the "exclusionary 'community of fate' transnationally", as Neuvonen (2019, 114–115) cautions.

In the context of mobility, it is therefore important to discuss who the 'people of Europe' with whom "Europe starts" (as in the EHL slogan) actually are. All mobility is not equally accepted, and our interviewees and respondents distinguish between travel, intra-European movement, and migration from outside the European continent into the EU. Nevertheless, mobility can help to deconstruct real and imagined boundaries and borders among EU citizens and residents and thereby create cohesion. Thus, it can promote recognition of Europe, characterized by transnational cultural and social dimensions with which it is desirable for EU citizens to identify, that equally shapes and inter-twines ideas about belonging to Europe and the EU.

6   The EU's Politics of Belonging: Opportunities for the Future

While EU cultural policy complicates the distinction between the EU and Europe, its transnational perspective on culture and heritage offers new ways of dealing with and negotiating what the EU and Europe actually are and who belongs to them. EU cultural initiatives may encourage people in Europe to exchange their views and experiences as well as helping both policy-makers and fellow citizens to listen to different 'voices'. With regard to the EU's cur-rent politics of belonging, we can note that in some areas and for some people it is very successful, but in other areas and for other people Europe does not evoke or enable feelings of belonging. Our book proposes a strong interrelation between belonging, identity, participation, and citizenship by foregrounding the importance of mobility. The interrelation of and interdependence between different and distinct spatial, cultural, and social dimensions manifest through mobility and situate citizens and residents of Europe between various 'spaces of places and flows'. Similarly, mobility contributes to a cultural and spatial discourse, in which Europe is constructed as a 'lived' cultural space, in and through which people meet, cooperate and manoeuvre in their everyday lives. Our book argues for the need to acknowledge the role of culture and cultural discourses for achieving equal participation also in other policy fields. How-ever, there is a need to research further the voices of migrants and non-EU citizens, as well as EU citizens who lack resources, means, and opportunities to engage in transnational interactions within the 'European space'. Future studies on how they receive EU cultural programmes and initiatives and expe-rience participation through them could shed new light on interpretations of belonging in the European context.

The politics of belonging always connect to issues of social inclusion and participation. Therefore, it is crucial to pay attention to whether and how EU cultural policy enables and encourages citizens' participation. This means more than consuming cultural products and services and taking part in cultural activities: it means a role in decision-making and knowledge production con-cerning culture as well as producing and experiencing culture through one's own citizen-driven grass-roots activities. Only if equal and democratic partic-ipation are adopted and implemented in the EU cultural policy can manifold notions of Europe and belonging to it constructed from below become visible in the context of EU cultural initiatives. Over the past decades, there have been signs of such a participatory approach from various actors of cultural policies and practices, the EU included, but in our fieldwork data, it was not a prominent feature.

A more participatory approach to the EU's politics of belonging could yield new ways of including and limiting the exclusion of mobile and immobile residents in Europe. It can also help us to find a new *modus operandi et vivendi* vis-à-vis migrants and refugees from other parts of the world and to engage with their belonging to and inclusion in Europe. Emphasis on participation in transnational cultural and heritage policies could transform views of belonging to Europe and the EU and favor the imagination of a transnational cultural and social community of Europe. The major challenge facing EU cultural initiatives is at the same time their greatest opportunity: to find new ways of reducing social and societal polarization and advancing social cohesion and social justice in order to make belonging to Europe equally accessible to all.

References

Bauböck, R. 2005. "Expansive Citizenship – Voting beyond Territory and Membership." *PS: Political Science & Politics* 38 (4): 683–687. doi: 10.1017/S1049096505050341

Bauböck, R. 2007. "Stakeholder Citizenship and Transnational Political Participation: A Normative Evaluation of External Voting." *Fordham Law Review* 75 (5): 2393–2447.

Bauböck, R. 2019a. "The New Cleavage Between Mobile and Immobile Europeans." In *Debating European Citizenship*, edited by R. Bauböck, 125–127. IMISCOE Research Series. Cham: Springer Open Access. doi: 10.1007/978-3-319-89905-3

Bauböck, R. 2019b. "Grab the Horns of the Dilemma and Ride the Bull." In *Debating European Citizenship*, edited by R. Bauböck, 245–256. IMISCOE Research Series. Cham: Springer Open Access. doi: 10.1007/978-3-319-89905-3

Bauböck, R. ed. 2019c. *Debating European Citizenship*. IMISCOE Research Series. Cham: Springer Open Access. doi: 10.1007/978-3-319-89905-3

Bauböck, R. ed. 2019d. "PART III: Should EU-Citizenship Be Duty-Free?" In *Debating European Citizenship*, 181–291. IMISCOE Research Series. Cham: Springer Open Access. doi: 10.1007/978-3-319-89905-3

Billig, M. 1995. *Banal Nationalism*. London, Thousand Oaks, CA: Sage.

Breakwell, G. M. 2004. "Identity Change in the Context of the Growing Influence of European Union Institutions." In *Transnational Identities. Becoming European in the EU*, edited by R. K. Hermann, T. Risse, and M. B. Brewer, 25–39. Lanham, Boulder: Rowman & Littlefield Publishers.

Bruter, M. 2004. "Civic and Cultural Components of a European Identity: A Pilot Model of Measurement of Citizens' Levels." In *Transnational Identities. Becoming European in the EU*, edited by R. K. Hermann, T. Risse, and M. B. Brewer, 186–213. Oxford: Rowman & Battlefield.

Castano, E. 2004. "European Identity: A Social-Psychological Perspective." In *Transnational Identities. Becoming European in the EU*, edited by R. K. Hermann, T. Risse, and M. B. Brewer, 40–58. Lanham, Boulder: Rowman & Littlefield Publishers.

Castells, M. 1999. "Grassrooting the Spaces of Flows." *Urban Geography* 20 (4): 294–302. doi: 10.2747/0272-3638.20.4.294

Castells, M. 2000. "Materials for an Exploratory Theory of the Network Society." *British Journal of Sociology* 51 (1): 5–24. doi: 10.1111/j.1468-4446.2000.00005.x

CoE (Council of Europe). 1953 [1950]. Convention for the Protection of Human Rights and Fundamental Freedoms and Protocols. Paris: Council of Europe.

Cram, L. 2012. "Does the EU Need a Navel? Implicit and Explicit Identification with the European Union." *Journal of Common Markets Studies* 50 (1): 71–86. doi: 10.1111/j.1468-5965.2011.02207.x

Čeginskas, V. L. A. 2015. *Exploring Multicultural Belonging. Individuals across Cultures, Languages and Places*. Annales Universitatis Turkuensis 411. Turku: University of Turku.

Čeginskas, V. L. A. 2016. "'I am Europe'. Experiences of Multiple Belonging." *Ethnologia Fennica* 43: 72–88. Accessed 23 March 2020. https://journal.fi/ethnolfenn/article/view/65636/26505

Delhey, J., E. Deutschmann, T. Graf, and K. Richter. 2014. "Measuring the Europeanization of Everyday Life: Three New Indices and an Empirical Application." *European Societies* 16 (3): 355–377. doi: 10.1080/14616696.2014.904916

EC (European Commission). 2012. "Charter of Fundamental Rights of the European Union." Official Journal of the European Union C 326: 391–407. Accessed 23 March 2020. http://data.europa.eu/eli/treaty/char_2012/oj

EC (European Commission). 2016. Consolidated Version of the Treaty on the Functioning of the European Union. Brussels: European Commission.

EC (European Commission). 2017a. European Heritage Label. 2017 Panel Report. 5 December 2017. Brussels: European Commission.

EC (European Commission). 2017b. White Paper on the Future of Europe. Reflections of Scenarios for the EU27 by 2025. COM (2017)2025. Brussels: European Commission.

EC (European Commission). 2017c. Commission Recommendation of 26. 4. 2017 on the European Pillar of Social Rights. C (2017) 2600 final. Brussels: European Commission.

EC (European Commission). 2018. Communication from the Commission to the European Parliament, the European Council, the Council, the European Economic and Social Committee and the Committee of the Regions. A New European Agenda for Culture. Brussels, 22.5.2018, COM (2018) 267 final. Brussels: European Commission.

Eurobarometer. 2015. Standard Eurobarometer 84. First Results (Autumn 2015). Brussels: European Commission.

Faist, T. 2014. "On the Transnational Social Question: How Social Inequalities are Reproduced in Europe." *Journal of European Social Policy* 24 (3): 207–222. doi: 10.1177/ 0958928714525814

Favell, A. 2008. *Eurostars and Eurocities. Free Movement and Mobility in an Integrating Europe*. Malden and Oxford: Blackwell Publishing.

Ferrera, M. 2019. "EU Citizenship Needs a Stronger Social Dimension and Soft Duties." In *Debating European Citizenship*, edited by R. Bauböck, 181–198. IMISCOE Research Series. Cham: Springer Open Access. doi: 10.1007/978-3-319-89905-3

Fine, S. 2019. "Whose Freedom of Movement is Worth Defending?" In *Debating European Citizenship*, edited by R. Bauböck, 129–132. IMISCOE Research Series. Cham: Springer Open Access. doi: 10.1007/978-3-319-89905-3

Fligstein, N. 2008. *Euroclash: The EU, European Identity, and the Future of Europe*. Oxford: Oxford University Press.

Hermann, R. K., T. Risse, and M. B. Brewer, eds. 2004. *Transnational Identities. Becoming European in the EU*. Lanham, Boulder: Rowman & Littlefield Publishers.

Koikkalainen, S. 2019. "Free Movement and EU Citizenship from the Perspective of Intra-European Mobility." In *Debating European Citizenship*, edited by R. Bauböck, 121–124. IMISCOE Research Series. Cham: Springer Open Access. doi: 10.1007/ 978-3-319-89905-3

Kuhn, T. 2011. "Individual Transnationalism, Globalisation and Euroscepticism: An Empirical Test of Deutsch's Transactionalist Theory." *European Journal of Political Research* 50 (6): 811–837. doi.org/10.1111/j.1475-6765.2011.01987.x

Kuhn, T. 2015. *Experiencing European Integration: Transnational Lives and European Identity*. Oxford: Oxford University Press.

Kuhn, T. 2019. "Grand Theories of European Integration Revisited: Does Identity Politics Shape the Course of European Integration?" *Journal of European Public Policy* 26 (8): 1213–1230. doi: 10.1080/13501763.2019.1622588

Lähdesmäki, T., and K. Mäkinen 2019. "The 'European Significance' of Heritage: Politics of Scale in EU Heritage Policy Discourse." In *Politics of Scale. New Directions in Critical Heritage Studies*, edited by T. Lähdesmäki, S. Thomas, and Y. Zhu, 36–49. New York: Berghahn's Books.

Lähdesmäki, T., V. L. A. Čeginskas, S. Kaasik-Krogerus, K. Mäkinen, and J. Turunen 2020. *Creating and Governing Cultural Heritage in the European Union: The European Heritage Label*. London: Routledge.

Lefebvre, H. 1991. *The Production of Space*. Oxford: Blackwell.

Neuvonen, P. J. 2019. "Free Movement as a Means of Subject-Formation: Defending a More Relational Approach to EU Citizenship." In *Debating European Citizenship*, edited by R. Bauböck, 113–116. IMISCOE Research Series. Cham: Springer Open Access. doi: 10.1007/978-3-319-89905-3

Paskalev, V. 2019. "Free Movement Emancipates, but What Freedom Is This?" In *Debating European Citizenship*, edited by R. Bauböck, 117–120. IMISCOE Research Series. Cham: Springer Open Access. doi: 10.1007/978-3-319-89905-3

Recchi, E., and A. Favell (eds.). 2009. *Pioneers of European Integration. Citizenship and Mobility in the EU*. Cheltenham and Northampton: Edward Elgar Publishing Inc.

Risse, T. 2004. "European Institutions and Identity Change: What have we learned?" In *Transnational Identities. Becoming European in the EU*, edited by R. K. Hermann, T. Risse, and M. B. Brewer, 247–271. Lanham, Boulder: Rowman & Littlefield Publishers.

Rodríguez, A. 2019. "Second Country EU Citizens Voting in National Elections Is an Important Step, but Other Steps Should Be Taken First." In *Debating European Citizenship*, edited by R. Bauböck, 69–72. IMISCOE Research Series. Cham: Springer Open Access. doi: 10.1007/978-3-319-89905-3

Sassatelli, M. 2010. "European Identity between Flows and Places: Insights from Emerging European Landscape Policies." *Sociology* 44 (1): 67–83. doi: 10.1177/0038038509351625

Swoboda, H. 2019. "Don't Start with Europeans First. An Initiative for Extending Voting Rights Should also Promote Access to Citizenship for Third Country Nationals." In *Debating European Citizenship*, edited by R. Bauböck, 55–56. IMISCOE Research Series. Cham: Springer Open Access. doi: 10.1007/978-3-319-89905-3

Thym, D. 2019. "The Failure of Union Citizenship Beyond the Single Market." In *Debating European Citizenship*, edited by R. Bauböck, 101–106. IMISCOE Research Series. Cham: Springer Open Access. doi: 10.1007/978-3-319-89905-3

Urry, J. 2003. "Social Networks, Travel and Talk." *British Journal of Sociology* 54 (2): 155–175. doi: 10.1080/0007131032000080186

Wiesner, C., A. Björk, H.-M. Kivistö, and K. Mäkinen 2018. "Introduction: Shaping Citizenship as a Political Concept." In *Shaping Citizenship: A Political Concept in Theory, Debate and Practice*, edited by C. Wiesner, A. Björk, H.-M. Kivistö, and K. Mäkinen, 1–16. New York and London: Routledge.

Witte, F. de 2019. "Freedom of Movement Needs to Be Defended as the Core of EU Citizenship." In *Debating European Citizenship*, edited by R. Bauböck, 93–100. IMISCOE Research Series. Cham: Springer Open Access. doi: 10.1007/978-3-319-89905-3

Annex 1

Research Participants and Their Background Information

European Capital of Culture (ECOC)

1,425 respondents at 3 ECOCS female 68% male 32%

Pécs on-site survey (n = 200)
female 58%, male 42%
Respondents living in the city: 64%
Respondents living somewhere else in Hungary: 35%
Respondents from abroad: 1% (from Austria and Germany)

Pécs online pilot survey (n = 532)
female 72%, male 28%
Respondents living in the city: 49%
Respondents living somewhere else in Hungary: 49%
Respondents from abroad: 2% (from Croatia, Germany, Romania, Slovakia, and the UK)

Tallinn (n = 293)
female 69%, male 31%
Respondents living in the city: 72%
Respondents living somewhere else in Estonia: 22%
Respondents from abroad: 6% (from Australia, Finland, Germany, Lithuania, Russia, Spain, the Netherlands, the UK, and Ukraine)

Turku (n = 400)
female 67%, male 33%
Respondents living in the city: 66%
Respondents living somewhere else in Finland: 29%
Respondents from abroad: 5% (from Austria, Belgium, Brazil, Denmark, Estonia, France, Germany, Italy, Latvia, Spain, Sweden, and the UK)

(cont.)

European Capital of Culture (ECOC)

Age of the respondents:
- All respondents: age range 15–82, mean age 34
- Pécs on-site survey: age range 17–80, mean age 37
- Pécs online pilot survey: age range 15–80, mean age 26
- Tallinn: age range 15–82, mean age 33
- Turku: age range 15–78, mean age 43

Educational background of all respondents:
- Comprehensive or elementary school: 3%
- Vocational course or degree or in-job training: 8%
- High school: 32%
- Polytechnic or other higher vocational education: 11%
- Higher education, bachelor's degree: 18%
- Higher education, master's degree: 24%
- Higher education, doctoral degree: 3%

European Citizen Campus

15 interviewees	*11 interviewees at Roots laboratory, Strasbourg:* 1 male, 10 female
female 73%	*4 interviewees at Home laboratory, Freiburg:* 3 male, 1 female
male 27%	*9 thematic writings:* 5 male, 4 female authors
20 written texts	*11 motivation letters:* 1 male, 8 female, 2 non-identifiable authors
	Participants were studying in Belgium, Germany, France, Italy, Luxembourg, the Netherlands, and Portugal.

Age and educational background of participants:
- All participants were in their early twenties and students in higher education

European Heritage Label (EHL)

271 interviewees	*225 EU citizens, representing 19 EU nationalities*:
at 11 EHL sites	Austria (n = 16); Belgium (n = 33); Czech Republic (n = 1);
female 52%	Denmark (n = 3); Finland (n = 3); France (n = 35);
male 48%	Germany (n = 37); Greece (n = 2); Ireland (n = 2); Italy (n = 22);
	Luxembourg (n = 1); the Netherlands (n = 35); Poland (n = 9);
	Portugal (n = 1); Slovakia (n = 1); Spain (n = 1); Sweden (n = 2);
	the UK (n = 15)
	Interviewees with dual or triple nationality (n = 6):
	Austrian-Polish (n = 1); French-German (n = 1);
	Russian-French (n = 1); Dutch-American (n = 1);
	Dutch-Swedish (n = 1); Hungarian-British-German (n = 1)
	46 interviewees from non-EU countries:
	Australia (n = 3); Canada (n = 8); Chile (n = 1); China (n = 1);
	India (n = 2); Japan (n = 2); New-Zealand (n = 1); Peru (n = 1);
	Russia (n = 1); Singapore (n = 2); South Korea (n = 1); Switzerland
	(n = 2); Ukraine (n = 2); USA (n = 19)

Age groups:

– Interviewees aged between 18 and 50: 52%
– Interviewees aged between 51 and 85+: 48%
– Group of young interviewees include age groups 1, 2, and 3: 36%
– Group of middle-aged interviewees include age groups 4, 5, 6, 7, 8, and 9: 41%
– Group of older interviewees include age groups 10, 11, 12, 13, and 14: 23%

Group 1	Group 2	Group 3	Group 4	Group 5	Group 6	Group 7
age 18–25	age 26–30	age 31–35	age 36–40	age 41–45	age 46–50	age 51–55
(n = 50)	(n = 27)	(n = 21)	(n = 11)	(n = 8)	(n = 8)	(n = 22)
Group 8	Group 9	Group 10	Group 11	Group 12	Group 13	Group 14
age 56–60	age 61–65	age 66–70	age 71–75	age 76–80	age 81–85	age 85+
(n = 21)	(n = 26)	(n = 27)	(n = 21)	(n = 9)	(n = 1)	(n = 3)

Educational background:

– High school diploma, secondary education: 9%
– Vocational training, apprenticeship, college: 12%
– University students: 12%
– Higher education – bachelor's, master's, PhD, equivalent diploma: 46%
– No information given: 4%

Annex 2

European Capitals of Culture up to 2020

1985	Athens	Greece
1986	Florence	Italy
1987	Amsterdam	Netherlands
1988	Berlin	West Germany
1989	Paris	France
1990	Glasgow	UK
1991	Dublin	Ireland
1992	Madrid	Spain
1993	Antwerp	Belgium
1994	Lisbon	Portugal
1995	Luxembourg	Luxembourg
1996	Copenhagen	Denmark
1997	Thessaloniki	Greece
1998	Stockholm	Sweden
1999	Weimar	Germany
2000	Avignon	France
	Bergen	Norway
	Bologna	Italy
	Brussels	Belgium
	Helsinki	Finland
	Kraków	Poland
	Prague	Czech Republic
	Reykjavík	Iceland
	Santiago de Compostela	Spain
2001	Rotterdam	Netherlands
	Porto	Portugal
2002	Bruges	Belgium
	Salamanca	Spain
2003	Graz	Austria
2004	Genoa	Italy
	Lille	France
2005	Cork	Ireland
2006	Patras	Greece

(cont.)

2007	Sibiu	Romania
	Luxembourg	Luxembourg
2008	Liverpool	UK
	Stavanger	Norway
2009	Vilnius	Lithuania
	Linz	Austria
2010	Essen	Germany
	Istanbul	Turkey
	Pécs	Hungary
2011	Turku	Finland
	Tallinn	Estonia
2012	Guimarães	Portugal
	Maribor	Slovenia
2013	Marseille	France
	Košice	Slovakia
2014	Riga	Latvia
	Umeå	Sweden
2015	Mons	Belgium
	Plzeň	Czech Republic
2016	San Sebastián	Spain
	Wrocław	Poland
2017	Aarhus	Denmark
	Paphos	Cyprus
2018	Leeuwarden	Netherlands
	Valletta	Malta
2019	Matera	Italy
	Plovdiv	Bulgaria
2020	Rijeka	Croatia
	Galway	Ireland

Annex 3

Sites Awarded with the European Heritage Label by 2020 Including Codes Used in the Interview Data in Chapter 6

2013	Archaeological Park Carnuntum (S2)	Petronell-Carnuntum	Austria
	Great Guild Hall (S6)	Tallinn	Estonia
	Peace Palace	Hooghalen	Netherlands
	Camp Westerbork (S3)	The Hague	Netherlands
2014	Heart of Ancient Athens	Athens	Greece
	Abbey of Cluny	Cluny	France
	Archive of the Crown of Aragon	Barcelona	Spain
	Union of Lublin	Lublin	Poland
	Münster and Osnabrück –Sites of the Peace of Westphalia (1648)	Münster and Osnabrück	Germany
	General Library of the University of Coimbra	Coimbra	Portugal
	The May, 3 1791 Constitution	Warsaw	Poland
	Hambach Castle (S7)	Hambach	Germany
	Charter of Law of Abolition of the Death Penalty	Lisbon	Portugal
	Student Residence	Madrid	Spain
	Kaunas of 1919–1940	Kaunas	Lithuania
	Franja Partisan Hospital	Cerkno	Slovenia
	Alcide de Gasperi House Museum (S1)	Pieve Tesino	Italy
	Robert Schuman House (S10)	Scy-Chazelles	France
	Historic Gdańsk Shipyard (S8)	Gdańsk	Poland
	Pan European Picnic Memorial Park	Sopron	Hungary
2015	Neanderthal Prehistoric Site and Krapina Museum	Hušnjakovo/ Krapina	Croatia
	Olomouc Premyslid Castle and Archdiocesan Museum	Olomouc	Czech Republic
	Sagres Promontory (S11)	Sagres	Portugal
	Imperial Palace	Vienna	Austria
	Historic Ensemble of the University of Tartu	Tartu	Estonia

(cont.)

	Franz Liszt Academy of Music (S5)	Budapest	Hungary
	Mundaneum (S9)	Mons	Belgium
	World War I Eastern Front Wartime Cemetery No. 123	Łużna – Pustki	Poland
	European District of Strasbourg (S4)	Strasbourg	France
2017	Leipzig's Musical Heritage Sites	Leipzig	Germany
	Dohány Street Synagogue Complex	Budapest	Hungary
	Fort Cadine	Trento	Italy
	Javorca Memorial Church and its cultural landscape	Tolmin	Slovenia
	Former Natzweiler concentration camp and its satellite camps	multiple	France-Germany
	Sighet Memorial	Sighet	Romania
	Bois du Cazier	Marcinelle	Belgium
	Village of Schengen	Schengen	Luxemboug
	Maastricht Treaty	Maastricht	Netherlands
2019	Archaeological Area of Ostia Antica	Rome	Italy
	Underwater Cultural Heritage of the Azores	Azores	Portugal
	Colonies of Benevolence	Veenhuizen, Frederiksoord, Wilhelminaoord, Willemsoord, Ommerschans, Wortel, Merksplas	Belgium, Netherlands
	Living Heritage of Szentendre	Szentendre	Hungary
	Kynžvart Castle – Place of diplomatic meetings	Lázně Kynžvart	Czech Republic
	Site of Remembrance in Łambinowice	Łambinowice	Poland
	Zdravljica - the Message of the European Spring of Nations	-	Slovenia
	Werkbund Estates in Europe	Stuttgart, Wroclaw, Brno, Prague, Vienna	Germany, Poland, Czech Republic, Austria
	Chambon-sur-Lignon Memorial	Le Chambon-sur-Lignon	France
	The Three Brothers	Riga	Latvia

Index

Printed in the United States
By Bookmasters